International Human Rights

Dilemmas in World Politics

Series Editor: Jennifer Sterling-Folker, University of Connecticut

Why is it difficult to achieve the universal protection of human rights? How can democratization be achieved so that it is equitable and lasting? Why does agreement on global environmental protection seem so elusive? How does the concept of gender play a role in the shocking inequalities of women throughout the globe? Why do horrific events such as genocide or ethnic conflicts recur or persist? These are the sorts of questions that confront policy makers and students of contemporary international politics alike. They are dilemmas because they are enduring problems in world affairs that are difficult to resolve.

These are the types of dilemmas at the heart of the Dilemmas in World Politics series. Each book in the Dilemmas in World Politics series addresses a challenge or problem in world politics that is topical, recurrent, and not easily solved. Each is structured to cover the historical and theoretical aspects of the dilemma, as well as the policy alternatives for and future direction of the problem. The books are designed as supplements to introductory and intermediate courses in international relations. The books in the Dilemmas in World Politics series encourage students to engage in informed discussion of current policy issues.

Books in This Series

International Human Rights

FIFTH EDITION

JACK DONNELLY
University of Denver

DANIEL J. WHELAN
Hendrix College

WESTVIEW PRESS

Westview Press
Hachette Book Group
1290 Avenue of the Americas
New York, NY 10104
www.westviewpress.com

Printed in the United States of America
Fifth Edition: July 2017

Published by Westview Press, an imprint of Perseus Books, LLC, a subsidiary of Hachette Book Group, Inc.

The Hachette Speakers Bureau provides a wide range of authors for speaking events. To find out more, go to www.hachettespeakersbureau.com or call (866) 376-6591.

The publisher is not responsible for websites (or their content) that are not owned by the publisher.

Library of Congress Cataloging-in-Publication Data has been applied for.

ISBNs: 978-0-8133-4948-0 (paperback), 978-0-8133-4949-7 (ebook)

LSC-C

10 9 8 7 6 5 4 3 2 1

Contents

PART TWO: MULTILATERAL, BILATERAL, AND TRANSNATIONAL ACTION

PART THREE: CONTEMPORARY ISSUES

List of Case Studies

List of Problems

List of Tables

Acronyms

ACHR	Arab Charter on Human Rights
AHRD	ASEAN Human Rights Declaration
AI	Amnesty International
AICHR	ASEAN Intergovernmental Commission on Human Rights
ANC	African National Congress
AQAP	Al-Qaeda in the Arabian Peninsula
AQIM	Al-Qaeda in the Islamic Maghreb
ASEAN	Association of Southeast Asian Nations
AU	African Union
CAT	Convention Against Torture
CED	Convention on Protection Against Enforced Disappearance
CEDAW	Convention on the Elimination of All Forms of Discrimination Against Women
CERD	Convention on the Elimination of All Forms of Racial Discrimination
CMW	Convention on the Protection of Migrant Workers
CRC	Convention on the Rights of the Child
CRPD	Convention on the Rights of Persons with Disabilities
CSO	Civil society organization
ECHR	European Convention on Human Rights
ECOSOC	Economic and Social Council (United Nations)
EU	European Union
FSLN	Sandinista National Liberation Front (Nicaragua)
HRC	Human Rights Committee (United Nations)
HRW	Human Rights Watch
IACHR	Inter-American Commission on Human Rights
IADC	Inter-American Democratic Charter
IC	Invisible Children, Inc.
ICC	International Criminal Court
ICCPR	International Covenant on Civil and Political Rights
ICESCR	International Covenant on Economic, Social, and Cultural Rights

ICISS	International Commission on Intervention and State Sovereignty
IDF	Israeli Defense Forces
IGO	Intergovernmental organization
ILO	International Labor Organization
IMF	International Monetary Fund
INGO	International nongovernmental organization
ISIL/ISIS	Islamic State (also known as Daesh)
JNA	Yugoslav National Army
LRA	Lord's Resistance Army (Uganda)
MNC	Multinational corporation
NATO	North Atlantic Treaty Organization
NED	National Endowment for Democracy (United States)
NGO	Nongovernmental organization
NLD	National League for Democracy (Myanmar)
NSS	National Security Strategy (United States)
OAS	Organization of American States
OAU	Organization of African Unity
OHCHR	Office of the High Commissioner for Human Rights (United Nations)
OSCE	Organization for Security and Co-operation in Europe
R2P	Responsibility to protect (doctrine)
SLORC	State Law and Order Restoration Council (Myanmar)
TMB	(Human rights) treaty monitoring body (United Nations)
UNAMIR	United Nations Assistance Mission in Rwanda
UNDG	United Nations Development Group
UNDP	United Nations Development Programme
UNESCO	United Nations Educational, Social, and Cultural Organization
UNPA	United Nations Protected Area (Bosnia; Croatia)
UNFPA	United Nations Fund for Population Activities
UNPROFOR	United Nations Protection Force in the Former Yugoslavia
UPR	Universal Period Review (United Nations)
URG	Universal Rights Group

Acknowledgments

I began working on the first edition of this book more than two decades ago. Over that time, I have had the help of literally dozens of friends, colleagues, students, research assistants, and editors. Any list would be both too long, losing the individuals in a stream of names, and too short, for I am sure that I would neglect mentioning at least a few people who contributed to the book. Thus, let me simply say: Thanks to all of you. (You know who you are.)

—Jack Donnelly

With the financial support of the Charles Prentiss Hough Odyssey Professorship, which I held from 2012 to 2015, I convened a small research team of Hendrix students to begin the process of updating this edition, including Zach Chastain, Nigel Halliday, Chirag Lala, Kay Beth Tyson, Janie Sanford, and Laela Zaidi, all of whom I would like to thank for their work. I would also like to convey my very special thanks to two other students who were in that group—Sarah Logan and Andrew McWard, who continued to work with me on the project over the summer and fall of 2016. They provided excellent updates and draft materials for the new case studies and problems that appear in this edition, especially for the chapters on multilateral mechanisms, regional mechanisms, and transnational advocacy, and the two foreign policy chapters. I am especially grateful for their outstanding support.

—Daniel J. Whelan

Preface

A Note to the Reader

This is a book about the international politics of human rights since the end of World War II; that is, the ways in which states and other international actors have addressed human rights. The topic, although broad, is narrower than some readers might expect.

Life, liberty, security, subsistence, and other things to which we have human rights may be denied by an extensive array of individuals and organizations. *Human rights,* however, are usually taken to have a special reference to the ways in which states treat their own citizens. For example, domestically, we distinguish muggings and private assaults, which are not typically considered human rights violations, from police brutality and torture, which are. Internationally, we distinguish terrorism, war, and crimes against humanity from human rights abuses, even though all lead to denials of life and security. Although the boundaries are not always clear, the distinction is part of our ordinary language and focuses our attention on an important set of political problems.

No single book can cover all aspects of the politics of human rights. Our concern is with the *international* politics of human rights, a vital and now well-established area of policy and inquiry. This does not imply that international action is the principal determinant of whether human rights are respected or violated. In fact, much of this book demonstrates the limits of international action, insofar as we maintain that, ultimately, human rights are respected and realized at the domestic, national level. In contrast to many other discussions of international human rights, we pay ample attention to the domestic politics of human rights throughout the book in a number of case studies.

Another distinctive feature of this book, along with the other volumes in the Dilemmas in World Politics series, is a relatively extensive emphasis on theory (and history), which forms the heart of Part 1. Chapter 1 examines the historical development of international human rights since World War II. Chapter 2 addresses philosophical issues of the nature, substance, and source of human rights; the place of human rights in the contemporary international society of states; and the theoretical challenges posed to the very enterprise of international human rights policy by arguments of radical cultural relativism and political realism (*realpolitik*, or power politics). Chapter 3 explores the important theoretical issue of the universality (and relativity) of human rights. And Chapter 4, which is completely new to this edition, explores the unity (indivisibility) of all human rights, with a particular emphasis on the two grand categories of civil/political and economic/social rights.

Part 2 looks at multilateral, bilateral, and transnational action, both separately and comparatively, with an emphasis on case studies since the end of the Cold War (with a few Cold War–era case studies from earlier editions). The chapters in this section consider global multilateral mechanisms, regional mechanisms, foreign policy action in general, U.S. foreign policy in particular, and transnational advocacy. All of these chapters have been significantly revised from the fourth edition, introducing new case studies and exploring the most recent human rights developments.

Part 3 turns to three contemporary issues: humanitarian intervention, globalization and human rights, and the challenges of (anti)terrorism and human rights. As with the chapters in Part 2, these chapters have been thoroughly revised and brought up to date with the latest developments in human rights policy and practice, including an examination of several new case studies.

We have tried to write a book that assumes little or no background knowledge. Most readers with an interest in the topic, regardless of age or experience, should find this book accessible, and we have highlighted **in bold** some key terms and concepts that are included in the glossary. However, we have tried not to write a textbook, a term that has justly acquired pejorative overtones. We have taken care not to write "down," either in style or in substance.

Textbook presentations of controversial issues—when they are not entirely avoided—tend to involve bland and noncommittal presentations of "the two sides" to an argument. Although we have made an effort to retain some balance in the discussion, we have not expunged our own views and interpretations. To some readers, it may seem like we often lay out and defend one interpretation and give little attention to alternative views. While we have made great efforts to be accurate and fair, we have no false pretense of objectivity.

With that in mind, we want to draw the reader's attention to the discussion questions for each chapter. There is almost a short chapter's worth of material in these questions, which often frame alternative interpretations and highlight controversial claims in the main body of the text. They thus provide at least a partial corrective to any "imbalance" in the main text.

We also draw your attention to the ten "Problems" spread throughout the volume. Each is, in effect, a discussion question, followed by our own answer, followed again by further questions or problems. They aim to provoke additional thought and discussion and to illustrate ways in which readers may take the material presented here and go beyond it.

Another central feature of this volume is the extensive use of case studies. These include recent (post–Cold War) as well as older cases, in order to provide historical context and depth to the discussion and to provide points of comparison between earlier periods and more contemporary ones.

Each chapter—as well as each case study and each problem—can be read independently, in any order. Teachers and students can thus easily customize this book. Our only strong suggestion is that those without a background begin with Chapter 1. From then on, follow your interests—or the instructions of your teacher. *And approach everything here with a critical mind.*

Our goal is to get you to think about why and how human rights are violated, what can (and cannot) be done about such violations through international action, why human rights remain such a small part of international politics, and what might be done about that. These are pressing political issues that merit, even demand, thought and attention. This book provides resources to help you think about these issues more broadly, more deeply, and more subtly—and thus to be a more informed, and perhaps even more effective, person and citizen.

PART ONE

History and Theory

1

Human Rights in Global Politics: Historical Perspective

There are many historically important precursors to the recognition of human rights as a matter of global concern. Only with the end of World War II and the establishment of the United Nations (U.N.), however, did human rights begin to take on an internationally obligatory nature.

The recognition of limited religious rights for some Christian minorities in the Peace of Westphalia (1648), which brought the Thirty Years' War to an end, is perhaps the earliest precursor of the idea of international human rights. Several treaties concluded in the aftermath of the Revolutionary and Napoleonic Wars, such as those affirming the sovereignty and independence of states such as Belgium (1815) and Greece (1832), included provisions protecting the rights of religious and linguistic minorities. In 1878, the major powers of Europe conditioned their recognition of the sovereignty and independence of Serbia on a guarantee of religious liberty. Nineteenth-century campaigns against the slave trade and slavery had clear overtones of what today we would call human rights advocacy. After World War I, workers' rights and minority rights were addressed by the newly created International Labor Organization and League of Nations. Nonetheless, prior to World War II there was near-universal agreement that human rights were *not* a legitimate concern of international relations. For example, the Covenant of the League of Nations, which is usually seen as an expression of the idealism of the immediate post–World War I era, does not even include the term *human rights*.

This reflected a particular understanding of sovereignty, which has been the organizing principle of international relations for the past three centuries. States, the primary actors in international relations, are seen as **sovereign,** that is, supreme authorities, and thus subject to no higher political authority in their own territories. The principal duty correlative to the right of sovereignty is **nonintervention,** the obligation not to interfere in matters essentially within the domestic jurisdiction of sovereign states (see §2.8). Human rights, which typically involve a state's treatment

3

of its own citizens in its own territory, were until relatively recently seen as such a matter of protected domestic jurisdiction. A major purpose of this book is to chronicle the ways in which, over the past seventy years, human rights have produced fundamental changes in understandings and practices of state sovereignty.

1. The Emergence of International Human Rights Norms

The contemporary human rights movement can be more directly traced back to the era between the two world wars. For example, the International Law Commission adopted the Declaration of the International Rights of Man in 1929. In the 1930s British novelist and activist H. G. Wells cast much of his advocacy for social reform in terms of a global regime committed to human rights. Such efforts, however, represented only a small fringe of civil society. Even those who believed that all human beings had an extensive set of equal and inalienable rights—a distinctly minority idea in an era that had little trouble justifying racism, sexism, and colonialism—did not suggest that other states had rights or obligations with respect to those rights. And not a single state endorsed the idea that governments had *international* human rights obligations to their own citizens.

This began to change during World War II. As the Allied powers reflected on the nature of their struggle with Hitler's Germany—and on how to justify the war to their own citizens and the rest of the world—respect for human rights became an increasingly central theme. In his January 1941 State of the Union address, nearly a year before the United States entered the war, President Franklin D. Roosevelt framed the Allied war effort in terms of securing four fundamental freedoms: of speech, of religion, from want, and from fear. This initial statement was further elaborated by Roosevelt and British prime minister Winston Churchill, who negotiated a statement of Allied war aims in the Atlantic Charter of August 1941. The January 1942 Declaration by United Nations claimed that "complete victory over their enemies is essential to defend life, liberty, independence and religious freedom, and to preserve human rights and justice in their own lands as well as in other lands." From late 1942 on, human rights were a part of postwar planning efforts within both the American and the British governments, the two leading Allied powers.

The immediate impetus for international action, however, came in 1945 as Allied governments and publics began to reflect on the Holocaust, Germany's systematic mass murder of millions of innocent civilians, a crime that the Polish lawyer Raphael Lemkin had recently named **genocide.** Before the war, little was done to aid Jews trying to flee Germany and surrounding countries. Some who escaped were even denied refuge by Allied governments, including the United States. During the war, no effort was made to impede the functioning of the death camps. The Allies did not even target the railway lines that brought hundreds of thousands to the slaughter at Auschwitz and other camps. The world watched—or, rather, turned a blind eye to—the genocidal massacre of six million Jews, a half-million Gypsies (Roma), and tens of thousands of communists, social democrats, homosexuals, church activists, and just ordinary decent people who refused complicity in the new politics and technology of barbarism. As the war came to an end, though, Allied leaders and citizens, previously preoccupied with military victory, finally began to confront this horror.

The Nuremberg War Crimes Trials, which began in 1945, introduced the novel charge of crimes against humanity. (These crimes were distinct from already-recognized violations of the laws of war, which had been codified at the beginning of the twentieth century in the so-called Hague Laws.) For the first time, officials were held legally accountable to the international community for offenses against individual civilians, not states, whether or not those civilians were citizens of the governments that committed the crimes.

These shocking crimes were crucial in mobilizing broad support for international action. But they were only the tip of the iceberg. Many organizations and individuals had already recognized that wartime atrocities had been preceded by, and built on, years of systematic state-imposed violations of fundamental rights. Prior to the instigation of the Final Solution, Jews and others perceived opponents and "deviants" in Germany had been stripped of many of the civil, political, and economic rights they held prior to Hitler's rise to power. In addition, there was general agreement that the worldwide economic depression and ensuing economic insecurity of the 1930s contributed significantly to the rise of rights-abusive regimes and to the unraveling of the international system, which precipitated the war. Proposals for the protection of fundamental rights thus become a central focus of postwar international institutions, leading to the incorporation of human rights into the Charter of the United Nations, which was adopted in San Francisco in the summer of 1945.

The Preamble of the U.N. Charter lists as two of the four principal objectives of the organization "to reaffirm faith in fundamental human rights, in the dignity and worth of the human person, in the equal rights of men and women and of nations large and small," and "to promote social progress and better standards of life in larger freedom." Likewise, Article 1 lists as one of the four purposes of the United Nations "to achieve international co-operation in solving international problems of an economic, social, cultural, or humanitarian character, and in promoting and encouraging respect for human rights and for fundamental freedoms for all without distinction as to race, sex, language, or religion."

These statements were in themselves revolutionary. Even more radical was the creation in 1946 of the Commission on Human Rights under the auspices of the U.N. Economic and Social Council (ECOSOC). The Commission quickly began to define these abstract statements of postwar optimism and goodwill. The original Commission was composed of eighteen elected members who were broadly representative of the (then fifty-one) members of the United Nations. Its first task was to draft an "international bill of rights," which would include a declaration of principles and a legally binding human rights convention (treaty), along with institutions and procedures for their enforcement. The Commission quickly decided to focus its attention on the first part of the bill, which in 1948 became the **Universal Declaration of Human Rights.**

The initial drafts were written by John Humphrey, a young Canadian member of the Commission's staff, and René Cassin, the French member of the Commission. There was widespread and essential participation, though, by non-Western representatives. The drafting committee included P. C. Chang of China (the vice chair of the

Commission), Charles Malik of Lebanon (the rapporteur of the Commission), and Hernan Santa Cruz of Chile. Each, along with the chair of both the Commission and the drafting committee, Eleanor Roosevelt of the United States, played a major role in shaping the Declaration.

2. The Universal Declaration

By the fall of 1948, after barely a year and a half of work, the Commission had completed a brief statement of principles. It was adopted as the Universal Declaration of Human Rights by the U.N. General Assembly on December 10, 1948. (December 10 is thus celebrated globally as Human Rights Day.) The vote was forty-eight in favor, none opposed, with eight abstentions. Saudi Arabia abstained principally because of provisions that allowed Muslims to change their religion. South Africa abstained because of the provisions on racial equality. The six Soviet-bloc states (USSR, Byelorussian SSR, Czechoslovakia, Poland, Ukrainian SSR, and Yugoslavia) abstained (ostensibly) because the document was insufficiently detailed, especially with regard to the specific duties of individuals toward their states.

Although most of Africa, much of Asia, and parts of the Americas were still under colonial rule, the Universal Declaration had global endorsement. It received the votes of fourteen European and other Western states, nineteen states from Latin America, and fifteen from Africa and Asia. And the countries that later achieved independence were at least as enthusiastic in their embrace of the Declaration as those who voted for it in 1948. In Africa in particular, the Universal Declaration was liberally referenced and frequently quoted in independence-era constitutions.

Article 1 of the Universal Declaration states its foundation: "All human beings are born free and equal in dignity and rights. They are endowed with reason and conscience and should act towards one another in a spirit of brotherhood." The substantive bookend is Article 28: "Everyone is entitled to a social and international order in which the rights and freedoms set forth in this Declaration can be fully realized." In between, Articles 2–27 lay out a comprehensive set of rights that have come to define what we mean by internationally recognized human rights. Article 2 recognizes the right to nondiscrimination. An extensive series of **civil and political rights** are recognized in Articles 3–15 and 19–21, including rights to life, liberty, and security of person; an array of legal protections and civil liberties; and the right to political participation. Articles 16–18 and 22–27 recognize a wide range of **economic, social, and cultural rights,** including rights to an adequate standard of living, social security, work, rest and leisure, family, education, and participation in the cultural life of the community. Article 29 indicates that people also have duties to their community that set parameters for the exercise of rights. Article 30, the final article, states that nothing in the Declaration may be interpreted as justifying any act that aims at the destruction of any of the enumerated rights in the Declaration.

Even today the Universal Declaration provides the most authoritative statement of international human rights norms. This vital document is reprinted in the appendix.

3. The Covenants

The Universal Declaration of Human Rights is not, in itself, legally binding. (It describes itself as "a common standard of achievement for all peoples and all nations.") The Commission thus moved immediately to drafting a treaty to give binding international legal force to international human rights norms. The initial draft "Covenant on Human Rights" was quite short—eighteen articles, focusing exclusively on civil rights. After quite a bit of debate, however, the General Assembly directed the Commission to include economic, social, cultural, and political rights as well.

The new draft, though, was unwieldy. Furthermore, there was significant disagreement over monitoring and adjudication mechanisms and a proposed reporting procedure for economic, social, and cultural rights. Many on the Commission—mostly Western states—believed that the new draft should be divided into separate Covenants. Others—mostly from the postcolonial global South—disagreed, arguing that the indivisibility of human rights was paramount. After much debate, in both the Commission and the broader United Nations, the General Assembly in 1952 directed the Commission to draft separate Covenants on civil and political rights and on economic, social, and cultural rights. (To guarantee the notion of unity, though, the two Covenants, once completed, were to be simultaneously adopted by the General Assembly.)

Many accounts of this period in the history of human rights erroneously blame the East-West ideological divide, the **Cold War**, for the division of the Covenant. The documentary record, however, tells a different story. There were differences of opinion and ideology between the West and the communist world over the nature of rights. But by far their biggest divide was over the role that the United Nations would play in monitoring the implementation of the Covenant(s) and adjudicating disputes between states over violations. Most countries agreed that the United Nations should play a role, albeit a weak one (see Chapter 4). The Soviet Union and its allies, however, rejected any form of monitoring or oversight by the United Nations.

The Cold War, though, did play a role in debates within the United States about different categories of rights and the supranational role of the United Nations. A coalition of cold warriors, isolationists, and racists (who did not want additional international scrutiny of legalized racial discrimination in the United States) forced newly elected president Eisenhower to agree not to support any human rights treaty that would emerge from the United Nations. On the Commission, the United States began to argue that perhaps the best way to ensure human rights would be through the provision of technical assistance and support to countries, rather than through binding treaties. Nonetheless, by 1954 the Commission finished its work on the Covenants and sent them to the General Assembly, whose Third Committee dithered over the drafts for nearly a dozen years, less because of Cold War wrangling than the wariness of most states of a legally binding treaty. In addition, the delay reflected a shift in focus of the growing bloc of postcolonial states toward fighting colonialism and racism.

The adoption in 1963 of the Declaration on the Elimination of All Forms of Racial Discrimination, followed quickly by a legally binding Convention two years later, indicated a renewed emphasis on human rights standard setting. A coalition of Third

Table 1.1 Internationally Recognized Human Rights

The International Bill of Human Rights recognizes the rights to:
Equality of rights without discrimination (Dl, D2, E2, E3, C2, C3)
Life (D3, C6)
Liberty and security of person (D3, C9)
Protection against slavery (D4, C8)
Protection against torture and cruel and inhuman punishment (D5, C7)
Recognition as a person before the law (D6, C16)
Equal protection of the law (D7, C14, C26)
Access to legal remedies for rights violations (D8, C2)
Protection against arbitrary arrest or detention (D9, C9)
Hearing before an independent and impartial judiciary (D10, C14)
Presumption of innocence (D11, C14)
Protection against ex post facto laws (D11, C15)
Protection of privacy, family, and home (D12, C17)
Freedom of movement and residence (D13, C12)
Seek asylum from persecution (D14)
Nationality (D15)
Marry and found a family (D16, E10, C23)
Own property (D17)
Freedom of thought, conscience, and religion (D18, C18)
Freedom of opinion, expression, and the press (D19, C19)
Freedom of assembly and association (D20, C21, C22)
Political participation (D21, C25)
Social security (D22, E9)
Work, under favorable conditions (D23, E6, E7)
Free trade unions (D23, E8, C22)
Rest and leisure (D24, E7)
Food, clothing, and housing (D25, E11)
Health care and social services (D25, E12)
Special protections for children (D25, E10, C24)
Education (D26, E13, E14)
Participation in cultural life (D27, E15)
A social and international order needed to realize rights (D28)
Self-determination (E1, C1)
Humane treatment when detained or imprisoned (C10)
Protection against debtor's prison (C11)
Protection against arbitrary expulsion of aliens (C13)
Protection against advocacy of racial or religious hatred (C20)
Protection of minority culture (C27)

Note: This list includes all rights that are enumerated in two of the three documents of the International Bill of Human Rights or have a full article in one document. The source of each right is indicated in parentheses, by document and article number. D = Universal Declaration of Human Rights. E = International Covenant on Economic, Social, and Cultural Rights. C = International Covenant on Civil and Political Rights.

World and Western states, with Soviet-bloc support, pushed the drafting process to completion. In December 1966 the International Covenant on Economic, Social, and Cultural Rights (ICESCR) and the International Covenant on Civil and Political Rights (ICCPR) were adopted by the United Nations. Although the Covenants make a few substantive revisions to the Universal Declaration of Human Rights, most notably adding a right of self-determination of peoples, they for the most part reaffirm and elaborate on the 1948 Declaration.

The U.N. Charter's human rights provisions, the Universal Declaration, and the Covenants are often referred to collectively as the **International Bill of Human Rights**. They state the minimum social and political guarantees recognized by the international community as necessary for a life of dignity in the contemporary world. Table 1.1 summarizes their content.

4. The 1970s: From Standard Setting to Monitoring

The comprehensiveness of the **International Human Rights Covenants** meant that further progress on international human rights would now depend primarily on implementing these standards—an area in which the United Nations had been, and still is, far less successful. The existence of international norms *alone* does not give the United Nations, or anyone else, the authority to implement them or even inquire about how states implement (or do not implement) them. However, by ratifying the Covenants, states agree to follow international human rights standards by complying with certain reporting procedures. But, as we will see in more detail in Chapter 5, these obligations do not even begin to provide international enforcement or implementation of the standards.

In the late 1960s, however, the United Nations began to move, very tentatively and in largely symbolic ways, from merely setting standards to examining how states implement these standards. In 1967 Economic and Social Council Resolution 1235 authorized the Commission on Human Rights to discuss human rights violations in particular countries. In 1969 the racial discrimination convention came into force, requiring parties to file periodic reports on implementation. In 1970 ECOSOC Resolution 1503 authorized the Commission on Human Rights to conduct confidential investigations of complaints that suggested "a consistent pattern of gross and reliably attested violations of human rights and fundamental freedoms."

The United Nations operates under severe structural constraints. It is an **intergovernmental organization** (IGO), established by a multilateral treaty (the U.N. Charter) among sovereign states, who are its members. Delegates to the United Nations represent states, not the international community, let alone individuals whose rights are violated. Like other IGOs, the United Nations has only those powers that states—which are also the principal violators of human rights—give it. Thus, perhaps more surprising than the limits on its human rights monitoring powers is the fact that the United Nations acquired even these limited powers. It may be of little comfort to victims, but we cannot ignore the limits imposed by state sovereignty in assessing the human rights achievements of the United Nations and other intergovernmental organizations. Although sovereign states have agreed to these norms and

Table 1.2 Key Dates in the Evolution of International Human Rights Norms and Institutions

1941 (January): Roosevelt's "Four Freedoms"

1941 (December): Atlantic Charter

1942: Declaration by United Nations

1945: United Nations Charter adopted

1946: Creation of the U.N. Commission on Human Rights

1948: Adoption of the Genocide Convention and the Universal Declaration of Human Rights

1950: Decision to include economic and social rights in the Covenant on Human Rights

1952: Decision to divide the Covenant into separate treaties

1954: Initial drafting of the Covenants completed by the Commission on Human Rights

1965: Adoption of the Convention on the Elimination of All Forms of Racial Discrimination (CERD)

1966: Adoption of the International Covenants on Economic, Social, and Cultural Rights (ICESCR) and Civil and Political Rights (ICCPR)

1968: International Conference on Human Rights held in Tehran, Iran

1969: CERD enters into force

1970: U.N. Economic and Social Council adopts 1503 Procedure (petitions mechanism)

1975: Helsinki Accords link human rights protections to security cooperation in Europe

1976: International Covenants enter into force

1977: Amnesty International wins Nobel Peace Prize; U.S. State Department makes human rights a foreign policy priority

1979: United Nations adopts Convention on the Elimination of All Forms of Discrimination Against Women (CEDAW)

1981: CEDAW enters into force

1984: United Nations adopts Convention Against Torture (CAT)

1987: CAT enters into force

1989: United Nations adopts Convention on the Rights of the Child (CRC); enters into force the same year

1990: United Nations adopts Convention on the Protection of Migrant Workers (CMW)

1993: World Conference on Human Rights held in Vienna, Austria

1993: Establishment of the Office of the High Commissioner for Human Rights

2003: CMW enters into force

2006: U.N. Human Rights Council replaces the Commission on Human Rights

2006: United Nations adopts Convention on Protection Against Enforced Disappearance (CED) and Convention on the Rights of Persons with Disabilities (CRPD)

2008: CRPD enters into force

2010: CED enters into force

procedures—they participated in drafting them and consented to them by ratifying human rights treaties—they designed them to be weak and highly circumscribed (see Chapter 5).

Modest progress on monitoring continued in the 1970s. In response to the 1973 military coup in Chile, the United Nations created the Ad Hoc Working Group on the Situation of Human Rights in Chile. In 1976 the International Human Rights Covenants entered into force, leading to the creation of the **Human Rights Committee** (HRC), which is charged with monitoring implementation of the International Covenant on Civil and Political Rights.

Human rights were also explicitly and systematically introduced into the bilateral foreign policies of individual countries in the 1970s, beginning in the United States. Although practice fell short of rhetoric, these bilateral initiatives helped to open space for new ways of thinking about and acting on international human rights concerns, as we will see in some detail in Chapters 7 and 8.

The 1970s also saw substantial growth in the number and range of activities of human rights **nongovernmental organizations** (NGOs), private associations that engage in political activity. Such groups act as advocates for victims of human rights violations by publicizing violations and lobbying to alter the practices of states and international organizations. Best known is Amnesty International (AI), which received the Nobel Peace Prize in 1977 and has an international membership of more than seven million people. Chapter 9 briefly examines transnational human rights advocacy.

5. The 1980s: Further Growth and Institutionalization

Multilateral, bilateral, and transnational nongovernmental human rights activity continued to increase, more or less steadily, through the 1980s. New treaties were adopted on discrimination against women (1979), torture (1984), and the rights of the child (1989). In 1985, ECOSOC established an independent Committee on Economic, Social and Cultural Rights that, along with the Human Rights Committee (which oversees implementation of the ICCPR), began to review periodic reports submitted by states (see §5.3). The Commission on Human Rights undertook thematic initiatives on disappearances, torture, and summary or arbitrary executions and a larger and more diverse group of countries came under Commission scrutiny.

The process of incorporating human rights into bilateral foreign policy also accelerated in the 1980s. The Netherlands, Norway, and Canada developed particularly prominent international human rights policies (see §8.7). The European Community (predecessor of the European Union [EU]) introduced human rights concerns into its external relations. A few Third World countries, such as Costa Rica, also began to emphasize human rights in their foreign policies.

The 1980s also saw a dramatic decline in the fortunes of repressive dictatorships. Throughout Latin America, military regimes that had appeared unshakable in the 1970s crumbled in the 1980s. By 1990 elected governments held office in every continental country in the Western Hemisphere (although the democratic and human rights credentials of some, such as Paraguay, were extremely suspect). In addition, there were peaceful transfers of power after elections in several countries in 1989, including Argentina, Brazil, El Salvador, and Uruguay.

In Asia the personalist dictatorship of Ferdinand Marcos was overthrown in the Philippines in 1986. South Korea's military dictatorship was replaced by an elected government in 1988. Taiwan ended four decades of imposed single-party rule. In Pakistan Benazir Bhutto was elected president in December 1988, ending a dozen years of military rule. Asia, however, also presented the most dramatic human rights setback of the decade—the June 1989 massacre in Beijing's Tiananmen Square.

The changes with the greatest international impact, however, occurred in Central and Eastern Europe. Soviet-imposed regimes in East Germany and Czechoslovakia crumbled in the fall of 1989 in the face of peaceful mass protests. In Hungary and Poland, where liberalization had begun earlier in the decade, Communist Party dictatorships also peacefully withdrew from power. Even Romania and Bulgaria ousted their old communist governments (although their new governments included numerous former communists with tenuous democratic credentials). And in the USSR, where glasnost (openness) and perestroika (restructuring) had created the international political space for these changes, the Communist Party fell from power after the abortive military coup of August 1991. The Soviet Union itself was dissolved four months later.

6. The 1990s: Consolidating Progress and Acting Against Genocide

The 1990s was a decade of gradual, but generally positive, change in most regions—punctuated by striking examples of the most retrograde barbarism (see Chapter 10). In Latin America and Central and Eastern Europe, the progress of the 1980s was largely maintained. In many cases, such as El Salvador and Hungary, liberalization substantially deepened. In a few countries, such as the Czech Republic, Argentina, and Mexico, full democratization was achieved. In most of the former Soviet republics, however, the human rights situation remained—and remains—discouraging.

In sub-Saharan Africa, where one-party and no-party states remained the norm throughout the 1980s, political liberalization was widespread in the 1990s. Progress, however, was inconsistent and often not very deep. Nonetheless, the November 1991 electoral defeat of Kenneth Kaunda, Zambia's president for the first twenty-five years of its independence, was an important democratic first for the region. And the end of apartheid in South Africa, which held its first elections under the principle of universal suffrage in 1994, was a dramatic change indeed. More typical, though, was Nigeria, Africa's most populous country, where the military annulled the results of elections in 1992 and 1993 and General Sani Abacha exercised particularly harsh military rule over the country from 1993 until his death in 1998.

In Asia the picture in the 1990s was also mixed but generally positive. South Korea and Taiwan consolidated democratic, rights-protective regimes. Cambodia, with a substantial assist from the United Nations, cast off Vietnamese occupation and freely elected a government that was by far the most liberal it had seen in decades.

Tentative and partial liberalization occurred in Vietnam. Indonesia saw limited political reform with the expulsion of the Suharto regime in 1998. And India, for all its problems, remained the world's largest multiparty electoral democracy.

China, however, despite its substantial economic opening and political reform, remained a highly repressive, Stalinist-party state. Burma continued to repress its internal democracy movement and rebuff international pressure for liberalization. Afghanistan suffered under the theocratic brutality of Taliban rule from 1996 to 2001. North Korea consolidated its position as the world's most closed and politically backward state. And many Asian governments and elites began to argue that international human rights standards did not apply in their entirety in Asia.

Sadly, though, the mixed picture in Africa and Asia was far more encouraging than that in the Middle East. Hafez al-Assad, Saddam Hussein, and Mu'ammar Gadhafi sustained their personalist dictatorships in Syria, Iraq, and Libya, respectively. Religious intolerance and the suppression of all dissent remained the norm in Iran. The Gulf states remained closed and undemocratic. Increasingly violent Islamic fundamentalist movements led to growing repression in Egypt and plunged Algeria into a shockingly brutal civil war. About the only examples of substantial progress in the 1990s were modest liberalization in the monarchies of Jordan, Morocco, and Kuwait.

International action showed a similar pattern of solidifying past gains and modest progress in selected areas. Perhaps most striking was the decisive rebuff of arguments by China and other countries at the World Conference on Human Rights in Vienna in 1993 against the full implementation of internationally recognized human rights in the short and medium terms. The Vienna Declaration and Programme of Action constituted a bold restatement of the fundamental tenets of human rights as "universal, indivisible and interdependent and interrelated." The Programme of Action set an ambitious agenda for strengthening the human rights system at the United Nations. And it declared unequivocally that many widespread and overlooked injustices—most notably violence against women—constitute violations of human rights. The creation at the end of 1993 of a high commissioner for human rights proved to be an important step in expanding both the scope and the depth of multilateral monitoring (see §5.2). Such events, particularly when coupled with the changes in national practices already noted, signified a deepening penetration of the international consensus on human rights norms.

Human rights also became a more deeply entrenched and less controversial concern of bilateral foreign policy. National nongovernmental human rights organizations and advocates became a significant part of the political landscape in a growing number of countries in the Third World and former Soviet bloc. Transnational human rights NGOs also increased their prestige and influence.

In one area, however, the 1990s saw not incremental growth but unprecedented change, namely, the development of a practice of legitimate military **humanitarian intervention** against genocide (see Chapter 10). This was a dramatic reversal of Cold War–era (and earlier) practice.

Although the 1948 Genocide Convention established genocide as an international crime, the almost universal practice during the Cold War era was international inaction. In places such as Burundi, East Pakistan (Bangladesh), Guatemala, Cambodia, and Uganda, genocide (killing large numbers of people because of their race, religion, ethnicity, or culture, with the aim of exterminating the group) and politicide (mass killing for other political purposes) were met by verbal expressions of concern but little concrete action, except by neighboring states such as India, Vietnam, and Tanzania with strong selfish interests in intervening.

Even with the Cold War at an end, the international community failed to take effective steps to stop the violence that accompanied the disintegration of Yugoslavia in the early 1990s, which included genocide, war crimes, and crimes against humanity. And, in 1994, the international community was paralyzed when three-quarters of a million Rwandans—about one-seventh of the population of the entire country (the proportional equivalent of more than 45 million Americans today)—were massacred in a mere one hundred days.

These dramatic failures, however, galvanized new efforts. Ad hoc international tribunals for the former Yugoslavia and for Rwanda, created in 1991 and 1994, respectively, revived the Nuremberg precedent—or, perhaps more accurately, began a process that transformed Nuremberg from an isolated exception into a precedent. The adoption of the Rome Statute in 1998, which led to the creation of the International Criminal Court (ICC) in 2002, marks an even deeper normative transformation. And the interventions in Kosovo and East Timor in 1999 consolidated an international practice of humanitarian intervention against genocide (see §§10.4 and 10.6).

7. Human Rights in the Twenty-First Century

The human rights record of the first decade and a half of the twenty-first century has been decidedly mixed. In many countries, the human rights progress of the 1980s and 1990s was maintained or even extended. This has been especially striking in Latin America. In sub-Saharan Africa as well, steady if limited and often fitful progress has been most typical, although the Congo, Sudan, and Somalia continue to suffer under decades-long humanitarian crises, and new crises, have emerged in Mali, Nigeria, and the Central African Republic. Elsewhere, however, efforts to improve human rights conditions, such Georgia's 2004 Orange Revolution, Ukraine's 2005 Pink Revolution, and Iran's 2009 Green Revolution, either failed or were ultimately reversed. And although the Arab Spring popular uprisings of 2011 resulted in the removal of long-entrenched dictators in Tunisia, Egypt, and Libya, human rights conditions in these countries (and across the Arab world more generally) remain discouraging—and Syria has descended into barbarous war waged by the Assad government against the bulk of its population (see Problem 7 in Chapter 10).

The "global war on terror" initiated in the aftermath of the September 11, 2001, terrorist attacks against the United States led many to fear that human rights would once again be pushed into the background in international politics, as had occurred during the Cold War. As we will see in Chapter 12, though, the reality has been much more complex. In a few instances, rights-abusive regimes (e.g., Pakistan) have been able to parlay antiterrorism into protection from international human rights pressures. In many countries (e.g., the Philippines and Russia), antiterrorism has added to existing rights-abusive practices. In many liberal democracies, some human rights have been subjected to limited infringements. And U.S. abuses of (often illegally held) prisoners in Iraq, Afghanistan, and Guantánamo, as well as the kidnapping and international transport (extraordinary rendition) of suspects, have provoked widespread national and international criticism. But there has not been the same kind of systemic negative impact as was seen in the Cold War. International human rights policies in general seem about as robust as at the turn of the millennium, and, at worst, the war on terror has produced only a modest downturn in global respect for some civil and political rights.

Globalization poses a much more serious new challenge to human rights. States are the central mechanism for implementing and enforcing internationally recognized human rights. Even if the threat to states posed by globalization is exaggerated, the relative capabilities of states are declining, especially when it comes to being able to extract revenues to support social welfare programs that realize economic and social rights. No alternative source of provision, however, seems to be emerging to fill the resulting gap. Therefore, as we suggest in more detail in Chapter 11, global markets are likely to be a much greater threat to human rights in the coming decades than either terrorists or the war against them.

8. The Global Human Rights Regime

In the decades since the end of World War II, a normatively robust global human rights regime has developed. (An **international regime** is conventionally defined as a set of principles, norms, rules, and decision-making procedures that states and other international actors accept as authoritative within an issue area.) States, however, have largely retained for themselves the responsibility—and the sovereign right—to implement these rights in their own territories.

Of the hundred or more treaties that address human rights issues, broadly understood, seven are usually taken to provide the core of international human rights law: the two 1966 International Human Rights Covenants; the 1965 Convention on the Elimination of All Forms of Racial Discrimination; the 1979 Convention on the Elimination of All Forms of Discrimination Against Women; the 1984 Convention Against Torture and Other Cruel, Inhuman, or Degrading Treatment or Punishment; the 1989 Convention on the Rights of the Child; and the 2006 Convention on the Rights of Persons with Disabilities.[1] As of December 2016, these treaties had an average of 175 state parties,[2] that is, states that had ratified or acceded to the treaties and thus were bound by them in international law. This represents an astonishing 89 percent ratification rate. We have come a *very* long way from the early 1940s, when even genocide was not legally prohibited.[3]

This extensive and substantively admirable body of international human rights law, however, is not matched by comparably strong international implementation procedures. As we will see in more detail in Chapters 5 and 6, states have largely reserved for themselves the right to interpret the meaning of their international human rights obligations and to implement them in their own territories. International law, in other words, has established a system of *national implementation of international human rights*. International human rights norms have been fully internationalized.

Implementation of international human rights obligations, however, remains almost entirely national.

There is, of course, an immense amount of national and international human rights advocacy. States, international organizations, nongovernmental organizations, and private individuals promote human rights every day in every country of the world. Their efforts, however, are focused ultimately on states, which still hold not only the duty but also the right to implement human rights in their own territories.

The shortcomings of this system of national implementation of international human rights are obvious and will be discussed in some detail in later chapters. Here, though, we want to emphasize the independent contribution of international human rights norms. International human rights law has been so widely endorsed because its normative force is seemingly inescapable in the contemporary world. Even states like North Korea and Belarus, which have never given any serious attention to implementing internationally recognized human rights, are parties to at least some core human rights treaties. And even cynical endorsements of these norms are of real practical significance for national and international human rights advocates.

Without an internationally agreed-upon list of human rights, national human rights advocates would be subject to charges of political or cultural bias, inauthenticity, and even treason. But when repressive governments today level such charges at their critics, those critics can reply that all they are doing is advocating rights that the government itself has repeatedly endorsed, including by accepting binding international legal obligations. This decisively shifts the burden of persuasion from the advocates of human rights to the governments that are violating those rights. Of course, might regularly triumphs over right, especially in the short run. But national human rights advocates are supported by international human rights norms. This makes a real practical difference in all but the most closed and repressive countries. And in countries with even merely not-too-bad human rights records, these protections are of immense day-to-day value to advocates and activists.

Similarly, when transnational human rights NGOs, foreign states, and regional and international organizations raise concerns about a state's human rights record, those states cannot credibly respond that it is none of their business. *All* states in the contemporary world have accepted that human rights are a legitimate subject of international politics, much as they hate to have their shortcomings brought to the attention of national and international audiences. And all states have agreed that the Universal Declaration of Human Rights and the International Human Rights Covenants provide an authoritative set of international human rights norms. As we will explore in more detail in Chapter 10 on humanitarian intervention, there is a widespread consensus among states that, at the most basic level, sovereignty cannot be invoked as a shield against criticism for the most serious of human rights violations: sovereignty is *conditional* rather than *absolute*.

International human rights law has taken off the table debates over whether there really are human rights and what belongs on a list of human rights. The scarce resources of human rights advocates thus can be focused on the real work of implementing internationally recognized human rights.

For all its shortcomings, the body of international human rights law rooted in the Universal Declaration of Human Rights has both armed human rights advocates and disarmed their opponents, at least normatively. This fundamental redefinition of the terms of national and international political legitimacy is the principal legacy of the global human rights regime.

The plan of the book expands upon many of the themes and issues that we've touched upon in this historical overview. Chapters 2, 3, and 4 explore in some depth key and foundational philosophical and historical questions. Chapter 2 examines theories of human rights, including sources and justifications for human rights, obligations for respecting and protecting human rights, and the problem of human rights versus state sovereignty. Chapter 3 explores the universality of human rights, the idea that all human rights are held equally by all humans, everywhere. Chapter 4 looks at the indivisibility, interrelatedness, and interdependence of different categories of human rights, providing a different perspective on the universality of human rights.

Part 2 of the book explores how human rights goals are achieved through international institutions (at the global and regional levels, in Chapters 5 and 6), state actors (through their foreign policies, in Chapters 7 and 8), and transnational, nonstate actors (through research and advocacy work, in Chapter 9). These are the major actors in the global human rights regime.

Finally, Part 3 looks at three contemporary challenges for international human rights: humanitarian intervention against genocide and other crimes (Chapter 10), globalization (Chapter 11), and terrorism (Chapter 12).

Discussion Questions

1. What explains the changes in human rights norms and practices over time? Consider the following possibilities:
   - Changing moral sensibilities. Are our moral views all that different from those of other generations? If so, what does that suggest about the universality of human rights? Or is it that we now feel freer to act on these values? If so, why? What is the relationship between changes in ideas and changes in policy?
   - Changes in the character of international relations. Have peace and prosperity changed our views of human rights? Growing international interdependence? The end of the Cold War? Decolonization? And then what about post-9/11 changes?
   - Changes in national human rights practices. Or is it that we are now doing better at home and thus want to project that progress abroad? Are we still doing better at home after 9/11?
2. How deeply have these changing views toward international human rights penetrated? We often talk about international human rights, but action regularly falls far short of rhetoric. Why? Is it due to a lack of real interest? Constraints on our ability to achieve our objectives? Competing objectives?
3. What accounts for the weakness of international human rights enforcement? What would be required to overcome the existing impediments?

How costly—economically, politically, and in human terms—would this be? Would these costs be worthwhile? Do you think that change is likely in the next few years? The next few decades? What factors would lead you to expect continuity? What factors suggest change?

4. What kind of actor is best suited to pursue the protection and promotion of international human rights: individuals, NGOs, states, or intergovernmental organizations? How do your assessments vary with the nature of the target of action? What are the strengths and weaknesses of each type of human rights advocate?

Suggested Readings

There are a number of good introductory overviews of international human rights. The best, in our opinion, is David P. Forsythe, *Human Rights in International Relations,* 3rd ed. (Cambridge: Cambridge University Press, 2012). Those with a somewhat more theoretical inclination might prefer Michael Freeman, *Human Rights: An Interdisciplinary Approach,* 2nd ed. (Cambridge: Polity Press, 2011). Micheline Ishay, *The History of Human Rights* (Berkeley: University of California Press, 2008) and Paul Gordon Lauren, *The Evolution of International Human Rights: Visions Seen,* 3rd ed. (Philadelphia: University of Pennsylvania Press, 2011) are good places to start for those with a historical bent. Samuel Moyn's *Last Utopia: Human Rights in History* (Cambridge, MA: Harvard University Press, 2010), which became an almost instant classic when it was published, argues that the contemporary human rights era did not really begin until the 1970s. Philip Alston and Ryan Goodman, *International Human Rights—Texts and Materials* (Oxford: Oxford University Press, 2013), is a massive compendium of excerpts from a wide range of legal and nonlegal sources that, although directed principally at law students, contains much of interest to those with little or no interest in international law.

There are also several good general readers. Patrick Hayden, ed., *The Philosophy of Human Rights* (St. Paul, MN: Paragon House, 2001), includes a large and excellent selection of international documents, extensive excerpts from important historical and contemporary theorists, and excellent essays on a wide range of contemporary human rights issues. Even after fifteen years it remains a fine book and a great value. Micheline Ishay, ed., *The Human Rights Reader,* 2nd ed. (New York: Routledge, 2007); and Jon E. Lewis, ed., *A Documentary History of Human Rights: A Record of the Events, Documents, and Speeches That Shaped Our World* (New York: Carroll & Graf, 2003), are complementary volumes that together provide good coverage of history and theory.

David P. Forsythe, ed., *Encyclopedia of Human Rights* (New York: Oxford University Press, 2009), is *the* general reference work. Attention should also be drawn to *Human Rights Quarterly.* This interdisciplinary journal is generally considered to be the best scholarly journal in the field, but its articles are typically quite accessible to the average reader.

The websites of Amnesty International (http://www.amnesty.org), Human Rights Watch (http://www.hrw.org), Minority Rights Group (http://www.minorityrights

.org), and other NGOs have much useful current information on human rights situations in individual countries. The site of the Office of the High Commissioner for Human Rights (http://www.ohchr.org/english/) is a superb resource for international law and activities of the U.N. system.

On the Universal Declaration of Human Rights, Johannes Morsink, *The Universal Declaration of Human Rights: Origins, Drafting, and Intent* (Philadelphia: University of Pennsylvania Press, 1999), is the standard study, offering a theoretically informed history of the drafting of the Declaration and a thoughtful analysis of its content (although many readers will find the level of detail on drafting somewhat ponderous). Mary Ann Glendon, *A World Made New: Eleanor Roosevelt and the Universal Declaration of Human Rights* (New York: Random House, 2001), is excellent and immensely readable, although, as its title indicates, it is somewhat more limited in its scope. John P. Humphrey, *Human Rights and the United Nations: A Great Adventure* (Dobbs Ferry, NY: Transnational, 1984), is a memoir by the most senior human rights official in the early years of the United Nations Secretariat. On the role of the smaller states in the drafting process, see Susan Waltz, "Universalizing Human Rights: The Role of Small States in the Construction of the Universal Declaration of Human Rights," *Human Rights Quarterly* 23 (February 2001): 44–72; and Mary Ann Glendon, "The Forgotten Crucible: The Latin American Influence on the Universal Declaration of Human Rights Idea," *Harvard Human Rights Journal* 16 (2003): 27–39. For a detailed account of the drafting of the two Covenants, see Daniel J. Whelan, *Indivisible Human Rights: A History* (Philadelphia: University of Pennsylvania Press, 2010), Chapters 3–5.

For critical perspectives on international human rights that see the entire enterprise as, at best, seriously distorted by hegemonic American dominance, see two books and one edited collection by Tony Evans: *U.S. Hegemony and the Project of Universal Human Rights* (Houndmills, UK: Macmillan Press, 1996); *The Politics of Human Rights: A Global Perspective*, 2nd ed. (London: Pluto Press, 2005); and *Human Rights Fifty Years On: A Reappraisal* (Manchester, UK: Manchester University Press, 1998). See also David Chandler, ed., *Rethinking Human Rights: Critical Approaches to International Relations* (Houndmills, UK: Palgrave Macmillan, 2002). For recent reappraisals of the overall effectiveness and legitimacy of the global human rights project, see Emilie M. Hafner-Burton's *Making Human Rights a Reality* (Princeton, NJ: Princeton University Press, 2013); and Stephen Hopgood, *The Endtimes of Human Rights* (Ithaca, NY: Cornell University Press, 2015). Stephen Hopgood, Jack Snyder, and Leslie Vinjamuri, eds., *Human Rights Futures* (Cambridge: Cambridge University Press, 2017), is a wide-ranging survey of past achievements and future challenges. Alison Brysk and Michael Stohl, eds., *Expanding Human Rights: 21st Century Norms and Governance* (Cheltenham, UK: Edward Elgar, 2017), emphasizes the need to expand the range and focus on contemporary human rights advocacy, a theme that is also thoughtfully explored in Alison Brysk, *Human Rights and Private Wrongs: Constructing Global Civil Society* (New York: Routledge, 2005).

2

◄○►

Theories of Human Rights

The preceding chapter reviewed major developments in the international politics of human rights over the past several decades. This chapter examines three sets of theoretical issues. Sections 1–7 consider philosophical theories of human rights. Sections 8 and 9 address the place of human rights in international society. Section 10 considers political realism, which challenges the very idea of international human rights policies. The following two chapters extensively address the universality and indivisibility of human rights.

1. Rights in General

Right in English has two principal senses. We speak of something being right; that is, in accord with a standard of righteousness. What makes something "right" depends on what standard we are using. Something may be right in the sense that it is fair or equitable, although the outcomes may not be equal. For example, most of us think that it is right that the rich be taxed at a higher rate than the poor, who may, rightly, pay no taxes at all.

A decision or outcome may also be right because a particular procedure was followed properly. In such cases the standard of righteousness is procedural. And this procedural standard may or may not conflict with substantive standards (which themselves may also conflict). For example, is it right that one can lose the popular vote but still be elected (by the Electoral College) president of the United States? It depends on the standard of "right" being applied—in this case, democracy, or the intentionally nondemocratic Electoral College (in which Wyoming, with a population of 555,000, has three electoral votes and California, with a population of more than 38 million, has fifty-five electoral votes, giving the average Wyomingan four times the impact on the outcome of the election as the average Californian).

We also speak of some*one having a right* to something; that is, being *entitled* to that thing. These two senses often overlap. For example, that someone has a right to

21

something is itself a standard of righteousness that makes it right that she have it. Here, however, we will emphasize their divergences.

Not everything that *is* right is something to which anyone *has* a right. For example, it may be right (good, desirable) that everyone be loved. But no one has a right to be loved—and not just because some people are unlovable. Even the lovable have no right to be loved.

Conversely, many things to which people have rights are not right under every standard of righteousness. For example, it may be wrong—that is, not right—that some people have immense wealth while others can barely survive. But, assuming that they obtained their wealth legally, even the unjustly wealthy have a right to their property.

Rights create special relationships between people and to things. "A has a right to x with respect to B." This paradigmatic statement of a right indicates that a right-holder (A) stands in a special relationship to a duty-bearer (B) with respect to the object(s) of A's right (x). Conversely, with respect to x, B has special duties to A.

Theories of rights generally emphasize the entitlement of the right-holder or the special claims that arise from having a right. Both claims and entitlements, though, are linked by the fact that they specially empower right-holders.

If A has a right to x, she is *entitled* to x. It is not merely good, desirable, or right that she have x. X belongs to her, in a particular and special way. She suffers a special harm if denied x. It is not merely unjust (wrong). Her rights have been violated by depriving her of something to which she is entitled.

Having a right also makes available to the right-holder special claims and related practices that seek to guarantee her enjoyment of x. Rights claims ordinarily take prima facie priority over—meaning that they trump—other types of claims. And, when rights are violated, the remedial claims of right-holders also have a special force.

In fact, a principal purpose of rights is to take things out of the domain where decisions are appropriately based on calculations of what is right, good, desirable, or otherwise acceptable. Appeals to rights, as it were, (1) stop discussion, at least for the moment; (2) shift the burden of proof to those who would infringe on a right; and (3) raise that burden substantially. Only rarely, when something else of relatively great importance is at stake, is it right to override a right.

2. Human Rights in Particular

The term **human rights** indicates both their nature and their source: they are the *rights* that one has simply because one is *human*. They are held by all human beings, irrespective of any differences that human beings have—for example, age, race, ethnicity, gender, religion, or residence—and regardless of any other rights or duties they may (or may not) have as members of states, families, or any other public or private group.

If all human beings have human rights simply because they are human, then human rights are held equally by all.[1] One cannot renounce, lose, or forfeit one's humanity. Therefore, human rights are also inalienable. Even the cruelest torturer and the most debased victim are still human beings. Not all people are able to *enjoy* all their human rights, let alone enjoy them equally. Nonetheless, all human beings *have* the same human rights, which they hold equally and inalienably.

Human rights are a special type of rights. They are paramount moral rights. They are also rights recognized in international law. Most countries also recognize many of these rights in their national legal systems as well. The same thing—for example, food or protection against discrimination—thus is often guaranteed by several different types of rights.

We need *human* rights principally when they are not effectively guaranteed by national law and practice. If you can secure food (through markets) or equal treatment (through national legal processes), you are unlikely to claim these as human rights. You still *have* those human rights, but they are not likely to be *used* (as human rights). For example, in the United States both constitutional and statutory law prohibit racial discrimination. Discrimination based on sexual orientation, however, is not prohibited in most jurisdictions (even though the right of same-sex couples to marry has been recognized by the U.S. Supreme Court). Therefore, gay rights activists frequently claim a human right to nondiscrimination. Racial minorities, by contrast, usually claim legal and constitutional rights, or civil, rights.

Human rights is the language of victims and the dispossessed. Human rights claims usually seek to alter legal or political practices. Claims of human rights thus aim to be self-liquidating. To assert one's human rights is to attempt to change political practices (and ultimately political structures) so that it will no longer be necessary to claim those rights (as human rights). For example, the struggle against apartheid in South Africa was a struggle to change South African laws and practices so that nonwhite South Africans could turn to the legislature, courts, or bureaucracy should they be denied, for example, their human right to equal protection of the laws or political participation.

Human rights thus provide a moral standard of national political legitimacy. (The Universal Declaration of Human Rights thus describes itself, as we saw above, as "a common standard of achievement for all peoples and all nations.") They are also emerging as an international political standard of legitimacy. More precisely, regimes that grossly and systematically violate human rights are widely seen as compromising their full legitimacy.

3. The Source or Justification of Human Rights

One common way to classify rights is according to the mechanism by which they are created, which also typically sets the range of their operation. Legal rights, for example, arise from, and operate within the domain of, the law. Constitutional rights arise from the constitution. Human rights, following this paradigm, arise from humanity.

Philosophically, it is not at all clear how humanity gives rise to rights. Nonetheless, international human rights law is clear and insistent that human rights are grounded in our shared humanity, understood as a matter of inherent human dignity. The Universal Declaration of Human Rights refers to "the inherent dignity . . . of all members of the human family." The International Human Rights Covenants proclaim that "these rights derive from the inherent dignity of the human person." The Vienna Declaration, adopted at the conclusion of the 1993 World Conference on Human Rights, likewise claims that "all human rights derive from the dignity and worth inherent in the human person."

Whatever the philosophical problems with such claims, we will take them as given. This simply is how human rights are generally understood today. Humanity or inherent dignity is presented as a "natural" attribute of all human beings, a feature of our nature as human beings. (What we today call human rights were in the seventeenth, eighteenth, and nineteenth centuries usually called natural rights.)

The human nature that underlies human rights is sometimes explained in terms of (basic) human needs. But any list of needs that can plausibly claim to be empirically established provides an obviously inadequate list of rights: life, food, protection against cruel or inhuman treatment, and perhaps companionship. Science simply is incapable of providing the appropriate theory of human nature. (As we will see in §3.5, an anthropological approach that seeks to ground human rights on cross-cultural consensus faces similar problems.)

We have human rights not to what we need naturally as animals for survival but to what we need for a life of dignity. The human nature that is the source of human rights is a moral account of human possibility. It reflects what human beings might become, not what they "are" in some scientifically determinable sense or what they have been historically.

Human rights rest on an account of a life of dignity to which human beings are "by nature" suited. In particular, international human rights reflect a vision of human dignity situated in contemporary economic, political, and social circumstances. If the rights specified by the underlying theory of human nature are implemented and enforced, they should help to bring into being the envisioned type of person, who is worthy of such a life. The effective implementation of human rights thus resembles a self-fulfilling moral prophecy.

However we understand the source of human rights, though, in what follows we will simply assume that there are human rights. This theoretical evasion is justified by the fact that almost all states acknowledge the existence of human rights. It is further supported by an emerging international consensus, based on overlapping moral and religious theories, on human rights (see §3.3). The assumption that there are human rights thus is relatively unproblematic for our purposes here, namely, studying the international politics of human rights.

4. Equal Concern and Respect

We will also take the list of rights in the Universal Declaration and the Covenants (see Table 1.1) as given and unproblematic. The principal justification for this is practical: to act internationally based on a different list would risk the charge of imposing one's own preferences instead of supporting widely accepted international standards. This list, however, can also be derived from a plausible and attractive philosophical account, namely, the requirement that the state treat each person with equal concern and respect. Consider the Universal Declaration (the full text is in the appendix).

One must be recognized as a person (Article 6) to be treated with any sort of concern or respect. Personal rights to nationality and to recognition before the law, along with rights to life and to protection against slavery, torture, and other inhuman or degrading practices, can be seen as legal and political prerequisites to recognition and thus respect (Articles 3–5, 15). Rights to equal protection of the laws and protection against racial, sexual, and other forms of discrimination are essential to *equal* respect (Articles 1, 2, 7).

Equal respect for all persons, though, is likely to be at most a hollow formality without the freedom to choose and act on one's own ideas of the good life. Freedoms of speech, conscience, religion, and association, along with the right to privacy, guarantee a private sphere of personal autonomy (Articles 12, 18–20). The rights to education and to participate in the cultural life of the community provide a social dimension to personal autonomy (Articles 26, 27). The rights to vote and to freedom of speech, press, assembly, and association guarantee political autonomy (Articles 18–21).

Rights to food, health care, and social insurance (Article 25) make equal concern and respect a practical reality rather than a mere formal possibility. The right to work is a right to economic participation very similar to the right to political participation (Article 23). A (limited) right to property also may be justified in such terms (Article 17).

Finally, the special threat to personal security and equality posed by the modern state requires legal rights to constrain the state and its functionaries. These include rights to the presumption of innocence until proven guilty; due process; fair and public hearings before an independent tribunal; and protection from arbitrary arrest, detention, or exile (Articles 8–11). Anything less would allow the state to treat citizens with differential concern or respect.

The idea of equal concern and respect certainly is philosophically controversial. It does, however, have a certain inherent plausibility. It is closely related to the basic fact that human rights are equal and inalienable. And it offers an attractive extension of the claim that internationally recognized human rights "derive from the inherent dignity of the human person."

5. The Unity of Human Rights

The Universal Declaration, which presents itself as "a common standard of achievement for all peoples and all nations," understands the rights that it enumerates as indivisible parts of an organic whole. As the 1993 Vienna Declaration of the World Human Rights Conference puts it, "All human rights are universal, indivisible and interdependent and interrelated," and the goal of international human rights action is "universal respect for, and observance and protection of, all human rights and fundamental freedoms for all."

In the next two chapters, we will examine in some detail the ways in which we can think about the universality and indivisibility of human rights, in theory and practice. In general, though, the conclusion that all human rights are essential to a life of human dignity reflects the idea that we are complex and multifaceted creatures who live in complex and multifaceted economic, social, and political situations. We thus require access to a relatively wide range of goods, services, opportunities, and protections in order to live a life of dignity in the modern world. International human rights thus are regularly described as interdependent and indivisible.

Unless (nearly) *all* internationally recognized human rights are respected, a life of full dignity is unlikely to be a realistic possibility. For example, a person is denied a life of dignity if she has enough to eat but is prevented from freely exercising her religion or faith. From this standpoint, the unity of human rights begins with the unity of human experience and human dignity.

We can also, though, think of the interdependence or interrelatedness of rights functionally. As a practical matter, one is much less likely to be able to enjoy a right to x if one does not enjoy a right to y. For example, a person who has the right to vote or assemble probably cannot effectively exercise that right if her freedom of movement is severely restricted. A person's freedom to seek out and receive information is hindered if his right to education has been violated to the extent that he is illiterate. The rights of poor rural children to education are often undermined by the needs of their families for their labor.

There is also an essential unity or interdependence of rights and their correlative obligations. Having a right to x is undermined if the duty-bearer is undefined or if the content of the obligations required to effectively fulfill the right is also unclear or insecure. Long-standing controversies on this point often serve to stall the progress of our enjoyment of human rights, because the question of who are the real duty-bearers for the promotion and protection of human rights—especially for economic and social rights—is a matter of unsettled political debate and disagreement. It does not help that these disagreements are reflections of long-standing debates among philosophers about the nature of the state and the proper constitution of political authority.

For example, a few philosophers, and a substantial segment of conservatives in the United States, have expressed skepticism about whether economic and social rights (other than the right to property) are really rights at all. Such arguments usually reflect the idea that only rights that have correlative duties that are negative—that require only inaction that avoids directly infringing the right—ought to be recognized as universal human rights. And, it is argued, such negative rights—"freedom from" rights—are restricted to civil and political rights (plus the right to property). Conversely, economic and social rights are held to be positive rights that require (often extensive) actions and expenditures to discharge the obligations that they impose.

The implied moral distinction here, however, is problematic. Is there really much difference between intentionally killing someone and intentionally leaving him to die? But even if we accept the moral distinction, many civil and political rights are in fact positive rights, and in many instances duties of forbearance (that is, the state refraining from taking an action) are sufficient to realize some economic and social rights.

Consider the right to "a fair and public hearing by an independent and impartial tribunal" or the right to "periodic and genuine elections." Providing for courts and elections are very positive, and expensive, endeavors that require significant action by the state, not mere inaction. Even the right to freedom from torture requires extensive and costly training and monitoring of police and prison personnel. Similarly, the right to property can only be protected by an robust legal system that assigns, registers, and adjudicates disputes over property rights as well as a well-developed criminal justice system to protect those rights.[2]

Conversely, the right to housing imposes both negative and positive obligations on the state, such as an obligation not to evict people onto the street. The right to education obligates the state to refrain from preventing students from attending school. And, in some rural areas, the best way to protect the right to food is for the government not to encourage (or even permit) land used for subsistence agriculture to be turned to the production of cash crops.

There are, of course, differences between economic and social rights and civil and political rights (see §§4.3 and 4.4). But there are equally significant differences within each broad class of rights, and there are important similarities across these classes. For example, the (civil and political) right to life and the (economic and social) right to food can be seen as different means to protect the same value. Categorical substantive distinctions—even when they are not motivated by other considerations—simply do not withstand scrutiny.

Internationally recognized human rights represent a comprehensive vision of a set of goods, services, opportunities, and protections that are necessary in the contemporary world to provide the preconditions for a life of dignity. No *systematic* deviations from the list of internationally recognized human rights can be theoretically justified.

6. Duties and Duty-Bearers of Human Rights

Rights in general and human rights in particular, as we have seen, have correlative duties that typically are both positive and negative. Extending a distinction originally drawn by Henry Shue, we can distinguish four types of duties: not to deprive, to protect from deprivation, to provide effective enjoyment, and to aid the deprived.[3] We can also rephrase this in terms commonly used in discussions of internationally recognized human rights as obligations to *respect*, to *protect*, to *promote*, and to *fulfill* human rights. Of special relevance to us here, these different types of duties typically have been allocated to different actors.

Every individual and all social actors are obligated to respect the human rights of every human being, in the sense of not depriving them of the enjoyment of those rights. Human rights are not merely held universally (by all human beings) but also apply universally (to all actors).

Nonetheless, most actions by individuals that deny someone the enjoyment of her human rights are not ordinarily thought of or talked about as human rights violations. For example, if you are shot and killed by your neighbor, we do not say that she has violated your human right to life. We call it murder, an ordinary crime.

Human rights are largely concerned with the duties and obligations that fall on those *in organized society* that are likely to be responsible for violating a right. Although the state is probably the first such agent that comes to mind, others are often just as important: for example, parents and families, social groups and organizations (which could be economic, social, or political in nature), and employers.

The duty not to discriminate provides a striking example of the importance of private groups. For example, employers (with respect to the right to work), landlords and homeowners (with respect to the right to housing), and many other social groups (in their own special spheres of social action) typically *are* considered to be violating human rights by engaging in invidious discrimination against members of protected classes of people. And in some areas, such as housing and employment, private actors in the public sphere are most likely to be the principal violators and therefore typically have been made the primary duty-bearers of the obligation to *respect* the right to nondiscrimination in these areas.

States also typically have a central—although often not exclusive, and sometimes not even primary—duty to promote and to fulfill human rights (or to provide for and aid the deprived). In international human rights law, the state has an obligation to ensure, for example, that everyone is housed, fed, and employed (or, in the case of employment, compensated for unemployment) and has access to health care. But in most societies these rights are guaranteed by a combination of public and private provision in which families and markets play a central role. In fact, in most societies most people enjoy their right to work by participating in markets and their right to food through the mechanisms of markets and families.

Nonetheless, it is true that when we think of human rights obligations we do tend to think first of the state. And the state, in the contemporary world, is the principal duty-bearer when it comes to duties to *protect* human rights through legal recognition and enforcement of those rights in the territory that it governs. For example, the state has a special obligation to prohibit invidious discrimination in housing and employment and to provide legal redress for those who are discriminated against. In many cases in contemporary societies, the state is not only the principal but the exclusive actor with duties to protect.

The resulting systems of provision can be quite complex. Consider health care in the United States. Most children get their health care through their families, most of whom purchase it (indirectly by buying insurance) with their own money, often combined with a financial contribution made by their employer. There is thus a substantial element of what might be called self-provisioning. Most elderly people, however, get most of their health care from the government through Medicare. And many low-income children and working adults also receive health care from the government through Medicaid. The Affordable Care Act (ACA, or Obamacare), as was intended, brought millions more Americans into the private insurance market.[4] In this mixed system, the state's obligations to different groups are quite different: direct provision to retirees and the very poor and ensuring market access at affordable rates for everyone else (as well as regulating those markets by, for example, prohibiting discrimination and other practices that impede access to coverage).

Mixed systems of provisioning can be found in other areas of human rights concern, throughout the world. For example, in India, Israel, Singapore, and Taiwan, adult children have certain legal obligations to support their aged parents. Employer-provided housing has sometimes proved successful. Privately funded schools are an important part of the educational system of many countries. Churches and charities are a significant part of the welfare systems of some states.

Turning to civil and political rights, in most countries legal services are obtained both by purchase on the market and through the state. Police protection is often substantially augmented by private security firms. Much of the burden of protecting property lies with property owners.

Different states may choose different mixes of public and private provision for different rights and at different times. The state, however, has ultimate responsibility for the system of provision, based on its special duties to protect and provide internationally recognized human rights and to aid the deprived.

Finally, there is the question of whether duties and obligations for respecting, protecting, and promoting human rights exist beyond states themselves. For example, does an American clothing company have a duty to respect the labor-related rights of garment workers in Bangladesh, who are in effect working for a third or fourth party within a complex supply chain within that country? (And if it does have such a duty, to what extent is it a *human rights* duty and to what extent is it a matter of righteousness?) What duties and obligations do international organizations, such as the United Nations, have to ensure that human rights are respected, protected, or fulfilled? What about the international community as a whole?

7. Human Rights and Related Practices

Human rights, as we have seen, are a particular type of social practice, founded on a particular conception of human dignity, implemented by particular kinds of mechanisms. They must not be confused with other values and practices.

Not all good things are human rights. People do not have a right to many good things: for example, love, charity, respect, talent, and beauty. Many things to which we do have rights arise not from mere humanity but from our actions (e.g., contractual rights) or from particular relationships in which we stand (e.g., the rights of members of families or the rights of citizens). And many actors other than individual human beings hold rights (e.g., states, corporations, and clubs).

Human rights do not even provide a comprehensive account of social justice. Justice is particular as well as universal. And it is not entirely a matter of rights.

Human rights are the minimum set of goods, services, opportunities, and protections that are widely recognized today as essential prerequisites for a life of dignity. No more. And no less.

8. Sovereignty and International Society

We turn now from philosophy to a broad theoretical consideration of the place of human rights in international relations. The modern international system is often dated to 1648, when the Treaty of Westphalia ended the Thirty Years' War. As we saw in Chapter 1, though, human rights have been an issue in international relations for fewer than seventy years. The absence of human rights from the first three centuries of modern international relations was the direct result of an international order based on sovereign states.

To be sovereign is to be subject to no higher authority (except those that the sovereign has voluntarily acknowledged, for example, by ratifying an international treaty). In early modern Europe, sovereignty was a personal attribute of rulers. In many other times and places, as in medieval Europe, no (earthly) power was considered to be sovereign. In any one place, varied actors exercised different kinds of authority with respect to a variety of aspects of civic and religious life. At any one time, a person might consider multiple powers—the Pope, the Holy Roman Emperor, a prince, the local ecclesiastical authority, a local baron—to exercise authority in complex, often crosscutting, ways.

In contemporary international relations, however, sovereignty is an attribute of states.[5] International relations is structured around the legal premise that states initially have exclusive jurisdiction over their territories, their occupants and resources, and the events that take place there and that states have the right to pursue their own affairs in relations with other states. Practice regularly falls far short of precept, as usually is the case with legal and political principles. Nonetheless, the fundamental norms, rules, and practices of contemporary international relations rest on state sovereignty and the formal equality of (sovereign) states.

Nonintervention is the duty correlative to the right of sovereignty. Other states are obliged not to interfere with the *internal* actions of a sovereign state. Because human rights principally regulate the ways states treat their own citizens within their own territories, international human rights policies would seem to involve unjustifiable intervention.

A principal function of international law, however, is to overcome the *initial* presumption of sovereign authority. International law, including international human rights law, is largely the record of restrictions on the exercise of sovereignty that have been accepted by states.

A **treaty** is a contract between states to accept mutual obligations, that is, restrictions on their sovereignty. For example, a treaty of alliance may oblige a state to aid an ally that is attacked. Such a state is no longer (legally) free to choose whether to go to war. Through the treaty, it has voluntarily relinquished some freedom of action. The same is true of international human rights treaties.

A system of sovereign states is, literally, anarchic—without *arkhē* (rule) or an *arkhos* (ruler)—a political arena without formal hierarchical relations of authority and subordination. But **anarchy,** the absence of hierarchical political rule, does not necessarily imply chaos, the absence of order. In addition to international law, states regulate their interaction through institutionalized practices such as diplomacy, balance of power, and recognition of spheres of influence. Although there is no international government, there is rule-governed social order. International relations take place within an anarchical **society of states.**[6]

The international society of states during the eighteenth, nineteenth, and early twentieth centuries gave punctilious respect to the sovereign prerogative of each state to treat its own citizens as it saw fit. Today, however, as we have seen, there is a substantial body of international human rights law. States have become increasingly vocal in expressing, and sometimes even acting on, their international human rights concerns. In addition, human rights NGOs, which seek to constrain the freedom of action of rights-violating states, have become more numerous and more active.

This reflects (and has helped to create) a transformed understanding of the place of individuals in international relations. States have traditionally been the sole subjects of international law, the only actors with international legal standing (the right to bring actions in international tribunals). The rights and interests of individuals were traditionally protected in international law only by states acting on their behalf. The International Bill of Human Rights does not empower individuals (or even other states) to act against states. Contemporary international human rights law, however, has given individuals, or at least their rights, a place in international relations.

It has also introduced a new conception of international legitimacy. Traditionally, a government was considered legitimate if it exercised authority over its territory and accepted the international legal obligations that it and its predecessors had contracted. What it did at home was largely irrelevant. Today, human rights provide a standard of moral legitimacy that has been (very incompletely) incorporated into the rules of the international society of states.

Consider the almost universal negative reaction to the Tiananmen Square massacre in 1989, when Chinese troops fired on unarmed demonstrators and brutally crushed China's emerging democracy movement. China's diplomatic isolation reflected this new human rights–based understanding of legitimacy. However, that isolation lasted only a year or two. Even the strongest supporters of sanctions were not willing to allow Chinese brutality to interfere with long-term economic and security interests.

This tension is characteristic of the current state of international human rights. The future of international human rights activity can be seen as a struggle over balancing the competing claims of sovereignty and international human rights and the competing conceptions of legitimacy that they imply.

9. Three Models of International Human Rights

The universality of human rights fits uncomfortably with a political order structured around sovereign states. Universal moral rights seem better suited to a cosmopolitan conception of world politics, which sees individuals more as members of a global political community (cosmopolis) than as citizens of states. Instead of thinking of international relations (the relations between nation-states), a cosmopolitan thinks of a global political process in which individuals and other nonstate actors are important direct participants. We thus have three competing theoretical models of the place of human rights in international relations, each with its own conception of the character of the international community.

The traditional **statist** model sees human rights as principally a matter of sovereign national jurisdiction. Statists readily admit that human rights are no longer the exclusive preserve of states and that the state is no longer the sole significant international actor (if it ever was). They nonetheless insist that human rights remain *primarily* a matter of sovereign national jurisdiction and (ought to continue to be) a largely peripheral concern of international (interstate) relations. For statists, there is no significant independent international community, let alone an international body with the right to act on behalf of human rights. According to this view, we have an international system but not much of an international society.

A **cosmopolitan** model starts with individuals rather than states—which are often "the problem" for cosmopolitans. Cosmopolitans see the state challenged both from below, by individuals and NGOs, and from above, by the truly global community (not merely international organizations and other groupings of states). International action on behalf of human rights is relatively unproblematic in such a model. In fact, cosmopolitans largely reverse the burden of proof, requiring justification for nonintervention in the face of gross and persistent violations of human rights. International society, in other words, is seen as a global or world society.

The space toward the center of the continuum defined by statism and cosmopolitanism is occupied by what we can call **internationalist** models. The international community, in an internationalist model, is essentially the society of states (supplemented by NGOs and individuals, to the extent that they have been formally or informally incorporated into international political processes). International human rights activity is permissible only to the extent authorized by the norms of the society of states. These norms, however, may vary considerably across particular international societies. (Consider, for example, the difference noted earlier between the late nineteenth and late twentieth centuries.) Therefore, we need to distinguish between strong internationalism and weak internationalism, based on the distance from the statist end of the spectrum.

Each of these three models can be read as making descriptive claims about the place that human rights have in international relations or prescriptive claims about the place they ought to have. For example, a statist might argue (descriptively) that human rights are in fact peripheral in international relations or (prescriptively) that they ought to be peripheral, or both.

Cosmopolitanism, however, even in this era of globalization, has little descriptive power. States and their interests still dominate world politics. The international political power of individuals, NGOs, and other nonstate actors is real and growing, but it is still relatively small—and power is a relative notion. The global political community—world society as opposed to the international society of states—is at best rudimentary. The cosmopolitan model, if more than a prescription about what is desirable, predicts the direction of change in world politics.

If the world envisioned by cosmopolitans has yet to come into being, that envisioned by statists is at least in part a thing of the past. Although accurate even into the 1970s, the statist model of international human rights today is at best a crude and increasingly deceptive first approximation. Furthermore, it misleadingly directs attention away from decades of significant, cumulative changes that typically go under the label of globalization.

Some sort of internationalist model—or a very heavily hedged statism—provides the most accurate description of the place of human rights in contemporary international relations. (The chapters of Parts 2 and 3 provide extensive evidence to support this conclusion.) Current descriptive power, however, is no guarantee of future accuracy. And it does not mean that internationalism is the best, or even a good, way to treat human rights in international relations. Nonetheless, as later chapters show in some detail, the international human rights reality that we face today is one of considerable state sovereignty, with modest limits rooted principally in the international society of states.

10. The Realist Challenge to Human Rights

Before leaving the discussion of theory, we need to consider a common theoretical challenge to even this limited concern with international human rights, namely, political **realism,** or *realpolitik* (power politics). The realist view stands in contrast to liberal, institutionalist, constructivist, and many other theories of international relations, which posit that, even under anarchy, there are various, often quite effective, mechanisms that allow states to cooperate. Most of what we have described accords with a broadly liberal and constructivist conception of politics, which gives considerable emphasis to the formation of norms, law, and institutions in a great variety of areas in international relations, such as trade, finance, peace and security, economic and social development, and protecting the environment—and also, of course, international human rights norms and institutions.

Realists, in contrast, emphasize the fear and uncertainty bred of anarchy that lead to conflict between states. *Realpolitik* is an old and well-established theory of international relations, typically traced back to figures such as Niccolò Machiavelli in the early sixteenth century and Thucydides, whose *History* chronicles the great wars between Athens and Sparta in the final decades of the fifth century BCE. Realism stresses "the primacy in all political life of power and security." Because people regularly are egoistic and often evil and because international anarchy requires states to rely on their own resources even for defense, realists argue that "universal moral principles cannot be applied to the actions of states."[7] To pursue a moral foreign policy would not only be foolishly unsuccessful but also leave one's country vulnerable to the power of (other) self-interested states.

Realists argue that only considerations of the national interest should guide foreign policy. And the national interest, for the realist, must be defined in terms of power and security. For example, George Kennan, one of the architects of the postwar U.S. foreign policy of "containment" (of the Soviet Union) and one of the most respected post–World War II realist writers, argued that a government's "primary obligation is to the *interests* of the national society it represents . . . its military security, the integrity of its political life and the well-being of its people." He maintained, "The process of government . . . is a practical exercise and not a moral one." As for international human rights policies, "it is difficult to see any promise in an American policy which sets out to correct and improve the political habits of large parts of the world's population. Misgovernment . . . has been the common condition of most of mankind for centuries and millennia in the past. It is going to remain that condition for long into the future, no matter how valiantly Americans insist on tilting against the windmills."[8]

Such arguments do contain a kernel of truth. The demands of morality often do conflict with the national interest defined in terms of power. But *all* objectives of foreign policy, not just moral ones, may compete with the national interest thus defined. For example, arms races may contribute to the outbreak of war. Alliances may prove dangerously entangling. Realists, however, rightly refuse to conclude that we should eschew arms or allies. They should also abandon their categorical attacks on morality in foreign policy. A valuable caution against moralistic excess has been wildly exaggerated into a general principle of politics.

Realist arguments against morality in foreign policy also appeal to the special office of the statesman. For example, Herbert Butterfield argued that although a man may choose to sacrifice himself in the face of foreign invasion, he does not have a "right to offer the same sacrifice on behalf of all his fellow-citizens or to impose such self-abnegation on the rest of his society."[9] But nonmoral objectives as well may be pursued by statesmen with excessive zeal—and equally deadly consequences. In any case, most moral objectives can be pursued at a cost far less than national survival. This certainly is true of many international human rights goals.

In addition, there is no reason that a country cannot, if it wishes, include human rights or other moral concerns in its definition of the national interest. Security, independence, and prosperity may be necessities of national political life. Governments, however, need not limit themselves to these necessities. Even if the primary obligation of governments must be to the national interest defined in terms of power, this need not be their sole, or even ultimate, obligation.

Finally, using the anarchic structure of international relations as a rationale will not rescue realist amoralism. For example, Robert Art and Kenneth Waltz claimed that "states in anarchy cannot afford to be moral. The possibility of moral behavior rests upon the existence of an effective government that can deter and punish illegal actions."[10] But even if we set aside the confusion of morality and law, this logic is clearly faulty. Just as individuals may behave morally without government to enforce moral rules, so moral behavior is possible in international relations.

The costs of moral behavior are typically greater in an anarchic than a hierarchical system. Nonetheless, states often can act on moral concerns without harm, and sometimes with success. There may be good policy reasons to pursue amoral, or even immoral, policies *in particular instances*. There are, however, no good theoretical reasons for requiring amoral policies or even accepting them as the norm.

Problem 1: Democracy and Human Rights

The Problem

Americans typically describe their form of government as a democracy committed to protecting basic human rights (especially those rights specified in the Constitution). Across the globe as well, the terms *democracy* and *human rights* are often used somewhat interchangeably. The analysis offered in this chapter, which emphasizes the differences between human rights and other moral, legal, and social practices, challenges this understanding.

One standard conception of democracy is government of, by, and for the people. This fits with the etymology of the term, *dēmokratia*, the rule (*kratos*) of the people (*dēmos*). But the people can, and regularly do, choose to do some very nasty things to some segments of the national population, including systematically violating their human rights. Think about the history of legalized racism, sexism, and religious discrimination in the United States.

Human rights require that democratic governments, no less than other forms of government, respect human rights. They demand what we can call a rights-protective regime. And that often requires acting in opposition to the will of the people, even if this requires substantial governmental expenditures or challenges traditional practices or beliefs.

How should we resolve the conflicts between democracy and human rights?

A Solution

Human rights set the boundaries of democratic decision making. A rights-protective regime will be democratic both for instrumental reasons (other forms of government, such as theocracy, aristocracy, monarchy, and vanguard party dictatorship have all proved to be systematically incapable of providing sustained protection of human rights) and for intrinsic reasons (self-rule is an important part of the conception of human dignity underlying internationally recognized human rights). But democratic government is desirable only to the extent that the rule of the people realizes the rights of all citizens (and in particular guarantees every citizen equal concern and respect).

Political scientists often describe such governments as "liberal democracies." Democracy operates within the constraints of the liberties (human rights) of the citizenry, which provide the justification and standard of legitimacy for any government. (The language of *democratic rights-protective regime* is clearer and more accurate—*democracy* is the adjective, rather than the noun—but clumsy and unlikely to gain wide acceptance.)

Whatever the verbal formula, though, human rights trump democracy when they conflict. (In the American legal context, the more limited set of constitutional rights performs exactly this role.) Even when elections are free, fair, and open—and especially when they are not—"democratic" regimes may fall far short of the demands of human rights. (Freely) elected governments are, on average, better than unelected governments. But human rights demand that all governments provide all their citizens (and others under their jurisdictions) all the goods, services, opportunities, and protections required by internationally recognized human rights.

Further Problems

How should we respond to foreign governments that plausibly claim that their rights-abusive actions reflect the will of the people?

How should we respond to our own government when it plausibly argues that the will of the people justifies or even demands infringements of internationally recognized human rights? For example, as a result of the Republican victories in the free, fair, and open democratic elections for national office in 2016, we can expect Obamacare to be repealed. This presumably will return the United States to a system of nonmandatory health insurance, less government support to pay premiums, and no requirement of substantial employer subsidies, leaving many more millions of Americans without effective access to nonemergency health care. Is this a case where human rights (see Article 25 of the Universal Declaration) ought to take priority over democracy?

For the sake of argument, let us assume that the answer is yes. How, then, do we deal with the fact that there is no legal means to advance such human rights claims in the United States? Health care is not a constitutional right, so the courts do not provide a remedy in the absence of congressional legislation. Furthermore, the United States is not a party to the International Covenant on Economic, Social, and Cultural Rights, and, even if it were, it is not clear what effect (if any) that would have on American law. What are human rights advocates to do when a national legal system is fundamentally incompatible with international human rights obligations?

Now realize that the conflict between democracy and human rights is only one of many such fundamental conflicts. Human rights and the demands of development often conflict in the short run. How should we deal with that conflict? With the conflicts between human rights and broader conceptions of social justice? Human rights and environmental protection? Human rights and the precepts of religion? Does it matter if it is a majority or a minority religion?

Discussion Questions

1. We emphasize differences between rights and other sorts of moral principles and practices. Do we overemphasize the differences? What are the ways in which rights are similar to considerations of righteousness?
2. Should we prefer to protect human rights when doing so conflicts with social utility? Should the rights of the individual or the few take priority over the happiness of the many? (Try thinking about different rights in answering this question.) In particular, should *governments* act on any principle other than social utility?
3. We assume that some sort of justification of human rights is possible. But does it not matter *why* people believe that there are human rights? For what purposes might it matter?
4. Why are many Americans reluctant to consider economic and social rights as fully legitimate human rights? Are the reasons philosophical? Are they a reflection of the generally poor performance of the United States in ensuring these rights? How different are such arguments from those made by some developing countries that civil and political rights are luxuries that first require the fulfillment of economic, social, and cultural rights?
5. Is there a moral dimension to the positive-negative distinction? Is there really no difference between killing someone and failing to help someone who is dying? Does your answer differ when you move from personal behavior to the activities of governments?

7. Sovereignty issues have impeded the acceptance of international human rights policies. Is that really such a bad thing? Do you want other countries and international organizations inquiring into the human rights practices of your country? International anarchy has its obvious drawbacks, but do you *really* want a higher political authority telling your country how to behave?

8. Which of the three models of international human rights—statist, cosmopolitan, or internationalist—do you find most attractive (issues of their current descriptive accuracy notwithstanding)? Why? What are the greatest strengths of your preferred model? Why might others find it defective?

9. Even if realists overstate their case, don't they have a legitimate one? How often do states have the political space and resources to be successful in pursuing international human rights concerns? Have the end of the Cold War, globalization, or 9/11 made it harder or easier? (In answering this question, consider a range of different rights.)

10. How often do states use realism as an excuse for not doing what they know they ought to do but don't want to be bothered with? Imagine personal moral relations if realist arguments were allowed. Are the differences between interpersonal and international relations really so great that we can allow radically different standards to apply? Conversely, are the similarities so great that we can apply the same standards without major modifications across the two realms?

Suggested Readings

Steven Lukes, "Five Fables About Human Rights," in *On Human Rights,* edited by Stephen Shute and Susan Hurley (New York: Basic Books, 1993), https://stevenlukes.files.wordpress.com/2012/06/3-sl-five-fables-about-human-rights.pdf, 154–169, provides a brilliant brief discussion of the difference that having human rights makes. The chapters in Part 3 of Patrick Hayden, ed., *The Philosophy of Human Rights* (St. Paul, MN: Paragon House, 2001), are well worth consulting. We have found that students particularly enjoy Martha Nussbaum's 1997 *Fordham Law Review* article, "Capabilities and Human Rights," http://www.palermo.edu/Archivos_content/2015/derecho/pobreza_multidimensional/bibliografia/Sesion3_doc1.pdf, which argues for rooting human rights in a notion of human capabilities (rather than the broader and vaguer idea of human dignity). For an excellent book-length discussion that emphasizes the similarities between rights and other grounds of action (in contrast to our emphasis on the special features of rights), see James W. Nickel, *Making Sense of Human Rights: Philosophical Reflections on the Universal Declaration of Human Rights,* 2nd ed. (Berkeley: University of California Press, 2006).

A powerful but brief and readily accessible version of the realist argument against pursuing moral issues, including human rights, in foreign policy is presented in George F. Kennan, "Morality and Foreign Policy," *Foreign Affairs* 63 (Winter

1985–1986): 205–218. A rather more nuanced version of a similar argument is provided in Chapter 4 of Hedley Bull, *The Anarchical Society*, 3rd ed. (New York: Columbia University Press, 2002). For a counterargument, see Chapter 6 of Jack Donnelly, *Realism and International Relations* (Cambridge: Cambridge University Press, 2000).

Henry Shue's *Basic Rights: Subsistence, Affluence, and U.S. Foreign Policy*, 2nd ed. (Princeton, NJ: Princeton University Press, 1996), provides a subtle and powerful argument for the equal and overriding priority of rights to security, subsistence, and liberty; an extended discussion of the duties that flow from these rights; and a sensitive (if now rather dated) application of these theoretical ideas to U.S. foreign policy. A shorter version of the core of the argument is available in Shue's essay "Rights in the Light of Duties," in *Human Rights and U.S. Foreign Policy: Principles and Applications,* edited by Peter G. Brown and Douglas MacLean (Lexington, MA: Lexington Books, 1979), Chapter 5. For attacks on the idea of economic and social rights, see Maurice Cranston, "Are There Any Human Rights?" *Daedalus* 112 (Fall 1983): 1–18; and Hugo Adam Bedau, "Human Rights and Foreign Assistance Programs," in the Brown and MacLean reader. Sandra Fredman, *Human Rights Transformed: Positive Rights and Positive Duties* (Oxford: Oxford University Press, 2008), is an interesting discussion. Daniel J. Whelan and Jack Donnelly, "The West, Economic and Social Rights, and the Global Human Rights Regime: Setting the Record Straight," *Human Rights Quarterly* (2007): 908–949, provides a detailed empirical refutation of the often-encountered idea that the West resisted including economic and social rights in the Universal Declaration and the Covenants. Daniel J. Whelan, *Indivisible Human Rights: A History* (Philadelphia: University of Pennsylvania Press, 2010), traces the history of the ideas of interdependence and indivisibility in discussions in the United Nations.

3

The Relative Universality
of Human Rights

Human rights are understood today to be universal rights, held by every human being, everywhere in the world. The foundational international legal instrument is the *Universal* Declaration of Human Rights. The 1993 World Conference on Human Rights, in the first operative paragraph of the Vienna Declaration and Programme of Action, insisted that "the universal nature of these rights and freedoms is beyond question." The universality of human rights is a central theme in diplomatic, political, popular, and academic discussions alike.

But if by human rights we mean equal and inalienable rights that hold against the state and society and that all human beings have simply because they are human, then almost all societies throughout almost all of their history not merely have had no idea (let alone practice) of human rights, but, had it occurred to them, they would have rejected it. How can such historically particular ideas and practices reasonably purport to be universal? And how does this purported universality relate to the undeniable cultural, political, economic, and historical diversity of our contemporary world? The answer proposed here is that human rights are *relatively universal*, a notion that, although initially paradoxical, captures the essential universality *and* the essential particularity of internationally recognized human rights.

1. Universality and Relativity

Human rights are often presented as either universal or relative. In fact, though, they are both. And this duality is built into the very notion of universality.

The first definition of *universal* in the *Oxford English Dictionary* is "extending over, comprehending, or including the whole of something." *Universal*, in this sense, is "relative" to a particular class or group, the "something" that is encompassed.

Universal, in this most basic sense, means "applies across all of a particular domain." For example, universal health care, universal primary education, and universal suffrage involve making health care, primary education, and voting rights available to all citizens, nationals, or residents of a country—not everyone on the globe (let alone anywhere in the universe). A universal remote control neither controls all possible entertainment devices nor works everywhere in the universe—only in the movie *Independence Day* are alien spaceships designed so that a Mac can be effortlessly plugged into their command consoles—but controls only those devices that are standard for us here and now. Most American universal remotes won't even work in Europe.

There is a second sense of *universal:* "Of or pertaining to the universe in general or all things in it; existing or occurring everywhere or in all things." In this sense, though, little if anything in the empirical world is universal. Thus, the *Oxford English Dictionary* goes on immediately to indicate that this sense is "chiefly poetic or rhetorical," to which we might add "or philosophical or theological." Human rights are definitely *not* universal in this "occurring everywhere" sense.

They are, however, universal in at least three important "across a class" senses. We will call these international legal universality, overlapping consensus universality, and functional universality.

2. International Legal Universality

Human rights are universal in the sense that they have been accepted by almost all states as establishing obligations that are binding in international law. As we saw in Chapter 1, the seven core international human rights treaties—the two Covenants plus the conventions on racial discrimination, torture, and the rights of women, children, and the disabled—have, on average, an 89 percent ratification rate. In this important sense, we can say that despite all the cultural, political, regional, and economic diversity in the contemporary world, there is near-universal agreement on both the existence and the substance of internationally recognized human rights.

International legal universality, however, is bounded. Although states have agreed that they have obligations with respect to these rights, there are, as we will see in more detail in later chapters, no significant international enforcement mechanisms. International legal universality is a universality of possession. It does not entail universal implementation, enforcement, or enjoyment.

Furthermore, international legal universality depends on the contingent decisions of states, international organizations, transnational actors, and various national groups to treat the Universal Declaration and the Covenants as authoritative statements of internationally recognized human rights. International actors may in the future no longer give as much weight to, or even continue to accept, such principles. Today, however, the overwhelming evidence is that they have chosen, and are continuing to choose, human rights—making those rights, for us, today, effectively universal for the purposes of international law and politics.

3. Overlapping Consensus Universality

The second kind of universality, overlapping consensus universality, relies on a useful distinction drawn by the American political philosopher John Rawls. Rawls identified what he called comprehensive doctrines: overarching or foundational philosophical, religious, or ideological perspectives or worldviews. He distinguished these comprehensive doctrines from what he called political conceptions of justice: narrower, constitutional accounts of the basic elements of political legitimacy, specified largely without reference to specific comprehensive doctrines.

Proponents of very different, and even irreconcilable, comprehensive doctrines may reach an overlapping consensus on a political conception of justice. This consensus is only partial; it is overlapping, not complete. It is restricted to a political conception of justice. But it can be real and important.

Human rights can be readily grounded in a variety of moral theories. For example, they can be seen as encoded in natural law, called for by divine commandment, political means to further human good or utility, or institutions designed to produce virtuous citizens. Since the end of World War II, and especially over the past three decades, more and more proponents of more and more comprehensive doctrines from more and more regions of the globe have come to see in human rights a political expression of their deepest values. Christians, Muslims, Jews, Buddhists, Confucians, and atheists; Kantians, utilitarians, neo-Aristotelians, Marxists, social constructivists, and postmodernists; and many others as well—all for their own very different reasons—have come to participate in an overlapping consensus on the rights of the Universal Declaration.

We are quite familiar with this process within Western liberal democracies. For example, neo-**Thomists** and **utilitarians** disagree about just about everything at the level of foundational moral theory. Thomists do not even consider utilitarianism to be a moral theory. Nonetheless, today most Thomists and most utilitarians, despite their irreconcilable differences at the level of comprehensive doctrines, endorse human rights as a political conception of justice. And much the same process is occurring today globally.

The implication of this argument is that human rights have no *single* philosophical or religious foundation. Rather, they have *multiple* foundations. And this multiplicity of foundations is essential to human rights (as we understand them).

Human rights *are* a (Rawlsian) *political* conception of justice. Human rights are a category of political, legal, and social theory—not moral theory. Human rights are not a moral "primitive" or foundation, an irreducible core that defines in the most basic possible sense what is right and wrong. They are one level removed from such foundations.

This remove, however, strengthens, rather than weakens, human rights—as they actually function in the world. Multiple foundations make human rights much more strongly rooted. They provide a wide-ranging, complex, interlocking network of roots that supports and grounds international human rights far more effectively than any single taproot could.

Overlapping consensus universality, besides its intrinsic interest and importance, also helps to explain international legal universality. The striking extent of the formal international legal endorsement of human rights reflects the fact that adherents of most leading comprehensive doctrines across the globe do in fact endorse internationally recognized human rights.

Again, we must carefully specify the limits of this universality. Not all of the comprehensive doctrines that today endorse human rights have done so throughout all or even much of their history. Quite the contrary. Consider the West.

The Greeks distinguished between civilized Hellenes (Greeks) and barbarians and among Greeks made a variety of categorical moral and political distinctions based largely on birth and virtue—both of which were understood in deeply inegalitarian ways. The Romans may have had a somewhat wider conception of who was capable of being civilized. For legal and political purposes, however, a sharp line was drawn between civilized and barbarian peoples. And both class distinctions and slavery were central to Roman society.

During the medieval era, Europeans drew a comparable distinction between Christians and heathens, practiced slavery and serfdom, and regularly ranked men by their birth (noble or common) or their work (ruling and fighting, praying, or working to provide sustenance for the community). And, of course, *men* meant males. Everyone, in both the ancient and medieval worlds, knew that women of whatever status were not entitled to the same rights as men of similar status.

Therefore, if we date Western history to the Persian Wars, in the first half of the fifth century BCE, then the West, for its first two millennia, had neither the idea nor the practice of human rights (understood as equal and inalienable rights that all human beings have and may exercise against society and the state). And, as we will see below, we cannot find much of an idea of human rights—or even a real hint of the practice—in early modern Europe either.

Much the same is true of all the great non-Western civilizations and almost all but the simplest nonstate societies. The international overlapping consensus on human rights largely emerged after World War II. This does not make the contemporary consensus any less real or important. It does, however, point to its historical particularity.

4. Functional Universality

Overlapping consensus universality can itself be explained, in part, by global social changes over the past three centuries. These social changes provide the basis for the functional universality of human rights. Human rights represent a set of best practices to respond to certain standard threats to human dignity posed by modern markets and modern states.

Natural or human rights ideas first developed in the modern West. Early inklings are clear in Britain by the 1640s. A full-fledged natural rights theory is evident in John Locke's *Second Treatise of Government,* published in 1689 in support of Britain's so-called Glorious Revolution of 1688. The American and French Revolutions used these ideas as the basis for constructing new political orders.

The essential point, however, is the modernity, not the cultural "Westernness," of human rights ideas and practices. Nothing in classical or medieval culture made the

West unusually conducive to the development of human rights ideas. Quite the contrary, in the thirteenth and fourteenth centuries, parts of the Islamic world, perhaps most notably Fatimid Spain, provided a much more tolerant cultural and religious environment that would on its face seem to have been more conducive to the development of human rights ideas and practices. The Catholic Counter-Reformation and the intolerance of most ruling Protestant regimes in the sixteenth and seventeenth centuries suggest that early modern Europe was in many ways a particularly *un*supportive cultural milieu for developing human rights ideas. The late sixteenth and early seventeenth centuries, it is important to remember, were an era of violent, often brutal, internecine and international religious warfare. No widely endorsed reading of Christian scriptures before the mid-seventeenth century supported the idea of a broad set of equal and inalienable individual rights held by all men—or even all Christian men.

At the risk of gross oversimplification, we can see capitalist markets and absolutist states lying behind both the rise of human rights ideas and practices and the modernization of Western economies, societies, polities, and cultures. Ever more powerful (capitalist) markets and (sovereign, bureaucratic) states disrupted, destroyed, or radically transformed traditional communities and their systems of mutual support and obligation—with traumatic consequences. Rapidly expanding numbers of (relatively) separate families and individuals faced a growing range of increasingly unbuffered economic and political threats to their interests and quality of life. New kinds of what Henry Shue called "standard threats" to human dignity provoked a variety of remedial responses.[1] By the late seventeenth century, claims of natural rights began to become a preferred mechanism for securing new visions of human dignity in these new social, economic, and political conditions.

At roughly the same time, the Protestant Reformation disrupted the unity of Christian Europe, often quite violently. By the middle of the seventeenth century, however, states, due more to exhaustion than conviction, began to stop fighting over religion. (The Westphalia settlement of 1648 is conventionally presented as the start of modern international relations.) Although full religious equality remained very far off, limited religious toleration for selected Christian sects became the European norm and provided an important foundation for broader ideas of human rights. If individual choice was permitted on the most important of all issues, the salvation of one's immortal soul, why not allow it on issues of lesser magnitude as well?

Add to this the growing possibilities for physical and social mobility, and we have the crucible in which contemporary human rights ideas and practices were formed. Privileged ruling groups faced a growing barrage of demands from an ever-widening range of dispossessed groups—first for relief from particular legal and political disabilities and eventually for full inclusion on the basis of equality. Such demands took many forms, including appeals to scripture, church, morality, tradition, justice, natural law, order, social utility, and national strength. Claims of equal and inalienable natural/human rights, however, became increasingly common.

These processes of threat and response occurred first in modern Europe. Modern markets and states, however, have spread to all corners of the globe, bringing with them roughly the same threats to human dignity. This has created a functional universality for human rights. Human rights represent the most effective response yet devised by human ingenuity to a wide range of threats to human dignity that have become nearly universal across the globe.

Although it was no coincidence that the idea and practice of human rights developed first in early modern Europe, this was, if not an accident, then an effect rather than a cause. Westerners, as we have already noted, had no special preexisting cultural proclivity to human rights. Rather, they had the (good or bad) fortune to be the first to experience the indignities of modern markets and states. These new forms of suffering and injustice called forth new remedies. One increasingly popular and effective response was claims of equal and inalienable individual human rights. And nothing better has yet been devised.

Human rights remain the only proven effective mechanism for ensuring human dignity in societies dominated by markets and states. The near-universal spread of the idea of human rights is rooted in the fact that they represent the record of a process of social learning about protections needed as preconditions for a life of dignity in a world of modern markets and states.

Although this universality is rooted in a particular time and place—or, more precisely, in a particular kind of social structure—human rights are (relatively) universal for us, now. And by *us,* we mean virtually everyone on this planet. Almost all of us live in a world of modern markets and modern states, which need to be tamed by human rights if those powerful institutions are to be made compatible with a life of dignity for all men and women.

5. Anthropological or Historical Relativity

The preceding sections clearly show that human rights are *not* universal either historically or anthropologically. Although it is often claimed that most cultures and civilizations have long-standing indigenous ideas and practices of human rights, such arguments are entirely without empirical support. We have just seen that the idea and practice of human rights is historically relatively recent in the West. The same is true of other areas of the world.

As we saw in Chapter 2, rights—entitlements that ground claims with a special force—are one mechanism for realizing social and political values. Human rights—equal and inalienable entitlements held by all individuals that may be exercised against the state and society—are a very distinctive way to seek to realize social values such as justice and human flourishing. The literature on so-called non-Western conceptions of human rights regularly confuses values such as limited government or respect for personal dignity with the practice of equal and inalienable individual human rights to realize such values. For example, Dunstan Wai argues that traditional African beliefs and institutions "sustained the 'view that certain rights should be upheld against alleged necessities of state.'"[2] This confuses human rights with limited government. Government has been limited on a variety of grounds other than human rights, including divine commandment, tradition, legal rights, and extralegal checks such as a balance of power or the threat of popular revolt.

Similarly, Hung-Chao Tai, discussing traditional Chinese views, argued that "the concept of human rights concerns the relationship between the individual and the state; it involves the status, claims, and duties of the former in the jurisdiction of the latter. As such, it is a subject as old as politics."[3] Not all political relationships, however, are governed by, related to, or even consistent with human rights. What the state owes those it rules is indeed a perennial question of politics. Human rights provide one answer. Other answers include divine-right monarchy, the dictatorship of the proletariat, the principle of utility, aristocracy, theocracy, and democracy.

Much the same confusion is evident in the extensive literature claiming that "Islam has laid down some universal fundamental rights for humanity as a whole, which are to be observed and respected under all circumstances . . . fundamental rights for every man by virtue of his status as a human being."[4] For example, the scriptural passages that Khalid M. Ishaque argued establish a "right to protection of life" are in fact divine injunctions not to kill and to consider life inviolable.[5] The "right to justice" proves to be instead a duty of rulers to establish justice. The "right to freedom" is a duty not to enslave unjustly (not even a general duty not to enslave). "Economic rights" turn out to be duties to help to provide for the needy. And the purported "right to freedom of expression" is actually an obligation to speak the truth.

Even the claim that because "different civilizations or societies have different conceptions of human well-being . . . they have a different attitude toward human rights issues" is misleading.[6] Other societies may have (similar or different) attitudes toward issues that we consider today to be matters of human rights. But without a widely understood concept of human rights that is endorsed or advocated by some important segment of that society, it is hard to imagine that they could have *any* attitude toward human rights. And it is precisely the idea of equal and inalienable rights that one has simply because one is a human being that was missing in traditional Asian, African, Islamic, Latin American, and (as we saw above) Western societies.

Most arguments of anthropological universality are rooted in an admirable desire to show cultural sensitivity, respect, or tolerance. In fact, however, they impose an alien analytical framework that misunderstands and misrepresents the foundations and functioning of those societies.

Just to be clear, we are *not* claiming that Islam, Confucianism, or traditional African ideas cannot support internationally recognized human rights. Quite the contrary, as we saw in §3.3, they not only logically can but in practice increasingly do. The point here simply is that Islamic, Confucian, and African societies, *like Western societies,* did not endorse human rights ideas or practices until rather recently.

6. Cultural Relativism

We have already seen that human rights are historically relative to the modern era and that their foundations are relative to a number of comprehensive doctrines that participate in the contemporary overlapping consensus on internationally recognized human rights. Human rights, however, are *not* culturally relative in any strong sense of that term. Their justification is not based on any particular culture. Neither is their endorsement or practice tied to a particular culture or set of cultures.

In particular, as we saw above, there is nothing special about the West or Western culture that made it particularly suited for human rights. For example,

Christianity, well into the nineteenth century, was harnessed to support forms of social and political life that were deeply hierarchical and organized people according to divisions—of culture, religion, gender, race, and occupation—rather than drawing political attention to what bound all human beings (or even all Christian men). And although there have always been mass movements from below inspired by Christian ideas, such elements were effectively repressed in the name of Christianity throughout almost all of Christian history.

Nonetheless, when men and women faced new social conditions—when traditional hierarchies were destroyed and modern ones built—these Christian and other Western cultural resources increasingly came to be appropriated by new groups, in new ways, on behalf of the idea of universal human rights. Thus, today we are all familiar with biblical texts that point in a universalistic and egalitarian direction. And, just as modernity and human rights transformed Western culture, so the same transformation not only can take place but is taking place throughout the non-Western world.

If the medieval Christian world of crusades, serfdom, and hereditary aristocracy could become today's world of liberal and social democratic welfare states, then it is hard to imagine a place where a similar transformation would be impossible. For example, Gandhi took Hinduism—on its face perhaps the least likely comprehensive doctrine to support human rights, given its traditional emphasis on qualitative caste differences and its denial of the moral significance of the category of human being—and transformed it into a powerful force in support of human rights.

No culture or comprehensive doctrine is by nature either compatible or incompatible with human rights. It is a matter of what particular people and societies make of and do with their cultural resources. Cultures are immensely malleable, as are the political expressions of comprehensive doctrines. Most if not all cultures have in their past denied human rights, both in theory and in practice. But that stops none of them from today finding human rights to be a profound expression of their deepest cultural values.

Denying that human rights derive from or are defined by culture implies neither the irrelevance of culture to human rights nor cultural homogenization. Quite the contrary, an overlapping consensus approach emphasizes the importance of people using their own local cultural resources on behalf of their own human rights. The universality of human rights is fully compatible with a world of rich cultural diversity. Although the problems that human rights were designed to remedy are today universal—as is the now almost hegemonic global endorsement of human rights as the best remedy—people and peoples across the globe come to universal human rights by a great variety of paths. And a central purpose of human rights is to protect the right of different individuals, groups, and peoples to make those choices of paths.

7. Universal Rights, Not Identical Practices

Although culture is not particularly relevant to the *definition* of human rights, it may be central to their *reception*. Different places at different times will draw on different cultural resources to provide support for human rights. And the different cultural idioms within and by which human rights are justified and explicated are of immense local importance. Therefore, effective advocacy of human rights requires knowledge of and sensitivity to how human rights fit with local cultures—and histories, and economies, and ecologies, and social structures.

Culture is also important to the details of implementation. We can think of three levels of universality and relativity.[7] Human rights are relatively universal at the level of the *concept*, the broad formulations characteristic of the Universal Declaration such as the claims in Articles 3 and 22 that everyone has "the right to life, liberty and security of person" and "the right to social security." Particular rights concepts, however, usually have different defensible *conceptions* (more detailed specifications of the overarching concept), introducing a very real element of relativity among universal human rights. Furthermore, any particular conception is likely to have many defensible *implementations*. At this level—for example, the design of electoral systems to realize the claim in Article 21 of the Universal Declaration that "everyone has the right to take part in the government of his country, directly or through freely chosen representatives"—the range of legitimate variation and relativity is substantial.

Functional and overlapping consensus universalities lie primarily at the level of human rights concepts; the arguments that support these kinds of universality usually operate at a high level of abstraction that rarely reaches very far into the level of conceptions, let alone implementations. The resulting, quite substantial, range of legitimate variability means that universal human rights do not require identical human rights practices. In fact, substantial second- and third-level variations, by country, region, or other grouping, are fully compatible with the relative universality of internationally recognized human rights.

Striking legitimate variations exist even within regions. For example, conceptions and implementations of many economic and social rights differ dramatically between the United States and the countries of Western Europe. Important variations exist even within Europe. For example, Robert Goodin and his colleagues demonstrated important systematic differences between the welfare states of Germany and the Netherlands.[8]

Even here, though, we should be careful not to overstate the significance of culture, which is not the only, or even obviously the most important, source of diversity in justifications and implementations of human rights. There are often immense philosophical and religious differences *within* a culture that are absolutely central to how human rights are understood and practiced. And historical, political, economic, and simply accidental factors are no less important than culture in explaining the different ways that societies implement human rights.

8. Universalism Without Imperialism

The universality of internationally recognized human rights clearly does not encourage, let alone require, global homogenization or the sacrifice of valued local practices. Quite the contrary, (relatively) universal human rights protect people from imposed conceptions of the good life, whether those visions are imposed by local or foreign actors.

The underlying purpose of human rights is to allow human beings, individually and in groups that give meaning and value to their lives, to pursue their own vision of the good life. Such choices deserve our respect as long as they (1) are consistent with comparable rights for others and (2) reflect a plausible vision of human flourishing to which we can imagine a free people freely assenting. Understanding human rights as a political conception of justice supported by an overlapping consensus *requires* us to allow human beings, individually and collectively, considerable space to shape (relatively) universal rights to their particular purposes—within the constraints at the level of the concept established by functional, international legal, and overlapping consensus universalities.

The legacy of imperialism does demand that Westerners in particular show special caution and sensitivity when advancing arguments of universalism in the face of clashing cultural values. Caution, however, must not be confused with inaction. Even if we are not entitled to impose our values on others, they are our values. They may demand that we act on them even in the absence of agreement by others, especially when that action does not involve force. If the practices of others are particularly objectionable, even strongly sanctioned traditions may deserve neither our respect nor our toleration. (Remember that slavery and sexism have been central parts of all the world's great civilizations throughout most of their histories.)

Such concerns are especially relevant to American foreign policy, which has often (and not unreasonably) been accused of confusing American interests with universal values. Even if there is no longer an American consensus that "what's good for GM is good for America," it does appear that most Americans today subscribe to the view that what's good for the United States is good for the world.

The proper solution to the false universalism of a powerful actor mistaking its own interests for universal values, however, is not **relativism** but *relative* **universalism.** Without authoritative international standards, what is there to hold the United States (or any other power) accountable to? If international legal universality has no force, it is hard to find a ground for saying that human rights are not whatever the United States says they are. This is especially true in international relations, where normative disputes that cannot be resolved by rational persuasion tend to end up being resolved by political, economic, and cultural power—of which the United States today has more than anyone else.

Consensus is no philosophical guarantee of truth. Nonetheless, insisting that the universality of internationally recognized human rights lies in significant measure in international legal and overlapping consensus provides important protection against the arrogant universalism of the powerful. The relative universality of human rights can be a significant resource for calling the powerful, including the United States, to account—especially because the principal problem with American foreign policy is not where it does raise human rights concerns but where it does not, or where it allows them to be subordinated to other concerns.

Universal human rights are hardly a panacea for the world's problems. They do, however, fully deserve the prominence they have received in recent years. The world is a better place than it would have been without the spread of universal human rights ideas and practices. And, for the foreseeable future, universal human rights are likely to remain a vital resource in national, international, and transnational struggles for social justice and human dignity.

9. The Relative Universality of Human Rights

Are human rights universal? Yes and no; it depends on the sense of *universal*. Are human rights relative? Yes and no; it depends on the sense of *relative*.

Sometimes the relativity of particular human rights practices and justifications deserves emphasis. Other times, the universality of internationally recognized human rights deserves emphasis. But both relativity and universality are essential to international human rights. There is danger both in treating the universal as if it were relative and in falsely universalizing contingent practices.

Human rights empower free people to build for themselves lives of dignity, value, and meaning. To build such lives anywhere in the contemporary world requires internationally recognized universal human rights. But one of the central purposes of universal human rights is to protect the free decisions of free people to justify and implement those rights in ways rooted in their own histories and experiences.

It is an empirical, not a logical, matter whether the legitimate demands of universality and relativity conflict or coordinate. Perhaps the most striking fact about the universality of human rights in the contemporary world, however, is how infrequently there is a truly fundamental conflict. And when there is indeed a real conflict, it is almost always restricted to a particular right or even just one part of an internationally recognized human right.

For example, one of us (Donnelly) has for more than three decades lectured overseas on issues of human rights and **cultural relativism.** He has often asked audiences to name the rights in the Universal Declaration that their society, culture, or religion rejects. Never has an audience objected to more than parts of two or three rights. For example, many Muslims reject the provision of Article 18 that allows anyone to change their religion. (Islam is ordinarily interpreted to prohibit Muslims from renouncing their faith.) But this is only one relatively small part of the internationally recognized right to freedom of religion, a right that Muslims strongly endorse. Another commonly encountered example involves some of the details of Article 16, which deals with family rights. But, again, the basic right to marry and found a family is always strongly endorsed by those who challenge details of the conception elaborated in the Universal Declaration.[9]

It is common to talk about universality and relativity as the end points of a continuum. We think, though, that a multidimensional conception of universality and relativity is both more accurate and more conducive to constructive dialogue. For example, international legal, overlapping consensus, and functional universalities are probably better seen not as parts of a single entity called "universality" but as qualitatively different dimensions of the universality of internationally recognized human rights. This formulation encourages us to appreciate the multiple forms that both universality and relativity take—and the fact that, in different contexts, different dimensions of both appropriately come to the fore.

However we conceptualize it, though, the universality of human rights is relative to the contemporary world. The particularities of implementation are relative to history, politics, and contingent decisions. But at the level of the concept, as specified in the Universal Declaration, human rights are universal. The formulation *relatively universal* is thus apt. Relativity modifies—operates within the boundaries set by—the universality of the body of interdependent and indivisible internationally recognized human rights.

Problem 2: Hate Speech

The Problem

Article 4(a) of the racial discrimination convention requires parties not just to prohibit violence and incitement to violence but also to "declare an offence punishable by law all dissemination of ideas based on racial superiority or hatred." This provision has been rejected by the United States, where the view that freedom of speech includes even "hate speech" is deeply embedded in constitutional history and jurisprudence. How should Americans respond to this conflict? What is the appropriate response for outsiders?

A Solution

Dealing with cases of conflicts between internationally recognized human rights can be facilitated by some general principles. In addition to the distinction among concepts, conceptions, and implementations introduced above, we suggest the following.

1. Important differences in the character of the threats being faced are likely to justify variations. For example, countries with a recent history of violent ethnic conflict might reasonably choose to deal with issues of discrimination in general, and hate speech in particular, differently than do countries with different histories.
2. Variations that appeal to important principles or precepts in underlying comprehensive doctrines involved in the overlapping consensus deserve special consideration. The case of apostasy in Muslim countries, mentioned above, may fall under this principle.
3. Arguments claiming that a particular conception or implementation is, for cultural or historical reasons, deeply embedded within or of unusually great significance to some significant group in society deserve, on their face, sympathetic consideration (but cannot be treated as decisive).
4. Variations from international standards are likely to be more acceptable the lower the level of legal and political coercion used to support them

(which suggests both a greater degree of popular support, or at least acquiescence, and relatively limited damage to those who suffer as a result of these practices).

How do these criteria apply to the case of hate speech in the United States? The first two are not particularly relevant, but the last two do seem to imply some toleration for this American peculiarity. Free speech has an especially important place historically among human and constitutional rights in the United States. And there is a long legal history of allowing even hate speech (or what used to be called "fighting words"), so long as it is restricted to speech that does not incite violence. Furthermore, even targets of hate speech are legally protected against not only violence but also incitement to violence. Many local and state jurisdictions have even increased the penalties for hate crimes. Hate *speech,* in other words, has been very narrowly understood and has been protected only so long as it remains unconnected to other criminal activity. And part of the underlying justification for the American practice is that prohibiting speech because of its content harms those whose speech is prohibited and in effect involves state support for particular viewpoints.

It thus seems relatively unproblematic for Americans to support this particular deviation from international human rights norms—especially because in ratifying the racial discrimination convention, the United States, as was its legal right, explicitly included a reservation that it would not be bound by this provision.

What about foreigners? Although they ought to have some appreciation for American arguments, there is no compelling reason for them to accept those arguments. Verbal pressure to criminalize hate speech is entirely appropriate. And those with a particular concern for the suffering it creates or an especially strong commitment to the general cause of international human rights standards may rightly feel compelled to draw critical attention to this internationally deviant American practice and to press for its change.

Further Problems

Suppose that we are talking about hate speech in, say, Rwanda or Bosnia, barely two decades after genocide. Or in Singapore, half a century after racial violence against Chinese helped to lead to its independence from Malaysia. These societies do in fact prohibit hate speech. But what if they were to move to allow it?

This example points to a very general problem, namely, different human rights regularly conflict with one another. (It also suggests that one of the ways in which societies differ is in how they handle such conflicts.)

What are some of the more prominent examples of conflicting human rights that you are familiar with? What are the implications of such regular and important conflicts for our understanding of the universality and relativity of human rights? Do such conflicts, when combined with the forms of relativity already noted above, leave much *as a practical matter* to the universality of human rights? Be careful to consider different types of countries in thinking about your answer.

Problem 3: Discrimination Based on
Sexual Orientation

The Problem

Many countries have in recent years taken more or less strenuous efforts to rem-edy discrimination based on sexual orientation or gender identity. In fact, LGBT (lesbian, gay, bisexual, and transgender) rights have been a major focus of human rights activism in most Western and many non-Western countries. But gender and sexual minorities are not explicitly protected in international human rights law. And many countries are strongly opposed to prohibiting discrimination against them. How should international human rights advocates respond given the silence of inter-national human rights law?

A Solution

Established nondiscrimination norms provide a strong prima facie case for interna-tional action on behalf of LGBT rights. Article 2 of the Universal Declaration reads, "Everyone is entitled to all the rights and freedoms set forth in this Declaration, without distinction of any kind, such as race, colour, sex, language, religion, political or other opinion, national or social origin, property, birth or other status." The lan-guage clearly says *everyone* is entitled to *all* human rights *without distinction of any kind.* And particular articles typically begin "Everyone is entitled . . . ," "Everyone has the right . . . ," or "No one shall be. . . . " *Everyone,* it would seem, would include those with a minority gender identity.

But "without distinction of any kind" does not really mean what it seems to say. For example, children and the mentally incompetent are, appropriately, excluded from the exercise of many rights. Those incarcerated for crimes are not permitted full liberty of person (as guaranteed in Article 3). In many countries, those who have not registered to vote may not exercise the right to participate in government through elected representatives (Article 21). And in many countries certain felons do not have equal access to public service (Article 21).

Furthermore, the phrase "such as race . . . " has typically been taken as some-thing like an authoritative list of impermissible grounds. More precisely, it is widely held that all countries are required to specify only these grounds as impermissible, although they are, of course, free to add additional grounds.

In addition, had the drafters of the Declaration (and the Covenants) been asked, they almost certainly would have said that sexual orientation was *not* an impermis-sible grounds for discrimination—and certainly the governments who voted for the Universal Declaration would have agreed. For example, when Article 16 states, "Men and women of full age, without any limitation due to race, nationality or religion, have the right to marry and to found a family," it was unquestionably assumed that this meant that men could marry women, and vice versa. Period.

Finally, we must consider the importance of consensus in the development of international human rights law. In the 1940s, 1950s, and 1960s there was a clear and strong international consensus that discrimination based on sexual orientation was permissible. Such a consensus has collapsed over the past two decades. But there is nothing even close to a consensus on positive protections for gender or sexual minorities. Therefore, advocacy for LGBT rights is *not* advocacy for *internationally recognized* human rights.

This does not mean that *all* advocacy for protections for sexual minorities is problematic from the perspective of international human rights law. In many countries, LGBT people are subjected to private violence that is not prosecuted by the authorities, who sometimes even condone it. Such treatment is a clear violation of basic internationally recognized human rights. The Human Rights Council (see §5.1) recognized that violence against people on the basis of their sexual orientation or gender identity was a grave concern and in 2011 commissioned a study on the problem. Denial of rights to vote, education, health care, or social security simply because one has a minority gender identity is similarly prohibited by international human rights law. Even accepting that homosexuality is a moral abomination, people cannot be denied the enjoyment of their human rights for private moral behavior.

Where to draw the line between permissible and impermissible discrimination will be a matter of considerable controversy. But the criminalization of consenting same-sex sexual activity is clearly *not* prohibited by international human rights law. And this is a powerful wedge that could be used to justify further discrimination—although homophobic governments rarely bother to prosecute offenders (except for political purposes), and thus justifiable discrimination against convicted felons is actually more a theoretical than a practical problem.

Furthermore, there is no reason that advocates of LGBT rights—individuals, NGOs, states, and even regional organizations—should not campaign on their behalf. But they should be careful to differentiate these activities from the defense of internationally recognized human rights.

Consider the most recent effort at the Human Rights Council to move more deeply into this area. Based on reporting on the situation of violence against LGBT people by the secretary-general, the Council debated a draft resolution that would have appointed an independent expert (see §5.6) to continue this work. But there was significant backlash from several conservative states around the world. The vote was 23 (yes) to 18 (no) with six abstentions.[10] The independent expert was appointed—but this is hardly consensus. And the move almost failed entirely. What kept the six abstainers from voting no were a series of amendments to the resolution, which repeated, in particular, the importance of respecting "regional, cultural and religious value systems on matters associated with historical, cultural, social and religious sensitivities." Perhaps more importantly, the resolution "deplores" the use of external pressure and coercion to influence what are essentially domestic matters and "is concerned" with attempts to "undermine the international human rights system" by "imposing concepts . . . that fall outside of the internationally agreed human rights legal framework." Although these are in principle legitimate concerns, and perhaps even legitimate grounds for opposing the development of new norms, suspicions that they are merely a pretext for protecting already prohibited discrimination and human rights violations also seem legitimate.[11]

We are far from comfortable with this "solution." But if we take seriously the commitment to international human rights law *as it is,* there seems to be no alternative. And we must remind ourselves of the larger context. Were we to open up the possibility of deviations from international standards, there will be a flood of demands for reducing existing protections—demands that advocates will be in a significantly weaker position to resist.

Further Problems

Can human rights advocates really allow systematic discrimination and suffering to be consistent with international human rights norms simply because a half century ago most people denied the full humanity of a particular group?

How are LGBT people different from disabled persons, who obtained their own convention? They, however, obtained their convention through the process of international consensus creation. What should LGBT people and others concerned with their plight do while they wait for international consensus?

Given all of these questions, do we really have a *human rights* issue here for which international human rights law provides no adequate solution? Just how authoritative should we take the list of human rights accepted in international human rights law? What are the benefits and risks of talking of human rights that are not internationally recognized?

Discussion Questions

1. Make a list of all the arguments you can think of that can be made for cultural relativism. Which of these actually involve *cultural* factors? And which involve political, economic, or ideological factors? Are arguments of political relativism as persuasive as arguments of cultural relativism? Why? What about economic relativism? Is the distinction among culture, politics, and economics helpful or revealing? Why?

2. *Are* human rights ideas truly universal today? Are the differences between contemporary cultures and countries really primarily concerned with secondary or peripheral human rights issues? Do recent changes in international relations have anything to tell us about the universality of human rights? Consider, for example, the fall of the communist bloc and democratization in much of the Third World. Then consider Islamic fundamentalism and the rise of nationalist ethnic hostilities.

3. Why do so many people, in the West and non-West alike, insist that their cultures have had human rights ideas and practices at times when they clearly have not? How much of this can be attributed to the notion that the legitimacy of cultures is somehow dependent on their conformity with "modern" Western ideas?

4. Is consensus morally important? Politically important? If so, why?

5. What are some of the principal threats to human dignity that are *not* connected with markets and states? How important is their absence from the list of internationally recognized human rights? If they are very

significant, how much does this undermine the claim for even the relative universality of human rights?

6. Just how malleable is culture? Even if it is immensely malleable across extended periods, is it relatively static over a few decades? Is that not the time frame of politics?

7. Should the United States be held to the same standards as everyone else? If not, how can Americans justify holding others to human rights standards?

Suggested Readings

The literature on human rights and cultural relativism is immense. Excellent short overviews can be found in Ann-Belinda S. Preis, "Human Rights as Cultural Practice: An Anthropological Critique," *Human Rights Quarterly* 18 (May 1996): 286–315; Andrew J. Nathan, "Universalism: A Particularistic Account," in *Negotiating Culture and Human Rights,* edited by Lynda Bell, Andrew J. Nathan, and Ilan Peleg (New York: Columbia University Press, 2001), 349–368; Abdullahi A. An-Na'im, "Towards a Cross-Cultural Approach to Defining International Human Rights Standards," in *Human Rights in Cross-Cultural Perspectives,* edited by Abdullahi A. An-Na'im (Philadelphia: University of Pennsylvania Press, 1992), 19–43; and Onuma Yasuaki, "Toward an Intercivilizational Approach to Human Rights," in *The East Asian Challenge for Human Rights,* edited by Joanne Bauer and Daniel Bell (Cambridge: Cambridge University Press, 1999), 103–123. See also Bhikhu Parekh, "Non-ethnocentric Universalism," in *Human Rights in Global Politics,* edited by Tim Dunne and Nicholas J. Wheeler (Cambridge: Cambridge University Press, 1999), 128–159.

Two superb books that treat the complexities of rights and related ideas in Chinese philosophy and political practice are Stephen C. Angle, *Human Rights and Chinese Thought: A Cross-Cultural Inquiry* (Cambridge: Cambridge University Press, 2002); and Marina Svensson, *Debating Human Rights in China* (Lanham, MD: Rowman and Littlefield, 2003). Both are extremely sympathetic to the similarities and the differences between Chinese and Western ideas and their significant changes over time. Even for readers with no special interest in China, these books are well worth reading. They offer careful and detailed understandings of complex issues that are far too often handled in glib generalities. Ann Elizabeth Mayer, *Islam and Human Rights: Tradition and Politics,* 5th ed. (Boulder, CO: Westview Press, 2013), does much the same for the Islamic world.

Classic statements of a rather radical relativism are Adamantia Pollis and Peter Schwab, "Human Rights: A Western Construct with Limited Applicability," in *Human Rights: Cultural and Ideological Perspectives,* edited by Adamantia Pollis and Peter Schwab (New York: Praeger, 1979), 1–19; and Alison Dundes Rentlen, "The Unanswered Challenge of Relativism and the Consequences for Human Rights," *Human Rights Quarterly* 7 (November 1985): 514–540. For a sharp response to such views, see Rhoda E. Howard, "Cultural Absolutism and the Nostalgia for Community," *Human Rights Quarterly* 15 (May 1993): 315–338.

The following are among the best arguments in support of indigenous non-Western conceptions of human rights: Adbul Aziz Said, "Precept and Practice of Human Rights in Islam," *Universal Human Rights [Human Rights Quarterly]* 1, no. 1 (1979): 63–80; Fouad Zakaria, "Human Rights in the Arab World: The Islamic Context," in *Philosophical Foundations of Human Rights* (Paris: UNESCO, 1986); Majid Khadduri, "Human Rights in Islam," *Annals* 243 (January 1946): 77–81; Dunstan M. Wai, "Human Rights in Sub-Saharan Africa," in Schwab and Pollis, *Human Rights,* 115–144; Kwasi Wiredu, "An Akan Perspective on Human Rights," in *The Philosophy of Human Rights,* edited by Patrick Hayden (St. Paul, MN: Paragon House, 2001); Timothy Fernyhough, "Human Rights and Precolonial Africa," in *Human Rights and Governance in Africa,* edited by Ronald Cohen, Goran Hyden, and Winston P. Nagan (Gainesville: University Press of Florida, 1993); Asmarom Legesse, "Human Rights in African Political Culture," in *The Moral Imperatives of Human Rights: A World Survey,* edited by Kenneth W. Thompson (Washington, DC: University Press of America, 1980), 123–136; Yougindra Khushalani, "Human Rights in Asia and Africa," *Human Rights Law Journal* 4, no. 4 (1983): 403–442; Ralph Buultjens, "Human Rights in Indian Political Culture," in Thompson, *Moral Imperatives of Human Rights*; James C. Hsiung, "Human Rights in an East Asian Perspective," in *Human Rights in an East Asian Perspective,* edited by James C. Hsiung (New York: Paragon House, 1985); and Lo Chung-Sho, "Human Rights in the Chinese Tradition," in *Human Rights: Comments and Interpretations,* edited by UNESCO (New York: Columbia University Press, 1949).

Finally, one of us (Donnelly) has written extensively on questions of universality and relativism. This chapter summarizes views that are developed in more detail in Part 2 of *Universal Human Rights in Theory and Practice,* 3rd ed. (Ithaca, NY: Cornell University Press, 2013).

4

The Unity of Human Rights

The previous chapter detailed the ways in which human rights are considered universal conceptually and practically. This chapter explores a second attribute of international human rights that is usually considered essential: their unity or indivisibility.

Paragraph 5 of the Vienna Declaration on human rights, adopted at the World Conference on Human Rights in 1993 and reaffirmed repeatedly ever since, states:

> All human rights are universal, indivisible and interdependent and interrelated. The international community must treat human rights globally in a fair and equal manner, on the same footing, and with the same emphasis. While the significance of national and regional particularities and various historical, cultural and religious backgrounds must be borne in mind, it is the duty of States, regardless of their political, economic and cultural systems, to promote and protect all human rights and fundamental freedoms.

In Chapter 2, we introduced a number of ways that we have come to think about the unity of the full range of human rights. This chapter explores these issues in greater detail. And, rather than emphasize concepts and theory, we stress processes of international political contestation in the history of the development of international human rights law. This chapter thus also provides a deeper and more explicit understanding of the relationship among theory, history, and politics.

1. Interdependent and Interrelated Rights

Despite the ubiquitous repetition of the formula "indivisible, interdependent, and interrelated," there is no agreed-upon definition of these terms. Most often, the terms are treated as interchangeable. But why, then, use three words instead of one? And on closer examination it becomes clear that the three terms are *not* interchangeable.

They describe different aspects of and different approaches to the unity of internationally recognized human rights.

A. Interdependent Rights

To say that rights are interdependent suggests that their effective enjoyment requires (is dependent on) other rights that may or may not belong to the same category. For example, freedom of movement (a civil right) is necessary for the exercise of other civil rights (such as freedom of assembly), political rights (e.g., the right to vote), and many economic and social rights (the right to work, for example).

The language of interdependence emphasizes that individual rights are parts of a larger whole. Divisions and categorizations are acknowledged and in some ways even highlighted. But the language of interdependency transcends these categories and divisions. And it stresses the fact that the whole is more than the sum of its parts.

Over the past several decades, human rights scholars and advocates have clearly demonstrated the empirical existence of these interdependencies (some of which we mentioned briefly in Chapter 2). There are limits, though, and the dependencies between rights are not necessarily symmetrical. The degrees of dependency vary as well. Furthermore, not all human rights are *equally* interdependent with all other human rights. As James Nickel pointed out, "Looking at relations between particular rights is illuminating and cannot be avoided, but fully realizing this perspective requires much tedious work. If there are 40 particular human rights then combining them in pairs will yield 1560 places where supporting relations may exist."[1]

Nonetheless, the complex web of dependencies among the full range of internationally recognized human rights justifies the language of interdependency, which stresses connections between parts of a whole. As a conceptual matter, the interdependence of human rights is relatively unproblematic, so long as we accept the validity of the rights in question as human rights. And politically it functions as one further argument against the relativist idea that states can pick and choose from the catalog of internationally recognized human rights.

B. Interrelated Rights

The idea that rights are interrelated can probably best be interpreted to mean that they are brought into a situation of mutual relationship or connectedness—early U.N. resolutions used the term *interconnected* instead of *interrelated*—as a result of international law (human rights treaties) and the institutions designed to monitor those international agreements (see §5.3). This suggests a certain permeability between rights and categories of rights.[2]

Relatedness, however, also suggests similarity. The grand categories of civil and political rights and economic, social, and cultural rights may be thought of as interrelated insofar as their legal foundations (like the Covenants) are similar. When the U.N. General Assembly voted in 1952 to divide the "Covenant on Human Rights" into separate treaties dealing with civil/political and economic/social/cultural rights, it insisted that the two Covenants (the ICCPR and ICESCR) have "as many similar provisions as possible," which helps to explain the identical preambles of the two

Covenants and the inclusion of a right to self-determination in both. Human rights thus can also be said to be interrelated insofar as they share common characteristics.

The question of interrelatedness—this sense of similarity—between the two Covenants came to the fore in the late 1980s and 1990s with respect to implementation and reporting obligations; the scope of monitoring authority held by the oversight committees for each; and the competency of those committees and other U.N. bodies to handle complaints, receive communications, and initiate inquiries (see §5.3). Some advocates of economic and social rights argued that, by design, the obligations and procedures for economic and social rights were weaker than those for civil and political rights, and, thereby, economic and social rights were considered to be less important than civil and political rights, as a matter of political action at the national and international levels.

Part of the problem stems from the differences between the general obligations clauses in the Covenants. Article 2 of the International Covenant on Civil and Political Rights requires states "to adopt such laws or other measures as may be necessary to give effect to the rights recognized in the present Covenant" and not only to provide "effective remedy" in the case of violations but to ensure that those remedies granted are enforced by the state. The parallel provision in Article 2 of the International Covenant on Economic, Social, and Cultural Rights, however, only requires a state to "take steps . . . to the maximum of its available resources, with a view to achieving progressively the full realization of the rights recognized in the present Covenant." And it allows developing countries the option not to guarantee these rights to "non-nationals."

For many years, these differences between immediate and progressive implementation were interpreted by some critics of economic and social rights to imply that civil and political rights were more important or fundamental—and that economic and social rights were merely programmatic aspirations. But this highly partisan reading confuses importance with ease of implementation. (And, even then, why not say that the more difficult to implement rights are the more important ones to focus on?) This reading also ignores the crucial fact that the ICESCR establishes *obligations* "to the maximum of [a state's] available resources." It also ignores the fact that in practice *full* implementation of the political, legal, and judicial reforms necessary for civil and political rights usually takes quite a long time. And the ICCPR in fact does *not* specify that its obligations are immediate.

The second major difference between the two treaty regimes, as they were originally established, concerns the monitoring mechanisms for each. The ICCPR established a monitoring body of independent experts, the Human Rights Committee, to review the reports of states-parties, consider disputes between states about compliance, and, where authorized by the state in question, to investigate petitions by individuals or groups alleging violations. The ICESCR only required states to submit periodic reports to the Economic and Social Council, which were transmitted to a Working Group for review.

The international community soon concluded, though, that these differing procedures not only had no basis in the nature of the rights but were fundamentally incompatible with the idea of interrelatedness. In 1986, the Economic and Social Council established a new Committee on Economic, Social, and Cultural Rights, which would review reports and be empowered to issue general comments (see §5.3.B) along the same lines as the Human Rights Committee. And in 2011, an optional protocol to the ICESCR allowed the Committee on Economic, Social, and Cultural Rights to adjudicate state-to-state complaints, receive individual and collective petitions, and initiate inquiries into alleged violations of the Covenant. This move toward greater institutional interrelatedness also strengthens the principle of the unity of all internationally recognized human rights.

2. The Indivisibility of Human Rights

Indivisibility is the term in the tripartite formulation that is the most difficult to pin down. And it carries especially great conceptual and symbolic weight.

The word itself—meaning "incapable of being divided, in reality or thought"—conjures powerful symbolic imagery. Consider the Catholic belief in the indivisibility of the Holy Trinity—God the Father, the Son, and the Holy Spirit. There is one God but in three instantiations: all are God. The American Pledge of Allegiance declares that Americans constitute "one nation, indivisible." For the early modern philosopher Thomas Hobbes, the awesomeness of the sovereign emanated from the indivisibility of sovereignty itself—that the making of, execution of, and adjudication of the law should remain in the sovereign's hands entirely.

The words *interdependent* and *interrelated* suggest bringing together two or more separate things into mutual harmony. *Indivisibility*, however, suggests that division destroys the thing in question. Applied to the relationship between civil and political rights and economic, social, and cultural rights, the language of indivisibility has usually carried this particular symbolic weight. Its meaning in international political practice, however, has changed over time.

A. One or Two Covenants?

The need to stress indivisibility arose when it came time to translate the principles embedded in the Universal Declaration of Human Rights into legally binding treaty commitments (see §1.3). The initial draft "Covenant on Human Rights" (presented to the Commission on Human Rights by the United Kingdom in 1949) was largely restricted to civil and political rights, which many states (including prominently India) saw as both more readily justiciable (capable of being guaranteed in law in any country) and more settled, both in the sense of being less controversial and clearer as to the obligations they implied.

Many other states, though, mostly from the postcolonial world, chafed at this idea. They argued that to exclude economic and social rights from the Covenant would be "anachronistic" and "unpardonable" and that it would harm the fundamental unity of the Universal Declaration. In a debate within the U.N. General Assembly's Third Committee (which deals with social, humanitarian, and cultural issues), the delegate from Argentina remarked that the United Nations should not attempt to "divide the indivisible." And so the rhetoric of indivisibility was born.

This debate, it should be emphasized, was not about whether the economic, social, and cultural rights were human rights. *That* question had already been settled by their inclusion in the Universal Declaration, which was adopted in 1948. Rather, the debate was over *the obligations of states to implement* those rights. In 1950, the U.N. General Assembly instructed the Commission to include "a clear expression of" economic, social, and cultural rights in the Covenant. The implications of this (probably intentionally vague) charge, however, were not at all clear.

When it went back to work in early 1951, the Commission drafted several new articles on economic and social rights. (Incidentally, Western states, rather than the Soviet/communist bloc, took the lead in drafting the articles that would form the core of the ICESCR.) It also drafted a reporting procedure to monitor their progressive implementation, with the hope that those reports would help to activate assistance mechanisms (as underdeveloped as they were at the time) both from the specialized agencies of the United Nations (for example, the International Labor Organization, the World Health Organization, and the U.N. Educational, Scientific, and Cultural Organization) and from other states.

The state-to-state complaint process initially included for civil and political rights, however, remained in the draft. Were those procedures supposed to apply to the new economic and social rights as well? Conversely, would the new reporting obligations apply to civil and political rights as well? In adding economic and social rights to the draft Covenant, the Commission had made little or no progress on determining how these two sets of rights were related.

Continuing to focus on monitoring and implementation issues, the General Assembly in 1952 instructed the Commission to draft two separate Covenants. It also, however, stipulated that they should have "as many common elements as possible" (to preserve the notion of indivisibility). Furthermore, they were to be completed and opened for signature and ratification at the same time, again, to preserve the idea of unity. And that is what was indeed done when both Covenants were adopted by the General Assembly in December 1966—although the International Covenant on Economic, Social, and Cultural Rights was adopted first, which, as twins (or at least the older twin) will tell you, remains of considerable importance.

B. Indivisibility, Decolonization, and Postcolonial Revisionism

Although the core of the debate over the Covenants was over different approaches to implementation and monitoring mechanisms, for most of the rapidly growing number of postcolonial states, there was a deeper, and different, meaning.

The West looked at human rights largely through the lenses of the era of the two world wars and the special problems of the interwar period (1919–1939). These included, prominently, the systematic violations of the rights of linguistic, religious, and ethnic minorities in Central and Eastern Europe and the rise of antidemocratic and antiliberal dictatorships. But they also included the devastating economic vulnerabilities suffered by millions of ordinary citizens as a result of the Great Depression. The decision to recognize both civil and political rights and economic and social rights thus was largely uncontroversial in the West, including the United States.

For the countries of what we today call the "global South"—which in the 1950s called themselves the Non-Aligned Movement and came to be most frequently referred to as the Third World (outside of both the Western world and the Soviet bloc)— the cause of human rights was much more centrally emancipatory in character. For these (mostly new) states, human rights was a call to bring an end to the injustices of colonialism and its remnants in the postwar international order. And the economic injustices of lingering neocolonialism and systematic international (North-South) inequality were a magnet for these states to appropriate human rights for their own entirely understandable economic- and development-related ends.

A legally binding Covenant that included economic and social rights would strengthen the arguments of postcolonial states not only for an immediate end to colonialism but also for greater resources from the global North—*as a matter of rights* (entitlement). Furthermore, this was seen less as a matter of the individual enjoyment of economic and social rights than of the enjoyment of economic and social rights by *peoples* in colonial or postcolonial states. The emphasis, in other words, was on *collective* rather than individual rights—and on the collective obligations of former colonizing and rich countries and the international community as a whole. This in large part explains the inclusion of the right to self-determination in both Covenants, and in particular its emphasis on the right to "permanent sovereignty over natural resources."

The right of peoples to self-determination, however, also reflected the broader legacy of colonialism. Whatever the fine-sounding justifications—*mission civilisatrice* (civilizing mission), white man's burden—the inescapable reality of colonial rule almost everywhere was systematic discrimination at best and usually violent repression of indigenous populations. In practice, self-determination *was* a necessary prerequisite to the effective enjoyment of all internationally recognized human rights. And also in practice, from the 1950s through the 1970s, self-determination continued to be widely denied in a (steadily declining but still significant) number of remaining Western overseas colonial holdings.

The newly emerging postcolonial world, in other words, tended to see more pressing concerns than securing the individual human rights of its own citizens. Ending colonialism, addressing colonial-era racism (including the practice of apartheid in South Africa), and addressing the pervasive problems of underdevelopment were the human rights issues of the greatest priority to the postcolonial world. Thus while the Covenants languished in the UN (between 1952 and 1966), the newly emerging majority in the global South was busy adopting resolutions calling for redress of these ongoing problems and concerns.

C. The Language of Indivisibility

To celebrate the twentieth anniversary of the Universal Declaration, the United Nations held its first International Conference on Human Rights in Teheran (now Tehran), Iran, in 1968. The Covenants had finally been adopted two years earlier. The Proclamation of Teheran in Paragraph 12 noted that "the widening gap between the economically developed and developing countries impedes the realization of human rights in the international community." And the following paragraph marked the first appearance of the word *indivisible* in an official U.N. human rights document:

> Since human rights and fundamental freedoms are indivisible, *the full realization* of civil and political rights without the enjoyment of economic, social and cultural rights *is impossible.* The achievement of lasting progress in the implementation of human rights is *dependent upon* sound and effective national and international policies of economic and social development.[3]

In this formulation, indivisibility is paired with a claim of the practical priority of the realization of economic and social rights—a very particular (and contentious) understanding of interdependence and interrelatedness.

By the mid-1970s, the global South's majority in the General Assembly was demanding the establishment of a New International Economic Order (NIEO). Such demands spread through all the organs of the United Nations, the Commission on Human Rights being no exception. Many on the Commission were now starting to argue, with increasing stridency, that the realization of economic and social rights took priority over civil and political rights—and that the realization of economic and social rights was dependent upon the implementation of the NIEO (and the new Charter on the Economic Rights and Duties of States, adopted in 1974).

This led in 1977 to the landmark General Assembly resolution Alternative Approaches to Human Rights (Resolution 32/130). In effect, every justice-related concern of the postcolonial world was brought under the umbrella of human rights by conditioning the enjoyment of individual human rights on the achievement of a host of other priorities that must be achieved first. The effort, for both principled and partisan reasons, was to shift the focus of the discussion of human rights from the relationship between the individual and the state that is commensurate with human dignity to the (alleged) practical priority of the achievement of social and economic justice *in the international system as a whole.*

Even in the 1970s and 1980s, however, other forces were already beginning to push back against this reorientation of priorities. A greater emphasis on civil and political rights was beginning to reappear, especially in Cold War Europe. The Helsinki Final Act (1975), which settled many Cold War political and territorial issues in Europe, also bound the Soviet Union to comply with basic human rights norms. There was the emergence of new NGOs like Helsinki Watch (today, Human Rights Watch), the rise of dissident movements in Eastern Europe (for example, Charter 77, founded by Czech writer and later statesman Václav Havel), and even the election of Karol Wojtyła of Poland as Pope John Paul II in 1978, all of which signaled the emergence of civil society in a part of the world that had been on lockdown for decades. In Latin America, civil society groups were instrumental in publicizing crimes committed during the "dirty wars" in the Southern Cone, prompting the Inter-American Commission on Human Rights to begin challenging repressive regimes in Latin America over enforced **disappearances** and torture. Many governments in the global North were beginning to include human rights (mostly civil and political) in their foreign policy priorities.

By the time the international community met again at the World Conference on Human Rights in Vienna in 1993, the Cold War had ended and a renewed commitment to something closer to the original understandings of indivisibility and universality began to (re)emerge. In particular, the Vienna Declaration and Programme of Action[4] noted that *indivisibility* means "fundamental equality." It also emphasized that, despite regional differences, historical particularities, or differences in levels of development, *all* states are obligated to fully protect and promote *all* human rights equally.

This framing remains predominant today. Therefore, it is worth requoting the relevant passage:

> All human rights are universal, indivisible and interdependent and interrelated. The international community must treat human rights globally in a fair and equal manner, on the same footing, and with the same emphasis. While the significance of national and regional particularities and various historical, cultural and religious backgrounds must be borne in mind, it is the duty of States, regardless of their political, economic and cultural systems, to promote and protect all human rights and fundamental freedoms.

3. Politics, History, Theory, and Consensus

This book takes the body of international human rights law as establishing the meaning of *human rights* for the purposes of international action. The preceding sections, however, show that this body of law was shaped as much by political controversy and historical circumstances as by conceptual or theoretical reflection. Doesn't that corrupt the results? Given the central role of politics and history in shaping international human rights law, *should* we really take international law as an authoritative statement of the meaning of human rights?

We suggest that we should, even setting aside the argument that there is no practical alternative. Despite the process, the results stand up pretty well to theoretical scrutiny. As the old saying goes, the making of laws, like the making of sausages, is not a pretty sight.

An important reason has been the centrality of the principle of **consensus** in the development of international human rights law. In the practice of the United Nations and other multilateral organizations, consensus procedures require the acquiescence of all participants in the outcome. In principle, any single participant can prevent action. In practice, any single major actor or significant group of minor actors can prevent action.

The process is slow and difficult, even when successful. But it both acknowledges political conflict and insists that it must be overcome (or at least be reduced to acceptable levels) before a decision is made. Consensus ensures that decisions are accepted rather than imposed. (We thus should expect the very high ratification rates of international human rights treaties that we in fact see.)

But many states have absolutely no intention of implementing their international human rights obligations. Why would they agree to treaties in the first place? Part of the explanation is the very weak implementation mechanisms of those treaties, which we will discuss in Chapter 5. Another part of the explanation, though, is the deep attraction of the idea of human rights in the contemporary world.

Few states are in a position to simply reject the idea of human rights. (North Korea is the exception that proves the rule.) Most feel a need to appear to support human rights, even as they go about systematically violating them. Hypocrisy is the compliment paid by vice to virtue. In the language that we introduced in the preceding chapter, international legal universality is rooted in overlapping consensus and functional universality.

Another part of the explanation of substantively good results achieved through suspect political processes is historical; namely, the Universal Declaration. A remarkable group of individuals, working in a moment of historical optimism and limited global political conflict, was able to craft an unusually good statement of the most progressive vision of human rights best practices. And this firm foundation has continued to set the parameters for the development of international human rights law right up to today.

Contemporary international human rights law elaborates and updates the Universal Declaration. It fills in a few gaps. But it continues to follow the Universal Declaration. And, in practice, the consensus principle always—eventually—has brought the international community back to the Universal Declaration.

The process of developing international human rights law thus has not only managed to transcend partisan politics but also maintain considerable substantive and theoretical integrity. And, as the preceding sections have shown, an important part of retaining that integrity has been the insistence that human rights are interdependent, interrelated, and indivisible—an insistence on the unity of human rights that was first embedded in the Universal Declaration.

4. Three Generations of Human Rights?

The Preamble to General Assembly Resolution 421 (V) of 1950, which called for the inclusion of economic, social, and cultural rights in the draft Covenant, stated that "the Universal Declaration regards man as a person, to whom civic and political freedoms and well as economic, social and cultural rights indubitably belong," and that, "when deprived of economic, social and cultural rights, man does not represent the human person whom the Universal Declaration regards as the ideal of the free man." This language could lead to the conclusion that it is the human person, or his or her needs in a modern society, that is an indivisible unity. Alternatively, the human person as a citizen (and not a subject) of the state must have his or her full range of rights protected and promoted *in order to be fully human*. This gets us a bit closer to some kind of deeper reading of unity or indivisibility.

But we must go further, considering that we are talking about rights. And if we are going to speak in the language of human rights, we must talk about the state. But

Table 4.1 Generations of Human Rights

	1st Generation	2nd Generation	3rd Generation
Principle reflected	Liberty	Equality	Fraternity
Types of rights	Civil/political	Economic/social	Solidarity/group
Target of claims	Antistate	Antimarket	Anticolonial
Prioritized by	First World	Second World	Third World

then we must ask ourselves what vision of the state—and its relations to individuals, markets, and civil society—is embedded within the Universal Declaration of Human Rights, which, we should remember, does not explicitly speak of indivisibility, interrelatedness, or interdependency.

One way these issues have been approached is to seek an historical synthesis of different "generations" of human rights. In 1977, Czech jurist Karel Vašák, then a lawyer at the United Nations Educational, Scientific and Cultural Organization (UNESCO), offered a still-influential formulaic model for explaining the historical development of human rights.[5] Vašák envisioned three generations of rights that, he argued, had been fully recognized by the international community by the late 1970s. Table 4.1 reflects our reading of Vašák's formula.

The generations model shows four different dimensions of the three generations of human rights. Each is based on one of the philosophical ideals of the French Revolution: liberty, equality, and fraternity. The categories of rights that reflect these historically bound ideals are civil and political rights (from classical liberalism); economic and social rights (from socialism/Marxism and workers' rights movements); and, finally, solidarity or group rights, such as the right to self-determination, sovereignty over natural resources, and the right to development. And, of central importance in understanding the attractions of this model, each generation was associated with each of the three principal geopolitical blocs of the Cold War era.

Table 4.1 also adds an additional dimension to Vašák's original formula, indicating the principal "enemy" of rights within each generation. First-generation rights view the state as the primary violator of rights. Second-generation rights seek to combat the power of the market. Third-generation rights were initially anticolonial but increasingly have become focused on the globalization of markets (see Chapter 11).

There are, however, at least three serious problems with this three-generations model. First, it is historically inaccurate. From the beginning, Western conceptions of natural (human) rights included economic rights. For example, John Locke's short and iconic list included life, liberty, and estates (property). Thomas Jefferson similarly emphasized rights to life, liberty, and the pursuit of happiness. The nineteenth-century development of more robust conceptions of economic and social rights, especially for working men who had little or no property, initially predated socialism and continued to proceed largely independently of (although sometimes in alliance with) socialism. (For example, the foundations of the German welfare state were laid by the archconservative Otto von Bismarck.) And in the interwar and post–World War II periods, when modern welfare states were created, Western states not only took the lead in elaborating and implementing economic and social rights but achieved results far surpassing those of socialist bloc states.

Second, the three-generations formulation gives wildly excessive emphasis to so-called third-generation rights, which make up only a tiny fraction of internationally recognized human rights—and, with the crucial exception of self-determination, have had little practical impact. Self-determination was an essential addition to the body of internationally recognized human rights. It is indeed qualitatively different from other human rights. And the Third World did play a central role in pressing for its recognition. (Although even here we should note that the right was in fact first introduced to international law by Westerners for application in Europe. Furthermore, by 1960 all the leading Western states had adopted the principle, and Western overseas empires—with the exceptions of the Portuguese and Spanish Empires—were well into the process of being dismantled.) The idea of a coequal third generation, however, has little basis in either theory or practice.

Sustainable development, poverty alleviation, responding to and ameliorating the environmental and ecological challenges of our times, and securing a life of peace and prosperity certainly are worthwhile endeavors that command the attention of states and the international community as a whole. We are wary, however, of ascribing to each of these important objectives the status of rights, let alone *human* rights.

Some of the conceptual distinctions introduced in Chapter 1 become central here. For example, what actors have which obligations with respect to these "rights"? How might individual citizens go about claiming them?

We are also concerned that proliferating such vague rights might actually detract from the realization of established rights. For example, rather than talk about a vague "right to development," it seems more profitable to focus on realizing the full range of internationally recognized economic, social, and cultural rights. This is an immensely difficult task, to be sure. But it is a much more concrete goal. We can readily measure its incremental achievement. And, unlike the pursuit of an amorphous abstraction, it promises real and immediate improvements in the quality of life of millions of people.

Third, and most immediately relevant to the issue of the unity of human rights, the three-generations model is fundamentally in tension with the ideas of interdependence, interrelatedness, and indivisibility. Political practice by states in the socialist bloc systematically denigrated civil and political rights (and did not even treat economic and social rights as inalienable entitlements of citizens). And, as we saw above, the leading advocates of solidarity rights similarly advanced them as prerequisites for, if not alternatives to, civil and political rights. In addition, the language of historically periodized generations risks driving permanent wedges between contemporary human rights categories. The generations approach also makes it difficult to consider the development of different rights, such as their extension to wider segments of the population, alongside the development of institutions (especially the modern regulatory welfare state) in which interdependent rights and freedoms take on new and important meanings.

We thus come back, again, to the idea that "all human rights are universal, indivisible and interdependent and interrelated." Or, phrased as an imperative for policy: all human rights for all.

Problem 4: Human Rights:
Hierarchical or Indivisible?

The Problem

This problem begins with an implicit hierarchy evident in much ordinary thinking about human rights. When someone speaks of human rights violations in a given country but does not specify which rights are being violated, what pops into mind? In our experience, most Americans tend to think of violations of what human rights theorists often call "personal integrity rights," such as torture, arbitrary arrest and detention, police brutality, enforced disappearances, or arbitrary executions. If the person clarified that he had in mind the lack of educational opportunities for girls or an out-of-control epidemic, this would, we think, strike most Americans as odd. That's just not what we ordinarily mean when we talk about human rights violations without some additional specification.

Even those of us convinced by the theoretical argument of indivisibility and deeply wary of the practical problems of the abuse of categorical distinctions between rights often find ourselves falling into hierarchical thinking. For example, many human rights advocates simply do not treat unemployment or even homelessness as if they were as significant violations of human rights as torture, let alone enforced disappearances or arbitrary executions. However deep our commitment to the maxim "all human rights for all" is, we are still reluctant to accept, in our unthinking practice, that all internationally recognized human rights really are equal.

How can we resolve such hierarchical thinking about human rights with the theoretically central idea of interrelated, interdependent, and indivisible human rights? Other hierarchies are encountered. (For example, above we encountered efforts to prioritize economic, social, and cultural rights and rights to self-determination and protection against racial discrimination.) Here, however, we will focus on the argument for hierarchy most commonly encountered in our own country, namely, the prioritization of civil and political rights over economic, social, and cultural rights.

One Solution

Much of the answer to this problem lies in distinctions that were developed in Chapter 2. There we saw that categorically dividing civil and political rights from economic and social rights as negative and positive rights respectively simply will not work. Most internationally recognized human rights impose both positive and negative duties (although not always on the same social actors). Furthermore, *all* internationally recognized human rights are subject to progressive implementation.

For example, what counts as adequate legal representation in criminal proceedings will vary at least as dramatically with the level of resources available in a society as will what counts as free and universal primary education.

Another distinction raised in Chapter 2 is also important. All states have three broad types of duties with respect to *all* human rights: duties to respect, protect, and promote or fulfill human rights. The duty to respect is often primarily negative. But duties to protect and promote or fulfill are fundamentally positive. And they clearly underscore the necessarily progressive realization of *all* human rights.

In other words, focusing on state obligations draws us away from haggling over the content of different categories of human rights. Instead, it focuses on the mechanisms and structures of making the state and society more just and more conducive to realizing the human dignity that underlies internationally recognized human rights. Interdependent and indivisible human rights reappear in the form of interdependent and indivisible state duties to allow people to live a life of dignity, respect, autonomy, and self-determination—across the full range of internationally recognized human rights.

Going Further

No one actually believes that all *violations* of every human rights are equally important. This does not, however, suggest any hierarchy of rights, because the importance of a violation is largely a matter of the circumstances of implementation rather than the content of the right. Again, let us focus on civil and political rights versus economic and social rights.

It is certainly true that most people, with some justification, would consider torture a more serious violation of human rights than unemployment or arbitrary arrest and detention a more serious violation than homelessness. But that is largely a function of the circumstances in which these violations typically present themselves.

Imagine a middle-income country in which the state arbitrarily detains and tortures a small number of people targeted for their political views and in which one-third of the adult population cannot find gainful work and half the population lives in temporary housing or on the streets. Here, from a quantitative standpoint (in terms of the number of people affected), the more serious violations would seem to concern economic and social rights, not civil and political rights. Yet, the smaller number of instances (victims) of torture or arbitrary arrest are likely to gain more of our attention.

Again, we need to focus on the underlying value of human dignity and on the impact of particular violations on the realization of human dignity, both of particular individuals and of the members of society collectively. And *that* impact has little to do with the particular content of the right. It is almost always dependent on contingent historical, material, and political circumstances.

More generally, the interdependence and indivisibility of human rights is a claim about the essential character of internationally recognized human rights. The gross and systematic denial of *any* of these rights is an unacceptable denial of human dignity. One cannot live a life of dignity unless one has at least some degree of enjoyment of nearly all these rights.

This is not incompatible with temporary and contingent decisions to prioritize progress on some rights rather than others. Quite the contrary, such decisions are inescapable in a world of limited material and political resources. And different societies, as well as the same society at different times, may legitimately make different decisions about priorities. (This is particularly true as we move down the levels identified in Chapter 3 toward detailed matters of implementation.)

The interdependence and indivisibility of human rights prohibits *categorical* priorities among rights. It does not deny that some human rights in some particular circumstances demand greater social and political attention than other human rights *in those particular circumstances.*

All human rights are always essential to a life of human dignity. That does not, however, mean that each right is equally important at every time. Much of the day-to-day struggle for human rights, in fact, involves choosing to prioritize progress in one area over other (equally important, in principle) areas. Such contingent priorities, however, must not be confused with categorical hierarchies of human rights. And, in the long run, the interdependence and indivisibility of human rights does require states and societies to strive to realize all human rights for all.

Discussion Questions

1. Even if you accept that economic and social rights are just as important as civil and political rights, is there still a difference between them? If so, what makes them different? Is one category, as a category, more important than the other? If so, why?

2. What is the basis, do you think, of the differences between these two categories of rights? Is it about the nature of the rights themselves (what they try to protect with respect to individuals), or are the differences rooted in what states' obligations are with respect to their protection? If it is about their nature as rights, can you say what that nature is? If it is about the obligations, what are the differences? Are those differences qualitatively important?

3. We have argued here that the historical generations approach to understanding human rights is problematic, even though, on some levels, it might make intuitive sense historically. Are you convinced? Why or why not?

4. Following from Question 3, would it make sense to talk about contemporary economic and social rights (guaranteed by the state), such as those related to work, working conditions, education, health, and social security, in the context of the eighteenth century (when core civil and political rights first emerged)?

5. The principle of indivisibility argues that both categories of human rights (civil/political and economic/social) are fundamentally equal, no matter the various details about how any specific right or rights must be respected or guaranteed. Yet some have also argued that one set of rights was more fundamental and therefore needed to be secured before the

other. Do you think there is any logic to either prioritization (i.e., that civil/political rights need to come first or that economic/social rights need to come first)? What is the reasoning behind each argument? How convincing is each?

Suggested Readings

This chapter is largely distilled from the work of one of this volume's coauthors (Whelan), whose book *Indivisible Human Rights: A History* (Philadelphia: University of Pennsylvania Press, 2010) explores these issues and the history in much greater detail. As we mention in the chapter, a major focal point about indivisibility has centered on the status of economic and social rights relative to civil and political rights. The literature reflecting those discussions began to emerge in the late 1980s, when the ICESCR's weak and ineffective reporting procedure was reformed and the U.N. Committee on Economic, Social, and Cultural Rights was established. These works are still worth reading, for they established the terms of the debates that we explore in this chapter.

Generally, in the realm of theory, philosophy, and the general politics of these questions, see David Beetham, "What Future for Economic and Social Rights?," *Political Studies* 43 (1995): 41–60; Antonio A. Cancado Trindade, "The Interdependence of All Human Rights—Obstacles and Challenges to Their Implementation," *International Social Science Journal* 50 (1998): 513–523; Isfahan Merali and Valerie Oosterveld, eds., *Giving Meaning to Economic, Social and Cultural Rights* (Philadelphia: University of Pennsylvania Press, 2001); Craig Scott, "The Interdependence and Permeability of Human Rights Norms: Towards a Partial Fusion of the International Covenants on Human Rights," *Osgoode Hall Law Journal* 27 (1989): 769–875; and "Reaching Beyond (Without Abandoning) the Category of 'Economic, Social and Cultural Rights,'" *Human Rights Quarterly* 21 (1999): 633–660; and James Nickel, "Rethinking Indivisibility: Towards a Theory of Supporting Relations Between Rights," *Human Rights Quarterly* 30 (2008): 984–1001.

On the legal obligations of the ICESCR and the establishment of the Committee on Economic, Social, and Cultural Rights, see Philip Alston and Gerard Quinn, "The Nature and Scope of States Parties' Obligations Under the International Covenant on Economic, Social and Cultural Rights," *Human Rights Quarterly* 9 (1987): 156–229; International Commission of Jurists, "The Limburg Principles on the Implementation of the International Covenant on Economic, Social and Cultural Rights," *Human Rights Quarterly* 9 (1987): 122–135; and Robert E. Robertson, "Measuring State Compliance with the Obligation to Devote the 'Maximum Available Resources' to Realizing Economic, Social and Cultural Rights," *Human Rights Quarterly* 16 (1994): 693–714.

On the adoption of "violations approaches" for economic, social, and cultural rights and the establishment of a petitions procedure for the ICESCR, see Audrey R. Chapman, "A 'Violations Approach' for Monitoring the International Covenant on Economic, Social and Cultural Rights," *Human Rights Quarterly* 18 (1996): 23–66; Scott Leckie, "Another Step Towards Indivisibility: Identifying the Key Features of

Violations of Economic, Social and Cultural Rights," *Human Rights Quarterly* 20 (1998): 81–124; International Commission of Jurists, "The Maastricht Guidelines on Violations of Economic, Social and Cultural Rights," *Human Rights Quarterly* 20 (1998): 691–704; Victor Dankwa, Cees Flinterman, and Scott Leckie, "Commentary to the Maastricht Guidelines on Violations of Economic, Social and Cultural Rights," *Human Rights Quarterly* 20 (1998): 705–730; Michael J. Dennis and David P. Stewart, "Justiciability of Economic, Social and Cultural Rights: Should There Be an International Complaints Mechanism to Adjudicate the Rights to Food, Water, Housing and Health?," *American Journal of International Law* 98 (2004): 462–515; and Catarina de Albuquerque, "Chronicle of an Announced Birth: The Coming into Life of the Optional Protocol to the International Covenant on Economic, Social and Cultural Rights—the Missing Piece of the International Bill of Rights," *Human Rights Quarterly* 32 (2010): 144–178.

Finally, three recent volumes cover current trends and research on the economic, legal, and political status of economic, social, and cultural rights: Katherine G. Young, *Constituting Economic and Social Rights* (New York: Oxford University Press, 2012); Lanse Minkler, ed., *The State of Economic and Social Human Rights* (New York: Cambridge University Press, 2013); and Sakiko Fukada-Parr, Terra Lawson-Remer, and Susan Randolph, eds., *Fulfilling Social and Economic Rights* (New York: Oxford University Press, 2015).

PART TWO

Multilateral, Bilateral, and Transnational Action

5

~<o>~

Global Multilateral Mechanisms

In this chapter we examine the multilateral global institutional mechanisms and procedures designed to facilitate greater compliance by states with global human rights law. We first consider the Charter-based bodies, that is, those that draw their authority from the U.N. Charter (§§5.1 and 5.2), followed by treaty monitoring bodies, whose authority derives from the various human rights treaties (considered in §5.3). We also briefly note the work of other global multilateral actors (§5.4) and efforts to **mainstream**—that is, incorporate—human rights concerns throughout the various agencies of the entire U.N. system (§5.5). We conclude with a case study on the special procedures of the U.N. human rights system (§5.6). The following chapter will consider regional human rights regimes.

1. The Human Rights Council

The Human Rights Council[1] was created in 2006 to replace the Commission on Human Rights. As we have seen, the Commission during its first two decades of work laid the foundations of the global human rights regime, doing the principal work on the drafting of the Universal Declaration of Human Rights and the International Human Rights Covenants. In the late 1960s and 1970s, it began very limited monitoring of state practices. In the 1980s and early 1990s, its monitoring activities expanded substantially, including many more countries and issues. But, in its final decade, the Commission became hopelessly politicized, as symbolized by the election in 2003 of Mu'ammar Gaddafi, the longtime military dictator of Libya, as its chair.

The Human Rights Council is composed of forty-seven member states, elected by secret ballot in the U.N. General Assembly, who serve staggered three-year terms. States may be reelected as long as it is not to a third consecutive term. Seats on the Council are distributed proportionally by region: thirteen to Africa, thirteen to the Asia-Pacific region, eight to Latin America, seven to Western European and other states (which includes Australia, Canada, Israel, New Zealand, and the United States), and six to Eastern Europe.

When considering nominees, member states are supposed to take into account the candidate-state's contribution to the promotion and protection of human rights, as well as its voluntary pledges (see below) and commitments to human rights in general. Despite these requirements, though, many states with poor human rights records make it onto the Council. For example, in the past few years, Bahrain, China, the Democratic Republic of the Congo, Cuba, Gabon, Kyrgyzstan, Pakistan, Qatar, Russia, Saudi Arabia, Venezuela, and Vietnam have been elected.

This has not, however, significantly diminished the value of the Council. It has been a largely nonpartisan forum for the consensual development of new international human rights norms. For example, it concluded work on the conventions on persons with disabilities and on disappearances and its wide-ranging resolutions are part of the global process of furthering the promotion and evolution of existing human rights norms, as well as the development of new ones. It undertakes significant efforts to promote implementation of internationally recognized human rights. It also engages in limited monitoring.

The implementation and monitoring activities of the Council have sometimes been less than impartial. Some countries, for political reasons, have received more attention than their human rights records warrant, while others receive less. (Israel and China, respectively, are often presented as examples.) The Universal Periodic Review process (explained below), however, has been much more evenhanded. Furthermore, partisan political considerations have become generally secondary considerations in the selection of states targeted for criticism in the Council's resolutions, which typically address important and well-documented violations.

The Human Rights Council meets for at least ten weeks annually, divided into three sessions held in March (four weeks), June (three weeks), and September (three weeks). If one-third of the members call for it, the Council may convene a special session at any time to address emergency situations. Through 2016, twenty-six special sessions have been held; that is, on average, two to three a year.

A. Universal Periodic Review

The most important task of the Council is the nearly continual Universal Periodic Review (UPR) process, under which all 193 U.N. member states undergo scrutiny of their human rights records every four years.[2] The Council not only created this mechanism but has turned it into a major, if somewhat complex, mechanism for mainstreaming human rights monitoring and promotion.[3]

A wide variety of information is gathered from independent human rights experts and groups both within the U.N. system and outside the United Nations, including national human rights institutions and NGOs. States also submit a national report on their efforts to promote and protect internationally recognized human rights.

When it is engaged in the UPR process, all forty-seven members of the Council form a Working Group to review these documents and engage in a conversation with the state under review that typically involves questions and comments and a series of recommendations, which states under review formally "accept," "note," or "reject." A group of three members of the Working Group (a "troika") prepares an outcome report, which typically summarizes discussions held with the state under review. The Working Group then adopts the report and sends it to the Council's plenary session to be adopted, following any clarifications, additional comments or questions, and comments or questions from observer states or NGOs present.

In November 2016, the Council wrapped up the second cycle of the UPR. The human rights records of all 193 U.N. member-states thus have been reviewed twice, giving us enough evidence to pose the question of the effectiveness of the UPR mechanism. Following an analysis that was recently conducted by the Universal Rights Group (URG; a Geneva-based human rights think tank),[4] here we will consider the question of effectiveness on three levels.

i. Quality of State Reports

The Council's guidelines specify that national reports should be prepared through a "broad consultation process" with relevant national stakeholders (especially elements from civil society) to ensure that the reports are as objective and reliable (accurate) as possible. Only a small minority of states, however, have taken this directive seriously. The norm continues to be that national reports are drafted by ministries of foreign affairs with little or no input from other groups (even within the government).

ii. Quality of Working Group Peer Review

The participatory nature of the UPR peer-review mechanism is in many ways remarkable. What, though, is the quality of this participatory process? The time allotted to the review of a particular country only permits each member of the Working Group two or three minutes for discussion, leading to Working Group sessions that tend to be formulaic and superficial, often amounting to a "rapid, almost metronomic delivery of recommendations by reviewing States . . . [followed by] a valedictory speech by the [State under review] to mark the end of the session."[5]

The total number of recommendations, however, has increased dramatically, from 430 at the very first Working Group session (in Round 1) to 1,804 by the fourth session. This increase largely reflects a growing number of states actively participating by offering recommendations—a sign of growing commitment to the peer-review mechanism. Furthermore, these recommendations are increasingly useful (i.e., specific and salient or germane) and measurable, allowing for follow-up in the next round. The URG analysis shows that in the second round only 12 percent of recommendations did not meet these criteria.

iii. Implementation of Recommendations

In a system of national implementation of international norms, the extent to which states actually implement recommendations of the Working Group would seem to be the most important metric of effectiveness of the UPR. An analysis of seventy-four countries from all regional groups, covering more than 5,000 recommendations, has found the following:

- Nearly half of all accepted recommendations were implemented; another 20 percent were partially implemented. Only 25 percent were not implemented.
- Generally, recommendations concerning women's rights and children's rights enjoy higher levels of implementation (54 percent and 62 percent, respectively) than those in other areas.
- Levels of implementation varied by the type of recommendation: for example, recommendations to accede to international human rights agreements or institutions had higher levels of implementation compared to those focusing solely on domestic-level reforms. This suggests that, as the low-hanging fruit recommendations are implemented, the overall level of implementation moving forward may begin to shrink.
- Interestingly, however, 30 percent of those recommendations that were noted by states under review (i.e., they were neither accepted nor rejected) nevertheless resulted in some domestic-level reforms— suggesting that the UPR process might be having a discernable impact at the national level.

Nearly half of all recommendations made in the first round of the UPR had been implemented by the second round. In some countries, the implementation rate was as high as 82 percent. This success is most likely due to the peer-to-peer, state-centric model of self-assessment embedded in the UPR.

The other side of the picture, though, is that the desire to avoid political confrontation in a peer-to-peer process unquestionably restricts the range of issues seriously addressed. Furthermore, even though the other "compilation reports" (by the U.N. system and other stakeholders) are part of the review dossier, only the national report is presented to the Working Group, which in many cases completely skews the review. Although this helps to explain some of the success of the recommendations— they are on issues that, because the state has included them in its report, it has implied that it is willing to address—this shortcoming is also a strength in that it increases the immediate productiveness and impact of the review.

A process that produces considerable positive impact, even on an often narrow range of issues, would seem to be one well worth keeping and trying to build on— which is a much more positive assessment than the many critics of the process (and the Council more generally) predicted when the UPR was instituted.

2. The Office of the U.N. High Commissioner for Human Rights

The Council's (and earlier the Commission's) activities reflect an information-advocacy model of human rights implementation. It seeks to acquire and disseminate authoritative information on violations to encourage (and if necessary shame) governments to improve their practices. It relies on the desire of states to be respected, both by their peers and by their citizens, and on the damage to state reputations that can be caused by well-publicized systematic human rights violations.

The U.N. Office of the High Commissioner for Human Rights (OHCHR), created after the 1993 Vienna World Conference, personifies this information-advocacy approach. The high commissioner has the global reach of the Council but without its cumbersome procedures and the inescapable politicization that goes along with the members of the Council being states, not independent experts. The high commissioner may deal directly with governments, any of whom he or she may approach, on any issue, at his or her discretion.

In practice, the high commissioner, who is directly accountable to (and appointed by) the U.N. secretary-general, has emerged as a prominent—probably the world's most prominent—global advocate for human rights. In particular, the second high commissioner, Mary Robinson (the former president of Ireland), turned the office into a major force during her tenure (from 1997 to 2002). The quality of the secretarial support work was brought to a high level, the budget increased substantially, and Robinson became a well-known public figure across the globe as a result of her difficult-to-resist intellectual brilliance, moral commitment, and hard work, combined with an unusual mix of diplomatic skill and a constant willingness to push the bounds of what her targets were willing to tolerate from an international public servant.

Robinson left her successor, Sérgio Vieira de Mello of Brazil, a completely transformed organization when she moved on to other work in 2002. Sadly, he was among the victims of the bombing of the U.N. offices in Baghdad in August 2003. The acting high commissioner, Bertrand Ramcharan of Guyana, a career U.N. official and a noted scholar of international human rights law, was succeeded in 2004 by Louise Arbour of Canada, another high-profile high commissioner. Previously, Arbour had served as the chief prosecutor for the International Criminal Tribunals for the former Yugoslavia and for Rwanda, and so exercised her mandate aggressively on behalf of human rights and victims of violations.

Arbour was succeeded in 2008 by Navanethem (Navi) Pillay of South Africa, a former judge of the International Criminal Court and former president of the International Criminal Tribunal for Rwanda. In 2012, Pillay's mandate was extended until 2014, when Ban Ki-moon appointed Prince Zeid Ra'ad Zeid Al Hussein of Jordan, who started his term on September 1, 2014. Zeid was previously Jordan's permanent representative to the United Nations and also served as Jordan's ambassador to the United States. He is the first Asian, Muslim, and Arab high commissioner.

Although the public activities of the high commissioner draw the most attention, the significance of the behind-the-scenes work of the office should not be underestimated. The OHCHR website[6] is a model of clarity and comprehensive coverage that is of great value to activists, scholars, ordinary citizens, and victims. The office also provides direct administrative support for the Council and the treaty bodies (which are discussed in the next section), engages in original research (with special attention to the Vienna Programme of Action and the right to development), and provides capacity-building and advisory services to governments seeking to improve their national practices.

The OHCHR staffs and maintains thirteen country offices (in Bolivia, Cambodia, Colombia, Guatemala, Guinea, Kosovo (Serbia), Mauritania, Mexico, the Occupied Palestinian Territories, Togo, Tunisia, Uganda, and Yemen) and ten regional offices for East Africa (Addis Ababa), Southern Africa (Pretoria), West Africa (Dakar), Central America (Panama City), South America (Santiago de Chile), Europe (Brussels), Central Asia (Bishkek), Southeast Asia (Bangkok), the Pacific (Suva), and the Middle East and North Africa (Beirut). It also supports a Regional Center for Human Rights and Democracy for Central Africa (Yaoundé, Cameroon) and a Training and Documentation Centre for South West Asia and the Arab Region (Doha, Qatar). In 2016, the Office of the High Commissioner had deployed nearly nine hundred international human rights officers and national staff placed in fifteen separate peace missions, as well as resident human rights advisers in twenty-nine countries—nearly double the number deployed in 2010.[7]

In 2015, the OHCHR budget was set at $229 million; 46 percent of that amount comes from the U.N. budget, with the remainder raised from voluntary contributions, most of which come from U.N. member states. The $126 million of voluntary contributions that were pledged in 2015 was the largest amount in the OHCHR's history.[8]

Compared to the resources devoted to development assistance, these budget numbers are very modest. For example, in 2015 the World Bank made loans totaling more than $60 billion. Its administrative budget for 2016 was $2.53 billion—more than ten times the total budget of the Office of the High Commissioner.[9] Nevertheless, the OHCHR has continued to expand its range of activities over the past several years, illustrating the possibilities for progressive cooperative action with governments that have some degree of openness to a combination of pressure and assistance from the outside world, especially when it comes through the politically less partisan mechanisms of multilateral organizations.

3. Treaty-Reporting Systems

An important cluster of global human rights institutions derive their authority from multilateral human rights treaties (see Table 5.1.) The principal activity of the committees created by these treaties (**treaty monitoring bodies,** or TMBs) is to review reports on compliance submitted by states-parties. Many also consider individual communications or petitions from alleged victims of violations. All TMBs regularly review the scope of their respective treaty's provisions and issue "general comments" that attempt to advance international human rights jurisprudence.

Unlike the Human Rights Council, whose members are representatives of their governments, the membership of the TMBs consists of individual experts who serve in their private and professional capacity. They do not represent their own national governments (although their governments may have been instrumental in putting their names forward in nomination to serve). The number of experts serving on the ten TMBs ranges from ten to twenty-five, with most (five) having eighteen members.

Table 5.1 Treaty Monitoring Bodies

Committee (Treaty Supervised)	Parties to Treaty	Established	Allows Petitions?	Year First Petition Received
Human Rights Committee (ICCPR)	168	1976	Yes, for the 115 that have ratified the Optional Protocol	1976
Committee on Economic, Social, and Cultural Rights (ICESCR)	164	1985	Yes, for the 22 states that have ratified the Optional Protocol	2013
Committee on the Elimination of Racial Discrimination (ICERD)	177	1969	Yes, under Article 14 of ICERD	1982
Committee on the Elimination of Discrimination Against Women (CEDAW)	189	1981	Yes, for the 108 states that have ratified the Optional Protocol	2003
Committee Against Torture (CAT)	160	1987	Yes, for the 67 states that have made a declaration under Article 22 of CAT	1987
Committee on the Rights of the Child (CRC)	196	1990	Yes, for the 29 states that have ratified the Optional Protocol	2013 (one petition; declared inadmissible)
Committee on Migrant Workers (CMW)	49	2004	Yes, for states that have made a declaration under Article 77 of the CMW (only three have done so; requires ten for the procedure to enter into force)	N/A
Committee on the Rights of Persons with Disabilities (ICRPD)	168	2009	Yes, for the 91 states that have ratified the Optional Protocol	2010
Committee on Enforced Disappearances (ICED)	53	2011	Yes, for the 19 states that have made a declaration under Article 31 of the ICED	None yet

A. Reporting

The principal and most important activity of the treaty bodies is to review periodic reports on compliance that parties are required to submit, usually every four or five years. Based on the report and additional information gathered by the committee, questions are prepared and submitted to the state in writing. A state representative participates in the committee's public discussion of the report. A follow-up written exchange often ensues.

The reporting process thus is an exchange of information that provides limited, noncoercive monitoring. The extent of state participation, beyond submitting its report, ranges from active cooperation to a largely nonresponsive presence. There are no sanctions of any sort associated with the reporting procedure, even if the country refuses to submit its report (as some do).

Complaints about the weakness of reporting systems assume that the goal is coercive enforcement. In fact, though, the aim is to encourage and facilitate compliance. Judged in these terms, reporting often has a significant positive effect. The most constructive part of the process is the preparation of the report. Much like the UPR, periodic reviews of national practice in the TMBs, if undertaken with any degree of conscientiousness, require states, agencies, and officials to step back from their day-to-day work and reflect on their processes, procedures, and institutions.

Reporting is especially valuable in countries with an active civil society. Issue-specific NGOs are sometimes directly involved in preparing the national report. Often they lobby the officials who draft the report. And they can use preparation of the report and its public review by the treaty body as occasions for campaigning. NGOs may also participate indirectly in the committee review through contacts with individual members. And the public hearing and comments by the committees often provide an occasion for amplified publicity. Paradoxically, then, reporting is most likely to have an impact where it is not critically needed: that is, where human rights records are relatively good. Nevertheless, any victim who is helped is a victory for international action, wherever that person resides.

One might even argue that the greatest virtue of treaty-reporting systems is their ability to address violations that are not sufficiently severe to merit scrutiny by the Council or a special procedure. Particularly for countries and violations that do not have a high international profile, reporting may actually provide greater scrutiny.

Furthermore, small-scale incremental progress, which is a realistic possibility in the case of any state that takes its reporting obligation seriously, is not to be sneered at—especially when we consider the typically modest impact of higher-profile inquiry or petition procedures. And even if stronger mechanisms are available, the periodic self-study that reporting requires is a valuable contribution.

Two major limits of reporting systems, however, deserve note. First, the positive effects of reporting depend ultimately on the willingness of the state to change—either because of a positive desire to improve or because of an openness or vulnerability to criticism (which all but the most repressive of regimes possess to some degree). Second, the changes produced by such mechanisms are limited and incremental.

As a general proposition, states typically engage in (massive) human rights violations only when they believe something of great importance is at stake. The national and international political costs of negative publicity and advocacy campaigns are almost never sufficient to overcome the political incentives to continue gross and persistent systematic violations. But where the violations are relatively minor or narrowly circumscribed—for example, particular rules on the treatment of prisoners, activities of a single part of the government bureaucracy, particular nondiscrimination policies, or the treatment of a single individual—all but the worst governments may be willing to consider improvements.

For all their limits, then, such modest improvements are not insignificant. And, over time, they may accumulate. This is especially true as the process is repeated in multiple treaty bodies—and as the reporting process interacts with other national, transnational, bilateral, and multilateral advocacy.

B. General Comments

Treaty bodies also regularly review the scope and content of their treaty and issue general comments. This practice, first developed and most effectively employed by the Human Rights Committee (which monitors implementation of the ICCPR),[10] attempts not only to improve the reporting process but also to influence the progressive development of international human rights law by offering quasi-authoritative interpretations of the obligations under the treaty.

Consider a more or less arbitrarily chosen example: General Comment 20 of the Human Rights Committee, adopted in 1992. It interprets Article 7 of the International Covenant on Civil and Political Rights, which states (in its entirety), "No one shall be subjected to torture or to cruel, inhuman or degrading treatment or punishment. In particular, no one shall be subjected without his free consent to medical or scientific experimentation." This pithy statement certainly could benefit from some elaboration, which General Comment 20 seeks to provide.

Paragraph 2 states that the aim of the article "is to protect both the dignity and the physical and mental integrity of the individual"—offering a relatively expansive reading that links the provision to the foundational claim in the Preamble of the Covenants that "these rights derive from the inherent dignity of the human person." Paragraph 2 also explicitly links this article to the provision in Article 10 that "all persons deprived of their liberty shall be treated with humanity and with respect for the inherent dignity of the human person." And it explicitly applies these obligations to agents of the state not just when acting in their official capacity but also when operating "outside their official capacity or in a private capacity."

Paragraph 3 draws attention to the fact that no exceptions are permitted in times of emergency. (Along similar lines, Paragraph 15 expresses concern over amnesties for torturers that have been granted by some states.) And, in holding that "no justification or extenuating circumstances may be invoked to excuse a violation of Article 7 for any reasons, including those based on an order from a superior officer or public authority," the committee in effect applies the provisions of the 1984 Convention Against Torture to the interpretation of the Covenant. (The prohibition of the use of evidence obtained by torture, advanced in Paragraph 12, does much the same thing.)

Paragraph 4 holds that it is neither necessary nor productive to draw up a list of prohibited acts. Nonetheless, Paragraph 5 emphasizes that mental suffering falls within the acts prohibited by Article 7 and that its protections extend to certain forms of corporal punishment, including protection of "children, pupils and patients in teaching and medical institutions." Paragraph 6 explicitly places prolonged solitary confinement within the coverage of Article 7.

Paragraph 8 claims that the state obligation is not simply to legislatively prohibit such actions but also to take positive steps of protection. Paragraphs 10–13 specify some of those steps, including widely disseminating information on the ban on torture, systematically reviewing interrogation practices, and prohibiting incommunicado detention.

Such observations and interpretations are not formally binding. They do, however, have considerable informal authority—and are especially useful for human rights lawyers and advocates who are seeking authoritative legal grounding for their human rights advocacy.

C. Communication/Petition Procedures

The nine core treaties also allow individual communications (sometimes called petitions). Four of the treaties allow for petitions within the text of the treaty itself (but states are required to opt in or opt out of these procedures); for the other five, this mechanism requires states-parties to accede to an "optional protocol" (see Table 5.1). Depending on the treaty, between one-third and two-thirds of states-parties do not allow individual petitions. Not surprisingly, some of the worst violators choose not to participate. In addition, the number of cases considered is tiny. And, in the end, petition procedures are not even binding in international law.

Although the details differ from body to body, there is a clear general pattern. Communications from individuals or groups are screened by the U.N. Secretariat. Those that show potential merit are registered. Registered petitions are then screened carefully for admissibility: the principal requirements are that the alleged violations fall under the scope of the treaty and that local remedies have been exhausted.

Once the procedural hurdles have been scaled, the relevant committee corresponds with the government in question and sometimes with the petitioner (or his or her representative). It also often carries out inquiries into public records and independent sources of information. It then states its views as to whether there has been a violation of the treaty and makes recommendations as to remedies. These findings are, explicitly, merely the view of the committee. They are not binding in international law (let alone national law). In fact, the state has no obligation even to respond to the committee's views. Nonetheless, many states, especially those with an active civil society, do take the findings seriously. Individuals often receive remedy as a result of their petitions. In some cases—prominent examples include complaints of discrimination on the basis of sexual orientation in Australia and against indigenous women in Canada—national legislation has been changed in response to the recommendations of the committee.

4. Additional Global Actors

At least four other global multilateral actors merit note: the International Labor Organization (ILO); the United Nations Educational, Scientific, and Cultural Organization (UNESCO); the International Criminal Court (ICC); and the U.N. Security Council. Each has a functional mandate that centrally includes, but is not limited to, human rights.

A. *International Labor Organization*

The International Labor Organization is the granddaddy of multilateral human rights organizations, founded in 1919.[11] Major ILO conventions (treaties) have dealt with freedom of association, the right to organize and bargain collectively, forced labor, migrant workers, and indigenous peoples, as well as a variety of issues of working conditions and workplace safety. Even nonbinding ILO recommendations provide an important international reference point for national standards.

ILO monitoring procedures, which date back to 1926, have been the model for other international human rights reporting systems. The Committee of Experts meets annually to review periodic reports submitted by states on their implementation of ratified conventions. If apparent problems are uncovered, the committee may issue a direct request for information or for changes in policy. Over the past two decades, more than a thousand such requests have brought changes in national policies. If the problem remains unresolved, the committee may make "observations," that is, authoritative determinations of violations of the convention in question.

The Conference Committee, which is made up of ILO delegates rather than independent experts, provides an additional level of scrutiny with greater political backing. Each year it selects cases from the report of the Committee of Experts for further review. Government representatives are called upon to provide additional information and explanation. Special complaint procedures also exist for violations of the right to freedom of association and for discrimination in employment.

No less important than these inquisitorial or adversarial procedures is the institution of "direct contacts," a program of consultations and advice, often initiated by a government concerned about improving its performance with respect to a particular convention. The ILO is a leader in cooperative resolution of problems before they reach international monitoring bodies.

Part of the ILO's success can be attributed to its unique tripartite structure. Intergovernmental organizations typically are made up solely of state representatives. NGOs often participate in deliberations but have no decision-making powers. In the ILO, however, workers' and employers' representatives from each member state are voting members of the organization, making it much more difficult for states to hide behind the curtain of sovereignty. The transideological appeal of workers' rights has also been important to the ILO's success. In addition, the Committee of Experts, the ILO's central monitoring body, deals principally with technical issues such as hours of work, minimum working age, workplace safety, and identity documents for seamen. In monitoring such technical conventions, the committee develops and confirms expectations of neutrality that can help to moderate controversy when more contentious political issues do arise.

B. United Nations Educational, Scientific, and Cultural Organization

UNESCO has addressed a variety of human rights issues explicitly.[12] Its 1960 Convention on Discrimination in Education was an important normative instrument during the doldrums while the Covenants languished in the U.N. General Assembly's Third Committee (see §1.3). Its 2005 Declaration on Bioethics and Human Rights has helped to globalize the discussion of this important topic. And UNESCO has done important normative and programmatic work on cultural rights, especially connected with preserving cultural heritages and languages. Most notably, UNESCO worked very closely with the International Criminal Court to bring charges against Ahmad al-Faqi al-Mahdi, who was indicted on charges of orchestrating the destruction of ancient mausoleums, medieval shrines, tombs of Sufi saints, and a fifteenth-century mosque in Timbuktu, Mali, in 2012. In issuing the indictment, ICC prosecutor Fatou Bensouda declared these acts to be war crimes under the Rome Statute. Al-Mahdi surrendered and was transferred to the Hague for trial in September 2015. At the trial's opening in August 2016, al-Mahdi admitted his guilt (the first person ever to do so in an ICC trial), and the case was closed. In September 2016 he was sentenced to nine years in prison.

C. International Criminal Court

The International Criminal Court was established by the Rome Statute, which was adopted in 1998 and entered into force in 2002. It is a permanent international tribunal that adjudicates individual criminal liability for genocide, crimes against humanity, and war crimes.[13] The symbolic significance of individual accountability for particularly egregious, systematic violations of human rights is undoubtedly great. However, the ICC is a "court of last resort," because of its extremely limited jurisdiction in terms of subject matter and also because states must agree to recognize the Court's jurisdiction (124 out of 193 U.N. member-states are parties to the Rome Statute). In rare instances the U.N. Security Council may refer situations in states that are not parties to the Rome Statute to the ICC for investigation.

The ICC handed down its first two judgments in 2012, against Thomas Lubanga Dyilo (sentenced to fourteen years) and Germain Kantanga (sentenced to twelve years) for several counts of war crimes and crimes against humanity committed in the Democratic Republic of the Congo. Two other guilty verdicts were handed down in 2016—in the al-Mahdi case (mentioned above) and against Jean-Pierre Bemba Gombo, who received eighteen years for crimes committed in the Central African Republic (his case is under appeal as of late 2016).

Currently, the ICC is conducting preliminary examinations into situations in ten countries. These examinations are to determine whether the Court has jurisdiction and whether the cases are admissible. Situations in nine other states (all but one—Georgia—are in Africa) have moved to the investigation phase. There are currently five trials that are open, for crimes committed in the Central African Republic

(Bemba et al.), the Democratic Republic of Congo (Bosco Ntaganda), and the case against the former president of Côte d'Ivoire, Laurent Gbagbo.

Although the establishment of a permanent international tribunal to investigate and try cases against individuals who have committed the most heinous of atrocities represents a significant development in the area of human rights and humanitarian law, it is not without its detractors, nor has it escaped political scrutiny, especially in the past few years. The ICC came under significant fire when it decided to issue an indictment against the sitting president of Kenya, Uhuru Muigai Kenyatta, for violence that erupted after the 2007 elections. The ICC ultimately had to drop the charges for lack of sufficient evidence. Many argued that the misstep was a result of an overzealous prosecutor. Ever since, the ICC has come under attack especially from several African states, some of whom have argued that the ICC is simply a tool of the West (in particular, they cite the failure of the ICC to open any investigations into war crimes they maintain were tied to the 2003 U.S.-led invasion of Iraq). In late 2016, Burundi, South Africa, and Gambia announced their decision to withdraw from the Court. Kenya and Namibia are also considering doing so. And in February 2017, at the close of a summit meeting of the African Union, leaders adopted a draft (but nonbinding) strategy to collectively withdraw from the Court. The strategy, however, has no timeline nor recommendations for further action. And some African states, including Nigeria, Congo (Brazzaville), and Senegal, continue to support the ICC.

D. U.N. Security Council

Finally, the U.N. Security Council regularly addresses human rights issues, which over the past quarter century have become a part of most peacekeeping and peace-building operations. It also has the authority to authorize the threat or use of force, which it has occasionally exercised in response to genocide—although its tragically limited response to the genocide in Rwanda was notorious, and its limited responses to genocide in the Darfur region of Sudan and to the atrocities committed by the al-Assad regime in Syria have provoked considerable international criticism. We will look more closely at these issues in Chapter 10.

5. Mainstreaming Human Rights
Throughout the U.N. System

Despite a clear commitment to human rights since its inception, the United Nations until recently tended to relegate human rights to the periphery of its work.[14] The end of the Cold War brought such a drastic change in the international political landscape that the United Nations was compelled to incorporate human rights across the board. We have already noted the roles of both Universal Periodic Review and the Office of the High Commissioner in mainstreaming human rights throughout the U.N. system. Here we note a few other examples of this important expansion of the United Nations' human rights work, focusing on increased interagency cooperation and the institutionalization of new norms.

Particularly notable was the 1998 partnership agreement between the OHCHR and the United Nations Development Programme (UNDP), which led to the United Nations Development Group's (UNDG) Human Rights Working Group (HRWG). It was established in 2009 with the goal of integrating human rights into the United Nations' development work.[15] The HRWG approaches this in three ways: providing a policy forum to ensure coherence in human rights mainstreaming efforts across the U.N. development system; making available human rights expertise to national development actors and processes; and taking the lead on the Human Rights Up Front initiative, which includes six action items:

1. Integrating human rights into the lifeblood of staff so that they understand what the U.N. mandates and commitments to human rights mean for their department, agency, fund, or program, and for them personally
2. Providing member states with candid information with respect to peoples at risk of, or subject to, serious violations of international human rights or humanitarian law
3. Ensuring coherent strategies of action on the ground and leveraging the U.N. system's capacities in a concerted manner
4. Adopting at Headquarters a "one-U.N. approach" to facilitate early coordinated action
5. Achieving, through better analysis, greater impact in the United Nations' human rights protection work
6. Supporting all these activities through an improved system of information management on serious violations of human rights and humanitarian law[16]

The impact of this push to put human rights up front has varied from agency to agency and case to case. At the very least, though, it has pushed human rights into the heart of many discussions where previously it had been ignored or treated largely as an afterthought.

Interagency cooperation has been further enhanced by the Common Human Rights-Based Approach to Development (the Stamford Common Understanding).[17] This Understanding stresses three essential attributes of development work: attention to international human rights treaties in development cooperation and programming in all sectors and all phases, a consideration of the impact on human rights realization of development cooperation programs, and attention to the impact of development cooperation on the capacities of states and other duty-bearers in regards to their international human rights obligations. The discussion on standards continues, but this agreement has led development teams to be more mindful in the case of social and economic rights and the situation of vulnerable populations.[18] Given the centrality of development work to the programmatic activities of the U.N. system and the reluctance of mainstream economists to address political issues and externalities such as human rights—as well as the near-complete separation of human rights and development assistance activities as recently as the mid-1980s—even a limited and relatively ritualized inclusion into development planning has been of real (if hard to measure) significance.

Mainstreaming in the security field has proved much more difficult, given the much more directly political nature of the issues addressed. Nevertheless, U.N. Security Council resolutions since the end of the Cold War have consistently demonstrated a real (if secondary) concern for human rights and regularly highlighted the effects of human rights violations on international peace and security. The rights of women and children in armed conflicts has been the subject of numerous resolutions. In addition, both the establishment of the ad hoc tribunals for Yugoslavia and Rwanda and referrals to the International Criminal Court demonstrate successful mainstreaming of at least some human rights concerns in the field of peace and security. Finally, every post–Cold War peacekeeping mission has included the protection of human rights as part of its mandate.[19]

6. Case Study: The Special Procedures

The special procedures (also called "special mandates") established by the Human Rights Council[20] involve either a single individual or a five-member Working Group of independent human rights experts tasked to report to and advise the Council on both thematic and country-specific human rights issues. In 2016, there were forty-two thematic mandates and fourteen country mandates. Examples of thematic mandates include Working Groups on arbitrary detention, enforced/involuntary disappearances, human rights and transnational corporations and other business enterprises, and discrimination against women in law and practice. The Council has appointed special rapporteurs on topics such as cultural rights, the rights of disabled persons, the right to food, and the situation of human rights defenders. Independent experts have been appointed to investigate matters such as the rights of older persons; the impact of foreign debt on the enjoyment of economic, social, and cultural rights; and violence and discrimination based on sexual orientation and gender identity (LGBTQ persons). Country-specific mandates as of 2016 included Belarus, Cambodia, the Central African Republic, Côte d'Ivoire, North Korea, Eritrea, Haiti, Iran, Mali, Myanmar (Burma), Palestine, Somalia, Sudan, and Syria.

Special procedures submit annual reports to the Human Rights Council. Many also report to the General Assembly. The Human Rights Council reviews country-specific mandates every year and thematic mandates every three years. Some mandates (such as the Working Group on enforced or involuntary disappearances) have operated continuously since the 1980s.

Mandate-holders work in their own capacity as independent experts. As such, they are not considered to be U.N. staff, receive no financial remuneration for their work, and are expected to remain impartial with respect to the United Nations and their own countries of citizenship. Individuals appointed as special rapporteurs, independent experts, or members of Working Groups are limited to a tenure of six years for each assignment.

The Human Rights Council appoints mandate-holders based on the candidate's overall expertise, experience in the mandate field, independence, impartiality, personal integrity, and objectivity. Gender balance, geographical diversity, and representation of different legal systems are also taken into account when the Council considers whom to appoint to carry out these mandates. Candidates may be nominated by governments, regional groups operating within the U.N. system, various international organizations, nongovernmental organizations, other human rights bodies, and even individuals.

Mandate-holders are empowered to undertake a wide range of activities in support of their mandate. They can visit countries, communicate with states regarding alleged violations, conduct thematic studies, convene expert consultations, engage in advocacy and raise public awareness, give advice on technical operations, receive information from individuals and civil society organizations, and overall contribute to the betterment of international human rights standards.

The stature of the mandate-holder (i.e., rapporteur or expert) can also be used to increase the impact of these special procedures. For example, Juan Mendez (from Argentina), who served as the special rapporteur on torture from 2010 to 2016, is the former head of Human Rights Watch and the International Center for Transnational Justice. Between 2005 and 2011, John Ruggie (from the United States) was the special representative of the secretary-general on human rights and transnational corporations and other business enterprises. Ruggie is one of the world's leading scholars of international relations (teaching at Harvard and having previously been a dean at Columbia), a former assistant secretary-general of the United Nations, and the founder of the Global Compact (a leading international actor in the field of corporate responsibility in the areas of human rights, labor, environment, and corruption). The groundbreaking work Ruggie undertook as special representative prompted the Council to transform this mandate into a Working Group on human rights and transnational corporations in 2011.

A. Growth and Development of the Special Procedures

In 1963—in response to alleged human rights violations in South Vietnam—the South Vietnamese government invited U.N. representatives to investigate the situation directly.[21] Although the subsequent mission to South Vietnam does not resemble the special procedures we have today, it was the first example of a country visit and established the tools mandates later would use to collect factual information on the ground.

In 1965 states from Africa, Asia, and the Middle East called for a U.N. response to alleged human rights violations related to colonialism, racism, and apartheid. This prompted the Commission on Human Rights to establish the first two special procedures mandates for a Working Group on the state of South Africa and a special rapporteur on apartheid.

In 1980 the first *thematic* special procedure was established by creating the Working Group on Enforced or Involuntary Disappearances. The thematic attribute was established in response to arguments that a country-specific mandate would be discriminatory, insofar as enforced disappearances plagued nations around the world. Over the next ten years, six thematic Working Groups were established to address enforced disappearances; extrajudicial, summary, or arbitrary executions; religious intolerance; mercenaries; torture; and the sale of children.[22] Since then, the number of thematic mandates has expanded to the forty-two we have as of 2016.

Despite their somewhat narrow scope, thematic mandates have the advantage of freedom from geographical limitations. A thematic mandate-holder can investigate her topic issue in any country and usually with little authorization needed. The comparative abundance of thematic mandates in contrast to country mandates showcases the current preference of the United Nations. Specific country mandates have proven more difficult to both establish and fulfill, in part because of the impression that country mandates are more political and the fact that they are reviewed every year instead of every three. (We should note that the number of thematic mandates surpassed the number of country mandates in 1998.)

The rapid growth (some use the word *proliferation*) of country and thematic procedures is quite remarkable. There were four mandates in 1980. By 1990, the number had grown to fourteen and by 2000 had increased to thirty-four. By the time the Human Rights Council replaced the Commission on Human Rights (in 2006), there were forty special procedure mandates. In May 2014, the number of active special procedure mandates reached fifty for the first time. The special procedures developed and grew on an ad hoc basis rather than by any grand design or structure. It is important to remember that it is states themselves—who constitute the membership of the Council—that have identified these gaps in human rights protections and have used the special procedures to fill them.

B. Impact of the Special Procedures

The special procedures mechanism has established itself as a core component to U.N. human rights protection and promotion and is perhaps the most important mechanism (along with the high commissioner) for addressing human rights violations on the ground. The recent and rapid expansion of the special procedures suggests that the United Nations as an institution believes the system has been and will continue to be effective in shaping state behavior regarding human rights. But has this mechanism actually initiated positive change regarding state behavior?

A 2014 report by the Universal Rights Group does not equate the numerical expansion of the mandates with an improvement in their effectiveness, defined as shaping or changing state behavior. While noting the rather impressive growth of the special procedures, especially since the 1993 Vienna Conference, the URG nevertheless has identified six core "determinants of influence" that U.N. policy makers must strive to strengthen and improve: independence and accountability; expertise and standing; flexibility, reach, and accessibility; cooperation; implementation and follow-up; and availability of resources and secretariat support.

In another assessment, Surya Subedi stated that most mandate-holders are overloaded with responsibility right from the start, as they are "expected simultaneously to become a human rights activist, a rallying point for human rights, an international diplomat, an academic, and a government adviser."[23] This work is also done without financial compensation and on the mandate-holder's own time. Subedi also believes the support that the OHCHR provides to its mandate-holders is meager (e.g., only providing one assistant and recommending only two country visits per year). Some mandate-holders who are based at academic institutions receive their support; however, this arrangement automatically favors the candidacy and selection of special mandate-holders from large, wealthy universities and research centers, most of which are based in the global North.[24] Subedi also cited the lack of effective follow-up procedures and overlaps in mandate duties (particularly between country and thematic mandates) as hindering the effectiveness of mandate-holders.

A more recent study by Rosa Freedman and Jacob Mchangama, which analyzed the proliferation of mandates, concluded pessimistically. First, the increase in mandates has not been paired with an appropriate increase in resources and funding. This has resulted in fewer country visits, fewer reports, and overall less time for mandate-holders to conduct their activities. Second, they found that new mandates are diverting resources away from traditional rights and the relationship between the individual right-holder and the state. The new mandates are instead focusing on criticizing state policy programs and foreign relations.[25]

However, for individuals suffering from human rights violations, these special procedures can make a real difference. Take, for example, the situation of enforced or involuntary disappearances. In 1980 the Commission on Human Rights created the Working Group on Enforced or Involuntary Disappearances to assist families and friends in determining the whereabouts of disappeared persons. After examining communications detailing a disappearance, the Working Group transmits the case to the government in question. If necessary, reminders are sent, at least once a year. More than 19,000 were handled in the group's first decade of work. Since its inception in 1980, the Working Group has inquired into the fate of more than 55,000 individuals in 107 countries around the world. In the period from May 2015 to May 2016, the Working Group was able to resolve 161 outstanding cases.

In close to 1 in 5 cases—around 10,000 cases in total—the whereabouts or fate of the individual has been clarified. Special urgent-action procedures for disappearances within the three months preceding the communication, when most victims suffer torture or execution but also when they are most likely to reappear, have resolved a somewhat higher percentage of cases. There is good reason to believe that a significant number of those identified by this procedure owe their lives to it.

The immediate impact of these bodies is ultimately a matter of the willingness of governments to engage in conversations with them, allow them to visit their countries, and listen to their concerns and advice. But particularly when either the body or the mandate-holder has a prominent international reputation, many states are willing to make improvements in the treatment of particular individuals. And some of the reports by these experts are important sources of information about abuses, used by national and transnational advocates.

Discussion Questions

1. Several U.N. treaty monitoring bodies have an interstate complaints mechanism where a state can report another state for an alleged human rights violation. However, this mechanism remains unused. Why might this be? Do you think states will continue to refrain from its usage? What are the potential effects of one state reporting another?

2. U.N. treaty monitoring bodies can conduct inquiries into a state's actions upon the body's own discretion. However, a state can opt out of this process by not recognizing the competence of the body. Does this render the inquiries mechanism useless? Or can you think of instances where an opt-out is justifiable?

3. We have suggested that international human rights procedures are likely to have their greatest impact where the human rights abuses are less egregious. What does this suggest about the most effective forms of international action? Are you comfortable with the idea of writing off the worst cases (which some may conclude is the central policy implication of this argument)? Is there a practical alternative?

4. Membership on the Human Rights Council has included states with traditionally good human rights records, like the Netherlands, as well as states with traditionally worrisome human rights records, like Nigeria. Is it better for human rights to attempt to include all states in this mechanism or selectively exclude states with troublesome records?

5. Multilateral institutions with a primary human rights mandate concentrate heavily on civil and political rights. What are the reasons for this? Is this a defensible allocation of resources and attention? What would have to change to bring about a more comprehensive system of international human rights monitoring?

6. As stated in the chapter, the number of thematic U.N. mandates has proliferated in recent decades, especially when compared to country-specific mandates. Why might this be? Are thematic mandates more likely to safeguard human rights, or are they simply easier to establish because they are not focused on a specific country? What are the potential pros and cons of this emphasis on thematic special procedures?

Suggested Readings

Primary source information on most of the bodies considered in this chapter is available on the comprehensive and easy-to-use website United Nations Human Rights (http://www.ohchr.org), run by the Office of the High Commissioner for Human Rights.

Among the extensive published scholarly literature, special note should be made of the recent second edition of Philip Alston, ed., *The United Nations and Human Rights: A Critical Appraisal* (Oxford: Oxford University Press, 2011). Two other wide-ranging readers are Gundmundur Alfredsson, Jonas Grimheden, Bertrand D. Ramcharan, and Alfred Zayas, eds., *International Human Rights Monitoring Mechanisms: Essays in Honour of Jakob Th. Möeller,* 2nd ed. (Leiden: Martinus Nijhof, 2009); and Geoff Gilbert, ed., *The Delivery of Human Rights: Essays in Honour of Professor Sir Nigel Rodley* (Hoboken, NJ: Taylor & Francis, 2010).

The standard work on treaty monitoring is Philip Alston and James Crawford, eds., *The Future of UN Human Rights Treaty Monitoring* (Cambridge: Cambridge

University Press, 2000). It covers the full range of venues and issues. Christof Heyns and Frans Viljoen, *The Impact of United Nations Human Rights Treaties on the Domestic Level* (The Hague: Kluwer International, 2002), provides considerable illustrative material on the domestic impact of international human rights treaties. The literature on individual bodies is immense.

The following recent books provide a good start for those interested in more details: Yogesh Tyagi, *The UN Human Rights Committee: Practice and Procedure* (New York: Cambridge University Press, 2011); Alex Conte, *Defining Civil and Political Rights: The Jurisprudence of the United Nations Human Rights Committee* (Farnham, UK: Ashgate, 2009); Hanna Beate Schöpp-Schilling and Cees Flinterman, eds., *The Circle of Empowerment: Twenty-Five Years of the UN Committee on the Elimination of Discrimination Against Women* (New York: Feminist Press at the City University of New York, 2007); Andrew Byrnes and Jane Connors, *The International Bill of Rights for Women: The Impact of the CEDAW Convention* (Oxford: Oxford University Press, 2008); Meena Shivdas and Sarah Coleman, eds., *Without Prejudice: CEDAW and the Determination of Women's Rights in a Legal and Cultural Context* (London: Commonwealth Secretariat, 2010); Fleur van Leeuwen, *Women's Rights Are Human Rights: The Practice of the United Nations Human Rights Committee and the Committee on Economic, Social, and Cultural Rights* (Antwerp: Intersentia, 2010); Catherine Rutgers, ed., *Creating a World Fit for Children: Understanding the UN Convention on the Rights of the Child* (New York: International Debate Education Association, 2011); Trevor Buck, *International Child Law,* 2nd ed. (Hoboken, NJ: Taylor & Francis, 2010); and Manfred Nowak, Elizabeth McArthur, et al., *The United Nations Convention Against Torture: A Commentary* (Oxford: Oxford University Press, 2008). The websites for all the individual treaty bodies can be accessed through http://www .ohchr.org/EN/HRBodies/Pages/HumanRightsBodies.aspx. Finally, Joel E. Oestreich, *Power and Principle: Human Rights Programming in International Organizations* (Washington, DC: Georgetown University Press, 2007), examines human rights in the work of UNICEF, the World Bank, and the World Health Organization.

6

~<o>~

Regional Human Rights Regimes

Regional human rights regimes run the gamut from a system of authoritative judicial enforcement in Europe to barely nascent regimes in Asia and the Arab Middle East. This chapter reviews these regimes and assesses their contributions to the multilateral promotion and protection of human rights.

1. The European Regional Regime

A. *The Council of Europe System*

The forty-seven-member Council of Europe operates a strong system of regional human rights enforcement.[1] Its normative core is the Convention for the Protection of Human Rights and Fundamental Freedoms (commonly known as the European Convention on Human Rights, or ECHR), which covers mostly civil and political rights; and the European Social Charter, which addresses a wide range of economic and social rights in considerable detail. The Council of Europe commissioner for human rights (Nils Muižnieks, a Latvian human rights scholar, became the third commissioner in 2012) has extensive powers to investigate and publicize human rights issues on either a thematic or a country basis. Special procedures exist in the case of torture, including the right of the European Committee for the Prevention of Torture to visit all places of detention in any member state.

The 1954 European Convention addresses core civil and political rights. In 2010, fifteen protocols were added to deepen and extend the list of rights protected by the Convention.

The original European Social Charter of 1961 includes nineteen enumerated rights. In 1996, the Revised European Social Charter greatly extended the range of recognized rights. Parties to the Revised Charter are bound by at least six out of nine core rights, of their own selection, and no fewer than sixteen articles total. (Parties to the original Charter agree to be bound by at least five of seven core articles and no fewer than ten articles total.) Forty-three of the forty-seven member states of the Council are parties to one of the Charters.

The most notable feature of the European human rights regime is the European Court of Human Rights, which exercises mandatory jurisdiction with respect to the European Convention, and whose decisions create binding legal obligations for states.[2] (The European Social Charter is not subject to judicial enforcement.) Since the reorganization and expansion of the Court in 1998, individuals in any member country have direct access to the Court, subject to minimal procedural restrictions (most notably the requirement that local remedies have been exhausted).

Since its founding in 1958, the European Court of Human Rights has issued roughly 18,500 judgments.[3] Some of its more prominent decisions have led to significant changes in national law. Most of its decisions, when in favor of the petitioner (as is the case about two-thirds of the time), have brought relief, including monetary damages. The system, however, has become a victim of its own success. In 2015, 40,650 petitions were received (down from 56,200 in 2014), and at the end of 2015 the Court had a backlog of 64,850 pending petitions.[4]

A small number of states find themselves continually before the Court. Roughly one-third of the Court's judgments involve three member-states: Russia, Turkey, and Romania. Nearly half of pending cases involve petitioners in Russia, Turkey, and Ukraine.

One of the most important features of the Court has been its adoption of the principle of "evolutive interpretation." Treaty provisions are interpreted not according to the understandings at the time of drafting (which is the norm in international law and many national legal systems) but in light of current understandings and practices. The Court thus serves as an important mechanism for the progressive evolution of regional human rights obligations.

The European Committee of Social Rights supervises implementation of the rights of the Social Charter, principally through a state reporting procedure similar to those in the U.N. system (see §5.3). Reports focus on four thematic areas: employment, training, and equal opportunities; health, social security, and social protection; labor rights; and children, families, and migrants. Each year, states-parties must report on one area. After the completion of a four-year cycle, the Committee issues its findings and recommendations to the member-state. Under a 1998 optional protocol, the Committee created a collective, rather than an individual, complaints procedure. Petitions or complaints may be filed only by "representative" organizations, such as trade unions and specific NGOs who have been officially recognized by the Committee to file petitions.[5]

B. The European Union and the OSCE

The twenty-eight member European Union (EU), although not primarily a human rights body, has further strengthened the European regime in at least three important ways. First, the 2007 Lisbon Treaty, a major constitutional revision of the European Union that amended the earlier Rome (1957) and Maastricht (1993) Treaties, made the Charter of Fundamental Rights of the European Union (adopted in 2000) legally binding on all member-states. Second, the Lisbon Treaty gave the Union's supreme judicial organ, the Court of Justice of the European Union, the powers to interpret the Charter of Fundamental Rights and to hear cases arising under its guarantees. (The United Kingdom and Poland secured protocols of dubious legal effect to exempt themselves from some aspects of this provision.) Third, the Lisbon Treaty committed the European Union *as an intergovernmental organization* to accede to the European Convention on Human Rights, thus making the Union itself and its institutions subject to the decisions of the European Court of Human Rights.

Important European regional mechanisms also exist under the Organization for Security and Co-operation in Europe (OSCE),[6] a group of fifty-seven states from Europe, Central Asia, and North America. Its work on minority rights has been especially significant: the OSCE high commissioner on national minorities is a leading regional actor on this topic of immense historical and contemporary importance. The OSCE also has notable programs to support free elections and rule of law (through the Office for Democratic Institutions and Human Rights) and media freedom (through the OSCE representative on freedom of the media) and to combat human trafficking (through the Office of the Special Representative and Coordinator for Combating Trafficking in Human Beings).

The citizens of Europe thus have a considerable array of regional multilateral mechanisms available to them not just to encourage their governments to implement their obligations but in many instances to make legally binding findings of violations. And given the context of extensive and intensive regional cooperation, most states usually comply with most decisions.

2. The Inter-American System

A. Regional Norms

The American Declaration of the Rights and Duties of Man was adopted by the General Assembly of the Organization of American States (OAS) in April 1948. Like the Universal Declaration, it is not legally binding. The 1969 American Convention on Human Rights, which is a legally binding instrument, came into force in 1978. It has been ratified by twenty-three of the thirty-five OAS members, including all Latin American states (except Venezuela, which denounced the Convention in 2012), but not the United States, Canada, and a number of Caribbean states.

The American Convention largely parallels the ICCPR, although it contains a few unusually robust guarantees. For example, Article 13 specifies that freedom of thought and expression includes the right to seek, receive, and impart information and Article 14 grants journalists and the media the right of reply. In its decisions and rulings, the Inter-American Commission and the Inter-American Court of Human Rights (discussed below) have ruled that transitional governments have an affirmative duty to investigate and prosecute human rights violations of prior governments, thus establishing a "right to truth" and the illegality of **amnesty** policies.

While the American Convention deals almost exclusively with civil and political rights, the Protocol of San Salvador addresses economic and social rights. It has been ratified by sixteen OAS member-states. There are also regional conventions on torture, violence against women, disappearances, and discrimination against persons with disabilities. And the OAS has adopted resolutions and declarations on a variety of topics, including freedom of expression, indigenous peoples, and racism and discrimination.

The other major normative instrument in the region is the 2001 Inter-American Democratic Charter (IADC), which today is arguably as important as the Declaration and the Convention. Unlike the American Convention, the IADC is legally binding on all thirty-five OAS member-states. It is aimed at promoting and defending democracy in the Americas. It defines democracy and the obligations of states when democratic rule appears to be under threat. The IADC was invoked at the behest of fourteen OAS heads of state for the first time in 2002, when elements of the Venezuelan military attempted to remove the late Hugo Chavez from power in a coup d'état. Although the short crisis led to only one declaration under the IADC, it inhibited recognition of the coup attempt. Later, in July 2009, the OAS General Assembly suspended Honduras after its elected government was deposed by a military coup. And in the summer and fall of 2016, as we were finishing drafting this chapter, the OAS used the Democratic Charter to push for dialogue in the political crisis emerging in Venezuela.

B. The Inter-American Commission and Court

The Inter-American Commission on Human Rights (IACHR) was established in 1959.[7] Much like the U.N.'s Human Rights Council, it operates independently of the Convention, in this case as an autonomous organization within the OAS (whose thirty-five members include all the independent states of the Western Hemisphere). Its seven members are elected by secret ballot by the OAS General Assembly and serve in a personal capacity.

The Inter-American Commission conducts country studies and examines thematic issues of regional concern. During the 1970s and 1980s, the Commission was particularly aggressive in using its independent authority to pressure repressive governments. Its reporting on Chile under military rule was particularly important to both internal and international human rights advocates (see the case study on page 104).

As the overall regional human rights situation has improved in the post–Cold War world, the reports of the Commission have become less prominent. Nonetheless, they remain significant. For example, Commission reports on Honduras in 2009 and 2010 drew attention to serious problems. And at the end of 2009, it issued an important report on citizen security and human rights. It also works to publicize prominent individual cases.

The Commission also plays a central role in processing individual petitions, which recently have numbered about 2,000 a year. After an initial procedural screening, the Commission conducts its own fact finding and typically attempts to facilitate a friendly settlement between the petitioner and her government. If this is not successful, it issues a report, indicating its findings and recommendations. And if the state does not accept those recommendations, the Commission may refer the case to the Inter-American Court of Human Rights (for the twenty-one states that have recognized the jurisdiction of the Court). Only about twenty cases a year, though, reach the stage of a report.

The Inter-American Court sits in San José, Costa Rica.[8] Its seven members are elected by state parties to the Convention (although nationals of any OAS member-state may serve, even if their state is not a party to the convention). Twenty-three of the twenty-five states-parties to the American Convention are also parties to the Court, and twenty of those recognize its **contentious jurisdiction,** meaning its power to declare a state-party to the Convention in breach of its treaty obligations and to order reparations. Individuals do not have direct access to the Court. Only the Commission and parties to the Convention can submit cases. One of the more interesting and innovative procedures of the Court is the use of provisional measures to attempt to protect persons in danger of irreparable harm or death. (Through November 2016, the Court had issued 575 provisional measures.) The Court also tries to serve as an active source of the progressive development of regional human rights law through its advisory opinions, twenty-three of which had been issued through September 2016.

The Court, however, has faced considerable criticism.[9] Through November 2016 the Court had issued only 317 judgments.[10] Furthermore, as with most international judicial institutions (including the International Court of Justice), the Court lacks the power to enforce its rulings. (By the Court's own reckoning, fewer than half of its decisions finding violations have been fully implemented.) A handful of states have quit paying their dues, recalled their ambassadors, threatened to leave, or suspended membership to protest judgments. (The bright side of this behavior is that it signals the Court's judicial independence.) The Court also faces a funding problem that prevents it from taking on a more robust role in the region. Finally, until recently, the Court tended to focus on remedying the violations of military or authoritarian governments. It thus has been criticized for not covering a wide enough range of human rights violations, such as indigenous rights, access to abortion, and LGBT rights.

This disappointingly small number of cases heard by the Court indicates the relative weakness of the Inter-American regime compared to its European counterpart. But we should be careful not to confuse cause and effect. As we will see in more detail below, strong multilateral measures are largely a consequence, not a cause, of a high level of national practice throughout the region.

3. The African Regional Regime

The African regional human rights regime is based on the 1981 African Charter on Human and Peoples' Rights (also known as the Banjul Charter). It includes the African Commission on Human Rights and African Court of Peoples' and Human Rights (see below). Although the regime is substantively much weaker than its European and American counterparts, the African Union (AU) has attempted to at least strengthen the institutional mechanisms for human rights on the African continent. Despite its shortcomings, the African system carries great symbolic significance in the region and has provided considerable encouragement and support to national activists in their struggle for human rights.

The African regime operates under the auspices of the fifty-four-member African Union, the successor organization of the original Organization of African Unity (OAU), of which every state on the continent (except Morocco, which in 2016 signaled its intention to join) is a member. All members are subject to the African Charter on Human and People's Rights. (Europe is the only other region in which all members of the regional organization are bound by the regional human rights treaty.)[11] In addition, Article 4(h) of the Constitutive Act of the African Union empowers the Union to intervene in a member state if the AU Assembly has made a finding of war crimes, genocide, or crimes against humanity. This is a significant departure from the African Union's predecessor, the Organization of African Unity, which adhered to a rigid and extreme principle of nonintervention that was regularly used as a shield by governments that committed grievous violations of human rights.[12]

The 1981 African Charter, which entered into force in 1986, is unique in several ways. It is the only regional instrument to include a full array of civil, political, economic, social, and cultural rights in a single document. It includes group rights as well as individual rights, which some observers believe creates significant tensions when the claims of individuals and groups clash. Article 29 outlines a number of individual duties—such as "not compromising the security of the State" and "to preserve and strengthen social and national solidarity," which again may clash significantly with individual (or even group) rights claims. Furthermore, and most significantly, many articles of the African Charter contain "clawback clauses" that weaken its protections. For example, Article 6 states, "No one may be deprived of his freedom except for reasons and conditions previously laid down by law." In other words, so long as a government bothers to pass a law first, it can deprive people of their freedom for pretty much any reason it chooses.

These departures from other regional systems are rooted in Africa's experience with imperial colonialism, which remained a powerful presence in the region into the 1970s (when nine of the African Union's fifty-four members finally achieved independence from colonial rule, following thirty-three of their colleagues who achieved independence in the 1960s). That experience fostered an unusual sense of solidarity and unity and a strong focus on issues of self-determination and racism (see also §4.2). And independence-era African governments regularly stressed the importance of the social unit and society, rather than the individual, in "African culture."

The Charter purports to combine different systems of justice, both individual and collective, and to balance rights with obligations toward the community and the state. And newly independent African governments, like their eighteenth- and nineteenth-century Western counterparts, gave perhaps understandable priority to state building and national consolidation over internationally recognized human rights.

The result, however, was increasingly dismal human rights records across the continent, with nearly all African states suffering under personalist or military dictatorships in the 1970s and 1980s. The post–Cold War era, however, has brought substantial (although quite uneven) democratic progress. And even the relatively weak institutions of the African regional regime have made a real if modest contribution to a greatly improved regional attitude toward human rights.

The African Commission on Human Rights was established to protect, promote, and interpret the African Charter. It is primarily a promotional and advisory body. Members of the Commission are elected by the Assembly of Heads of State and Government of the African Union, from a slate of nominees put forth by member-states.[13] The Commission's members thus are much less independent than are their European and American counterparts, who serve in their own capacities as independent experts. The reporting system is plagued by poor reports—a reflection of both lack of resources in most states and lack of interest by many—and by underfunding of the Commission. As for the investigation of complaints, few states cooperate, and the decisions of the Commission have been criticized for their vagueness with respect to suggested remedies. In addition, the Commission's members work under confidentiality clauses that prevent the public's awareness of its work.[14]

The African Court of Peoples' and Human Rights sits in Arusha, Tanzania, and is composed of eleven judges who are elected by secret ballot from nominees put forth by member-states. The African Court resembles its Inter-American counterpart in that its jurisdiction is optional—twenty-nine states have accepted its jurisdiction. The protocol establishing the Court stipulates that the Court may hear cases brought to it by the Commission, other states-parties, and African intergovernmental organizations. The protocol also allows NGOs that have consultative status with the Commission, as well as individuals, to bring cases to the Court, provided they have satisfied the rules of admissibility and that the state involved has made a "special declaration" (under Article 34.6) that it will allow such petitions. Only seven states have done so.

The Court first met in July 2006. After a slow start, since 2011 the Court has issued twenty-six rulings and six advisory opinions. An additional five are pending, and sixty cases are awaiting disposition. The Court has also embarked on "sensitization visits" to African Union member states to promote the Court's activities and to lobby states to adopt the Court's protocol and especially the special declaration allowing for individual and group petitions.

The African Commission and the Court are leading regional voices for human rights. The meetings of the Commission provide the occasion for valuable networking by NGOs from across the continent. Its activities have helped to socialize African states to the idea that their human rights practices are legitimately subject to regional scrutiny—a not insignificant achievement given the radical notions of sovereignty and nonintervention that dominated the continent in the 1970s and 1980s. And there is an infrastructure in place that African states can build on in the future.

However, the future of the Court remains in question. In June 2004, a proposal was made to merge the stillborn African Court of Justice with the African Court of Peoples' and Human Rights to form a new institution, the African Court of Justice and Human Rights. This new Court would thus have two sections: one dealing with general violations of international law (e.g., piracy, terrorism, drug trafficking) and the second dealing with human rights (as is now the case with the current African Court of Peoples' and Human Rights). A protocol to this effect was opened for signature at the AU Heads of State summit in June 2008. To date, however, only five states have signed (fifteen ratifications are required for the protocol to enter into force).

Further complicating matters, the 2014 Malabo Protocol adopted by the African Union would further amend the new Court's statute to include jurisdiction over crimes under **international humanitarian law,** for example, genocide, war crimes, and crimes against humanity. The effect of all of this would be to create a hybrid super-Court such as has never been seen before in international or regional politics. The potential case load of such a Court, which would include cases under three branches of law (public international law, international human rights law, and international criminal law), especially in a region that suffers from significant institutional capacity deficits, is troublesome to some observers.[15] Nevertheless, this proposal points to a significant development in regionalism, with African leaders essentially seeking out robust regional solutions and institutions that are more appropriate to their circumstances and the regional context.

4. Asia

The Asian region has been very slow to develop human rights institutions, although the pace of development has begun to quicken in the past several years. Only recently has the region considered a highly circumspect declaration on human rights. There is no legally binding convention on human rights and no formal monitoring or enforcement mechanisms.

Part of the reason for this is that Asia is largely a geographical entity, not a true cultural, economic, or political region. But even at the subregional level, organizations that might include a human rights dimension to their mandates are rare. Only the Association of Southeast Asian Nations (ASEAN) enjoys region-wide participation and has a long tradition of collective multilateral consultation.

ASEAN is notorious for its extreme deference to state sovereignty, understood in almost absolutist terms. Nevertheless, building on more than a decade of advocacy by the Working Group for an ASEAN Human Rights Mechanism, member-states in the region finally agreed to the creation of the ASEAN Intergovernmental Commission on Human Rights (AICHR) in 2009.

The first task of the Commission was to draft the ASEAN Human Rights Declaration (AHRD), which member-states unanimously adopted in 2012. Despite this watershed achievement, the AHRD was heavily criticized by human rights NGOs, the U.S. State Department, and even the U.N. high commissioner for human rights.[16] Many of the Declaration's provisions, which were drafted without collaboration with the public or nongovernmental organizations, act as a shield for ASEAN member states against already established international human rights standards. It does not include fundamental rights such as freedom of association or protection against enforced disappearance. Many of the rights it does recognize are subordinated to national law. The Declaration is heavily skewed toward group rights and limitations on human rights demanded by "Asian culture." And in many cases the enjoyment of rights is secondary to the fulfillment of duties to the community or the state.

The AICHR uses the ASEAN Charter and its own Terms of Reference (TOR, from 2009) as its core governing documents. The AICHR is merely a consultative organ—it has no power to investigate human rights violations or monitor the human rights situations within the region. Upon close inspection of the TOR, one can easily find evidence of ASEAN's relativistic approach to human rights, which privileges state interests and preferences over the fulfillment of universal human rights standards. The TOR promotes principles such as the "independence, sovereignty, equality, territorial integrity and national identity of all ASEAN Member States," "non-interference in the internal affairs of ASEAN Member States," and "respect for the right of every Member State to lead its national existence free from external interference, subversion and coercion." In comparison to the European, Latin American, and even African regional systems, these guiding principles characterize the AICHR as a fundamentally toothless organization that places state preferences over human rights within the region.

Nevertheless, the AICHR has released two 5-year plans (2010–2015 and 2016–2020). The first plan's goals were not fully realized, but the new plan accounts for this and expands the Commission's duties somewhat. So although progress in the establishment of a regional human rights system in Asia has been painfully slow, it is still moving forward. (The section on the ASEAN system in the previous edition of the book covered just three short paragraphs!)

5. The Arab World

We turn finally to human rights in the Arab Middle East. In some respects the Arab regime is the least developed of the regional systems. Its legal foundation, however, is somewhat more firm than the ASEAN regime.

The League of Arab States (known commonly as the Arab League) created the Permanent Arab Commission on Human Rights in 1968, largely in response to the 1967 occupation of Palestinian territory in the West Bank and Gaza. The League adopted the Arab Charter on Human Rights (ACHR) in 2004, which entered into force in 2008. The Charter includes a full array of civil, political, economic, social, and cultural rights. The monitoring mechanism is the Arab Human Rights Committee, which is composed of seven members who serve in their own capacity. Each is elected by secret ballot from a slate of candidates nominated by states-parties to the Charter.

As of 2016, seventeen out of the twenty-two member-states of the League have signed, and thirteen have ratified, the Arab Charter. The Charter does not include complaint or petition procedures. It does, however, include a state-reporting obligation, although there is little cooperation with civil society organizations.[17]

Indicative of the state of regional human rights efforts is the Arab League's website, which can only be described as atrocious. The site (http://www.lasportal.org/Pages/Welcome.aspx) does not even come up on the first page of a Google search. The English-language link is broken. And most of the limited information on the Commission's recent activities is largely ceremonial, which seems sadly accurate.

There are some recent developments that suggest improvements are coming, or at least possible. The General Secretariat of the Arab League proclaimed 2016–2026 the Decade of Arab Civil Society Organizations. There have also been recent efforts to establish a human rights court for members of the Arab League in accordance with the Arab Charter on Human Rights.[18]

6. Assessing Regional Human Rights Regimes

Strong regional human rights regimes are more an effect than a cause of good human rights performance. If a state has a good human rights record, then not only will a strong regime appear relatively unthreatening, but the additional support it provides for national efforts is likely to be welcomed. Conversely, states with bad records are unlikely to support strong regional monitoring mechanisms, let alone systems of authoritative legal remedy.

Several states in Central and Eastern Europe, however, have poor human rights records and yet agree to subject themselves to the strong regional procedures. Part of the explanation is the normative and emotional significance of being part of "Europe." (This active sense of regional identity also supports the Inter-American and African regimes and helps to explain the ASEAN exception in Asia.) The participation of Ukraine, Belarus, and Russia, however, also reflects the fact that the European Court of Human Rights deals only with individual cases. A finding of a violation only requires the state to provide restitution to the individual victim, not change the law or administrative practice that produced the violation.

This brings us back to the importance of national commitment (political will). States with a real commitment to human rights usually will take the findings of a court, committee, commissioner, or expert to heart. Those without such a commitment can get by nicely, even in the European system, with formalistic compliance with a reporting process, court decision, or visit by monitors. Thus the impact of the European and Inter-American regimes varies greatly among countries within the region.

Regional mechanisms, however, do have the special advantage of greater cultural community. This may give the organization special credibility. And it undercuts arguments about the imposition of inappropriate alien standards. Furthermore, the expectation that there should be regional human rights regimes may exert some modest but perhaps not entirely insignificant pressure for progress even in Asia and the Arab world.

Regional regimes can also be valuable simply by providing another set of eyes. This additional scrutiny, because it is regional rather than global, may even be better attuned to or better able to address some issues, although on other issues the regional perspective may be constraining. And, in practice, there is considerable synergy, and even interaction, between regional and global multilateral mechanisms. Regional human rights regimes thus are significant players in the global human rights regime.

7. Case Study: Chile and the Inter-American Commission

In Chile, military rule had been rare since the mid-nineteenth century. After World War II, a stable three-party democratic system emerged. In 1970, Salvador Allende became the world's first freely elected Marxist president. Allende dramatically intensified the economic and social reforms begun under his Christian Democratic predecessor, Eduardo Frei. Large agricultural estates were expropriated. Key private industries and banks were nationalized, including Chile's (largely U.S.-owned) copper industry. Social services were expanded. These changes were both lavishly praised and reviled, both within Chile and abroad. The resulting ideological polarization helped to set the stage for a military coup in September 1973, which installed a repressive military regime under the dictatorial rule of Augusto Pinochet, who remained in power until 1990.

Within a week of the coup on September 11, 1973, the Inter-American Commission cabled Chile expressing its concern and asking for information. In October, its executive secretary, Luis Reque, visited Chile. His report advised a formal onsite visit by the Commission, which took place July 22–August 2, 1974.

During its visit, the Inter-American Commission interviewed government authorities, received 575 new communications, and took statements from witnesses to support previously submitted communications. Commission members also observed military tribunals, studied trial records of military and civil courts, and gathered information on the junta's legislation. Their visits to detention centers led to some minor changes and helped to identify facilities where torture was being practiced.

The Commission's report concluded that the government of Chile was guilty of a wide range of human rights abuses, including systematic violations of the rights to life, liberty, personal security, due process, and civil liberties. In October 1974, this was hardly news. Nonetheless, the report was thorough and tough. It also provided authoritative confirmation of the charges that had been made against the Chilean junta. This made it much more difficult for sympathetic foreign governments to dismiss the complaints of exiles and human rights activists as partisan or unsubstantiated. For example, the report was a standard source of information in U.S. congressional hearings.

Over the next two years, the Commission focused on individual communications. In 1975 it considered more than six hundred cases of torture and 160 disappearances. The government, however, was uncooperative. Furthermore, as noted earlier, individual communications are not well suited to handling systematic, gross violations. Not much came of these investigations—beyond added publicity and greater detail on individual violations.

The Commission's second report on Chile, in 1976, applied new pressure on the Pinochet regime. Although noting a decline in some violations, it documented continuing systematic abuses and concluded that government actions and policies continued to be an impediment to the restoration of respect for human rights in Chile. This helped to undercut arguments made by and on behalf of Chile that the situation was returning to normal.

The political organs of the OAS, however, refused to follow the Commission's lead. The first report on Chile provoked an innocuous resolution that did little more than ask for additional information. The OAS was so little moved that in 1975 the members overwhelmingly accepted Chile's offer to host the next session of the OAS General Assembly. Following the Commission's second report, Chile was asked "to continue adopting and implementing the necessary procedures and measures for effectively preserving and ensuring full respect for human rights in Chile." By implying more progress than had in fact occurred, this resolution was in some ways worse than nothing. And after the third report, in March 1977, the OAS General Assembly did not even extend the formal courtesy of asking for a further study.

This icy reception underscores the limits of even aggressive and independent monitors in an organization with little concern for human rights. Nonetheless, the Commission persisted. Its annual reports for 1977, 1978, and 1979–1980 included sections on Chile. The reports for 1980–1981 through 1982–1983, in a concession to the generally hostile organizational environment, contained no references to particular countries. But the 1983–1984 report returned to a tougher stand, with a chapter on violations in several states (including Chile).

In May 1984, in response to the worsening situation in Chile, the Commission began work on a new country report, issued in 1985. A resolution criticizing Chile by name failed by a single vote in the OAS General Assembly in December 1985. And the IACHR continued to pressure the Pinochet government until it was finally removed from office.

What can we conclude from all this? A cynic can point to the bottom line, namely, the persistence of military rule in Chile. If a state is willing to accept the costs to its reputation, which rarely exceed strained relations and reduced foreign aid, it can flout international human rights regimes.

But to expect recalcitrant states to be forced to mend their ways is wildly unrealistic. The Inter-American Commission, like most other multilateral human rights agencies, works primarily with the power of publicity. It can promote the regional implementation of human rights norms. It can monitor and publicize violations and try to persuade states to improve their practices. But it cannot, and is not intended to be able to, force a state to do anything. Sovereignty remains the overriding norm in the Inter-American human rights regime—as in all other international human rights regimes (except Europe).

Nonetheless, in summarizing the Commission's work on Chile, Cecilia Medina, who herself was forced into exile by the military government, has argued that "in a situation of gross, systematic violations, the constant attention of the international community is of the highest importance; it serves as a support and encouragement for those suffering and opposing repression within the country, and at the same time prompts, and serves as a basis for, further international action by other governmental and nongovernmental international organizations."[19] This is particularly true when a state is subject to scrutiny in multiple intergovernmental organizations and by several national and international NGOs.

Perhaps the strongest evidence for the importance of international publicity is the diplomatic effort states exert to avoid it. In the late 1970s and early 1980s, both Argentina and Chile devoted much of their diplomacy—in the United Nations, the OAS, and the United States—to avoiding public criticism.[20] If rights-abusive regimes take international condemnation seriously enough to struggle to avoid it, the work of international human rights agencies is unlikely to be entirely pointless.

We must also remember that the bottom line includes individuals who are helped. States often respond to international pressure by releasing or improving the treatment of prominent victims. These small victories for international action are victories nonetheless—and of immense significance to individual victims.

In rare cases, there may even be a systematic impact. For example, the 1978 IACHR report on Nicaragua increased the pressure on the dictatorial Somoza government. Furthermore, the OAS call for Somoza to resign in June 1979 shook his political confidence and seems to have hastened his departure.

Reports, though, are only reports. Decisions on individual cases are only nonbinding resolutions. Real change requires additional action by states. This is an inherent shortcoming of almost all international human rights regimes.

Nonetheless, the Inter-American Commission has aggressively exploited its powers to at least some effect. Its activities have improved the treatment of many thousands of victims of human rights violations. If we compare it not to Europe but to global mechanisms discussed in the preceding chapter, the record of the Inter-American regime, even in the difficult environment of the Cold War, appears in a relatively good light.

Discussion Questions

1. ASEAN has been accused of drafting its own human rights language that allows member-states to circumvent certain rights. Would such a rights framework be preferable to no framework at all? Or could faulty frameworks cause harm to international human rights fulfillment overall?
2. Is there a risk that regional human rights bodies could subvert international human rights bodies? Does the example of the European system support this possibility? What about the example of the Asian system?
3. Do regional human rights conventions have the capability to complement international human rights law, or do they merely conflict with it, as in the case of the African Charter's usage of clawback clauses?
4. Do any distinct differences stand out when comparing the different regional organizations? What about when compared to global mechanisms?
5. Do you think states are more likely to follow a global or regional human rights framework? Why?
6. Is it better to have a stronger system where countries threaten to leave, such as the Inter-American system, or a weaker system, like the African example, that might have greater participation by all states?
7. A number of the regional treaties that serve as the normative cores for regional human rights mechanisms include provisions that reflect unique regional conceptualizations of human rights. What are the positives or negatives of this approach? How does this relate to international human rights mechanisms?
8. As discussed above, the European Union has put forth serious effort to become a party to the European Convention on Human Rights. Should this be a model for other IGOs? What implications might this have for the international system?

Suggested Readings

Dinah Shelton, *Regional Protection of Human Rights* (Oxford: Oxford University Press, 2008), provides an exhaustive survey of regional regimes. Recent works on particular regional mechanisms include the following: Council of Europe, *The European Court of Human Rights in Facts and Figures* (Strasbourg: Council of Europe, 2010); Jonas Christoffersen and Mikael Rask Madsen, eds., *The European Court of Human Rights Between Law and Politics* (Oxford: Oxford University Press, 2011); Thomas Hammarberg, *Human Rights in Europe: No Grounds for Complacency; Viewpoints by the Council of Europe Commissioner for Human Rights* (Strasbourg: Council of Europe, 2011); Malcolm Evans and Rachel Murray, eds., *The African Charter on Human and Peoples' Rights: The System in Practice, 1986–2006* (Cambridge: Cambridge University Press, 2009); and Monica Serrano and Vesselin Popovski, eds., *Human Rights Regimes in the Americas* (New York: United Nations University Press, 2010).

7

Human Rights and Foreign Policy

The preceding chapters examined how the international community collectively addresses human rights and how states interact within multilateral and regional human rights mechanisms and institutions. This chapter and the next look at how states include human rights concerns in their relations with other states. We consider both the ways that human rights concerns interact with other foreign policy goals and the means available to states for acting bilaterally on their international human rights goals. We also consider undesirable unintended consequences of human rights foreign policies and criticisms of states that target other states' human rights practices.

In the contemporary world, states of different capabilities have varied and often complex bilateral relationships. Security is typically at the heart of national foreign policy—and thus of many bilateral relationships. This is especially true of the United States, which (not implausibly) considers itself to be the leading global power. For example, the United States is especially concerned about the growing influence of China, both in Asia and globally. Therefore, it maintains and has tried to strengthen its ties and influence with other nations in the region such as Vietnam and Myanmar along with traditional allies such as Japan and South Korea.

Economic ties are also often important in bilateral relationships. We live in a globalized world economy (see Chapter 11). Most states are more or less reliant on trade with other states to access the resources they need for their own economic growth and development. Whether trade and investment relationships are balanced or lopsided, they often color the ways in which states will consider the importance of other foreign policy priorities, including human rights.

Virtually all states, however, also pursue a great variety of other interests in their bilateral foreign policies. This is where human rights enter the picture: as one of many interests that states pursue in their foreign policies.

1. Human Rights and the National Interest

We have come a long way since the 1970s and 1980s, when discussions about human rights and foreign policy often centered on *whether* states ought to have an international human rights policy. And the answer given to that question was as often no as yes. Today, it is largely uncontroversial—and perhaps even expected—for states to pursue human rights objectives in their bilateral and multilateral foreign policies. In liberal democratic countries, the questions have become what should be included in a country's human rights foreign policy, where should it be pursued, and how aggressively. Such a change reflects a fundamental redefinition of the national interest.

In an earlier era, a distinction was often drawn between the "high politics" of security in contrast to other international concerns of states (low politics). The theoretical and policy perspective of *Realpolitik*—political realism, power politics—largely considers *any* interests beyond security (including economic security) to be inconsequential. In such a world, human rights is a (merely) moral concern. Although states may choose to pursue international human rights objectives out of a sense of compassion or justice, they must be rigorously subordinated to vital material national interests.

In fact, though, the national interest is whatever states and their citizens are interested in. If states consider it in their interest to expend some of their foreign policy resources and attention on the rights of foreigners, there is no reason they should not. And the reasons for doing so need not be instrumental (e.g., the idea that rights-protective regimes are more peaceful or better trading partners). An intrinsic interest in living in a more just world fully justifies including international human rights in a country's definition of its national interest. And, in fact, many countries have done precisely that.

Today, most democratic countries in all regions of the world have more or less ambitious international human rights objectives in their bilateral foreign policies. Most nondemocratic regimes support (or at least tolerate) the multilateral mechanisms discussed in Chapter 5. With very few exceptions, though, none of them include human rights concerns as part of their bilateral relations with other states.

The rise of human rights in the foreign policy agendas of democratic states has both internal and international dimensions. Democracies tend to identify themselves internally with the pursuit of human rights. Carrying this pursuit over into their foreign policies thus seems natural. It also gives expression to a sort of universal solidarity based on a common humanity (without challenging the system of national implementation of international human rights).

Democratic regimes, though, long predate international human rights norms. Bilateral human rights policies emerged along with the maturing of the global human rights regime. The expression of a "natural" internal inclination to pursue human rights in foreign policy was in fact greatly facilitated, and in some senses even created, by changes in international norms. States define their national interests as the result of the intersection of national and international influences. The deepening of the commitment to human rights in the national foreign policies of democratic states is in some ways as much the result of an active international human rights policy as a cause of such policies. It was no coincidence that Jimmy Carter was elected president of the United States in the same year that the International Human Rights Covenants came into force, and that he took office in the same year that Amnesty International won the Nobel Peace Prize.

Foreign policy is about how a state sees itself, the world around it, and its place in that world. The global human rights regime has created a world in which a government's commitment to human rights is seen as essential to full national and international legitimacy. That has not only enabled the expression of existing tendencies to address human rights in national foreign policies but also created additional support for such policies. The transformation of the national interest represented by the rise of bilateral human rights policies is thus both a cause and a consequence of the domestic preferences of states and the global human rights regime's mutual interactions with one another to push policy in a particular direction.

2. Means and Mechanisms of Bilateral Action

As an objective of foreign policy, human rights can be legitimately pursued using all the means of foreign policy—short of the threat or use of force, which contemporary international law reserves for self-defense (but see Chapter 10). We can think of policy responses along a continuum, with persuasion through "quiet" diplomacy on one end and military, economic, and political sanctions on the other. We should not, though, think of a simple persuasive-coercive dichotomy. For example, diplomatic measures often are primarily persuasive but may sometimes serve to signal coming coercion. Sanctions, by contrast, tend to be relatively coercive. When they involve carrots rather than sticks, though, they are fundamentally persuasive. And action may be neither coercive nor persuasive but primarily expressive: for example, passing judgment, supporting values, or taking a stand with no expectation of altering the world.

A. Persuasion Through Diplomacy

Human rights diplomacy tends to have three principal targets: the treatment of specific individuals (usually dissidents and political prisoners), particular policies, and the character of the regime (with a focus on patterns of gross and systematic violations of internationally recognized human rights). These objectives are pursued through both public and private means.

Although most attention is rightly focused on public human rights diplomacy, private diplomatic initiatives—**quiet diplomacy**—can be important. This is particularly true when dealing with individual victims or attempting to change laws, policies, or practices. Nonetheless, private action alone, without at least the plausible threat of public action, rarely helps even in the most limited cases. And when gross and systematic violations are at issue, quiet diplomacy rarely is an adequate response to such severe provocations.

Public human rights diplomacy has at least three important dimensions: gathering and disseminating information, communicating opposing views, and mobilizing pressure. Although mobilizing pressure certainly is of central importance, we should not underestimate the importance of information gathering and the diplomatic exchange of views.

The international politics of human rights is largely a matter of mobilizing shame. Reliable information about national human rights practices thus is essential to human rights advocacy of any sort. Professional diplomats are well positioned to develop and disseminate such information, both through their own direct inquiries and through contacts with human rights advocates in their host country.

The United States in particular has made a major contribution through its annual Country Reports on Human Rights Practices.[1] Especially since the end of the Cold War, these reports have become a major source of reliable information about national human rights practices that are used not only by foreign policy decision makers in numerous countries but also by national and transnational human rights advocates across the globe.

The private and public exchange of views, especially among friendly countries, is a frequently overlooked means of exerting influence. This is often particularly effective in countries that have fair to good human rights records and where foreign policy initiatives support the work of local activists. Knowing that one's international allies—especially powerful friends—are watching and will raise an issue sometimes influences a government's actions. This is rarely the case when addressing gross and systematic violations. But when dealing with particular individuals or practices, it can be of considerable help. Especially when undertaken in concert with other national, international, and transnational action, persuasive diplomacy can make a difference. Sometimes it may even provide the decisive element that tips the balance.

But, just as quiet diplomacy depends on the possibility of escalation to public pressure, the efficacy of exchanging partially diverging and partially converging views often depends on the public mobilization of shame. Escalation to direct public criticism may be used as a threat. No less important, though, the retreat to less publicly contentious means may allow a country to save some face. It may also facilitate the often-difficult internal and international negotiations associated with changes in policy.

B. Coercive Diplomacy

Diplomacy, however, can be, and often needs to be, coercive, not merely persuasive. Rarely will the privately expressed views of other countries, or even polite public disagreements among friends, be sufficient to improve even very specific human rights practices. States in their relations with other states often may reasonably choose to allow other actors, both national and transnational, to bear the burden of vocal public criticism. But such criticism is almost always necessary to win even incremental improvements in human rights practices. And when confronting severe and systematic violations, anything less than public criticism will appear to be, if not complicity, then at least acquiescence to practices that simply should not be borne in silence.

Words are the principal tool of bilateral human rights policy. The same is true of multilateral action, as we saw earlier, and of transnational action, as we will see in the next chapter. States, however, typically have more material means at their disposal that can be utilized on behalf of internationally recognized human rights than most multilateral human rights actors and transnational human rights NGOs.

One strategy that has often been employed is to link foreign aid to the human rights practices of recipients. Two different kinds of strategies have been pursued. Many countries have reduced aid in response to human rights violations (and, to a somewhat lesser extent, increased aid to reward improved human rights performance). However, as we will explore in the next chapter, "like-minded" "middle powers" such as Canada, the Netherlands, and the Nordic countries have gone further, choosing aid recipients in significant measure on the basis of good or improving human rights records.

C. Sanctions

States also have a variety of other relations that they can manipulate to support their bilateral human rights policies. At the lowest level, which shades into diplomacy, states may engage in symbolic gestures, such as recalling an ambassador for consultations or delaying the nomination of a new appointee to a vacant ambassadorial post. Cultural contacts can be expanded or curtailed, as can joint military or political actions. Trade relations have occasionally been curtailed. Very rarely, diplomatic relations may be broken. The use of material means of persuasion and coercion, however, is often problematic. As a result, there has been a general move away from most (but not all) sanctions over the past two decades.

Cutting development assistance, assuming that it had previously been effectively employed, perversely punishes people for being oppressed by their government. Major economic sanctions, although relatively rare, have also typically had such perverse results, particularly in the case of Iraq in the 1990s. (South Africa under apartheid is the one clear exception, in part because there was considerable support from the majority of South Africans for the sanctions but also because sanctions proved, in the end, not to be particularly punishing.)

There has thus been a move toward targeted sanctions. For example, rather than seek to block investment in a country, the overseas bank accounts of rights-abusive foreign leaders and officials are targeted. In rare cases, though, such as North Korea, where a brutal government has insinuated itself in all areas of the economy and society, suspending all but the most narrowly defined humanitarian aid may prove the right course, all things considered (we will look at the case of Myanmar below).

But even—or, rather, especially—in these cases, the coercive power of sanctions is limited. Where human rights violations are so severe and systematic that comprehensive material sanctions seem appropriate, perhaps even demanded, they are unlikely to have much effect. Governments like North Korea's need little from the outside world—because they are willing to make their people suffer the consequences of being denied access to external resources. Comprehensive sanctions thus are likely to have little direct or immediate impact on changing the behavior of the most abusive regimes.

Nonetheless, to most human rights advocates, sanctions often still seem to be the most appropriate course of action, even though they have little prospect of altering the behavior of the target government. This raises the important question of what we expect international human rights policies to achieve.

3. The Aims and Effects of Human Rights Policies

The most obvious aim of international human rights policies and initiatives is to improve the human rights practices of the targeted government. This is indeed an important objective. But it is not the only aim. In fact, as the discussion of comprehensive sanctions has suggested, sometimes it is not even the principal purpose.

International human rights policies that do not eliminate or even reduce the violations directly addressed may nonetheless be important in preventing further deterioration or deterring similar future violations. States may be reluctant to appear to be bowing to external pressure. That pressure, though, may be factored into calculations in the future, especially if there is a reasonable prospect that it will be repeated. This seems to have occurred in the 1980s in El Salvador. It did not eliminate violations, but it seems to have moderated them.

Human rights initiatives that bring no direct change in a government's practices may nonetheless have positive effects by supporting local human rights advocates or delegitimating repressive regimes. By subtly altering the local human rights environment that a rights-abusive regime faces, human rights initiatives may have significant long-term effects. Consider Myanmar (Burma).

Myanmar had been under military rule since 1989, when the government changed the name of the country from Union of Burma to the Republic of the Union of Myanmar. The United States and the European Union adopted economic and military sanctions against Myanmar starting in the 1990s. These actions, coupled with significant transnational pressure, put the military regime under a fairly harsh spotlight, especially with respect to the twenty-one-year period of nearly continuous detention and house arrest of democracy activist Aung San Suu Kyi, whose notoriety as a prisoner of conscience helped to earn her the Nobel Peace Prize in 1991.

According to many observers, these sanctions had little direct effect; they were targeted sanctions, mostly aimed at the military leaders. Although they did help to discredit the regime, they had little impact on changing its practices. However, one indirect effect of the sanctions was to push Myanmar into a closer relationship with China, which had no qualms about the form of government in Myanmar but wanted concessions of its own. Some observers believe that the combination of this uncomfortable, neocolonial relationship with China plus the international pressure to free Suu Kyi from her house arrest led to the relaxation of military rule in Myanmar and the eventual elevation of Suu Kyi and her political party to democratic legitimacy.

In 2016, the United States and the European Union lifted the majority of their sanctions on Myanmar, to much fanfare. For the United States, this was as much a strategic move as it was a victory lap for democracy and human rights: the Asian pivot (a reorientation of American foreign policy under the Obama administration, to prioritize relations with Asia) and hemming in rising Chinese power. And although this was a victory for democracy, the overall human rights situation in Myanmar is still very dicey, especially for the minority Muslim Rohingya and other refugee communities in Myanmar, who suffer significant levels of discrimination in this officially Buddhist nation. Unfortunately, Suu Kyi has largely remained silent about these problems, as she is trying to consolidate a very fragile democracy in her country (in §8.5, we consider the case of Myanmar with respect to U.S. foreign policy).

Altering the broader normative environment is another possible impact for international human rights policies. For example, the 1975 Helsinki Accords, which sought to reduce tensions in Europe between the West and the Soviet Union, included a set of human rights provisions that the Soviet Union agreed to in exchange for the West's recognition of its sphere of influence in Eastern Europe. (Even the archrealist Henry Kissinger hailed this human rights breakthrough.)[2] Later in the 1970s and 1980s, sanctions imposed on governments in Central and South America usually had little impact on the behavior of the target governments. Nonetheless, they were crucial elements in altering international expectations and giving new force to the norms of the Universal Declaration and other international instruments. Some of the most striking differences between Cold War and post–Cold War international human rights politics owe as much to these normative changes as to changes in the global balance of power.

In addition, actions directed by Country A against Country B may have an impact on Country C. Knowing that one is likely to be subject to international pressure, because pressure has been applied elsewhere in a comparable case, may have a deterrent effect. This is especially true when the violations are not seen as crucial to the survival or prosperity of the regime—that is, when they are more of a convenience, against which the inconvenience of international pressure needs to be weighed—or are considered a practice that is preferred, all other things being equal, and international pressure makes other things no longer equal.

Actions with no direct effect on the target country may also alter the direction of foreign policy in the sending state. For example, the initial decision of the Carter administration to suspend aid to Guatemala in 1977 established a precedent that influenced policy in a number of later cases in the Americas and elsewhere.

International and bilateral human rights policies may also be undertaken primarily to satisfy domestic constituencies (the case of American policy toward Cuba prior to the Obama administration being among the most obvious). There certainly is something troubling in the notion of a "successful" policy that satisfies national political constituencies while having no effect on the target country. If that is what it is designed to do, though, that reality must be acknowledged. For example, periodic changes in American support to the U.N. Fund for Population Activities (UNFPA) seem driven mostly by the abortion debate in the United States.

We can also note that international and bilateral human rights policies may have punitive effects even when they have no remedial effect. Making the lives of human rights violators less pleasant is a good thing, even if it does not improve the lives of their present or future victims.

Even where there is no discernible direct impact—immediately or in the future, remedial or punitive, in the direct target or in other countries engaging in similar violations—there may be a diffuse impact. International human rights policies reinforce and help to further disseminate international human rights norms. Over time, the cumulative effect of policies that reinforce both the substance and the binding nature of international human rights norms may subtly but significantly change the context of national or international action. In the most optimistic scenario, new generations of leaders and citizens may, as a result of regular and aggressive international human rights policies, internalize human rights norms to a much greater extent than have their predecessors.

Finally, even if we have reason to believe that our policies will have no discernible impact on the world, they may nonetheless be appropriately undertaken simply because they are right: our values demand that we act on them. Taking a stand is something that we owe ourselves, and those who share our values.

4. Drawbacks, Problems, and Criticisms

A. Foreign Policy Priorities and Trade-Offs

The foreign policies of most states can, in a highly stylized fashion, be said to include security, economic, and other goals. Most states tend to rank these classes of goals in roughly this order. But there are also gradations within each category. High-order security interests usually take priority over all other objectives of foreign policy, including human rights. And there is nothing wrong with that *as a matter of national foreign policy*. Low-level security interests, however, often are, appropriately, sacrificed to major economic or other concerns, including human rights. And this too is entirely appropriate.

Issues of trade-offs are regularly raised in discussions of international human rights policies. Some human rights advocates are uncomfortable with—even critical of—the idea that human rights are often balanced against competing foreign policy objectives. Such criticisms fail to take seriously the idea that human rights are but one of many interests pursued in foreign policy. Human rights interests *should* be balanced against other national interests—which sometimes appropriately take priority.

Moralists may see the demands of human rights as categorical. Foreign policy decision makers, though, are not independent moral actors. Their job is not to realize personal, national, or global moral values but to pursue the national interest of their country. They are officeholders, with professional and ethical responsibilities to discharge the duties of their office.

There certainly are moral and legal constraints on the pursuit of the national interest. But the principal aim of national foreign policy is the national interest. The national interest includes many objectives. And those varied interests regularly conflict and thus must be balanced against one another.

Many countries today include fostering the broad goal of the international realization of human rights in their definition of the national interest. But the national interest, and thus the goals of foreign policy, are not reducible to human rights. The issue then is not whether human rights are appropriately balanced against other objectives of foreign policy—there is no viable alternative to such balancing—but the weights assigned to the values being balanced.

Setting priorities among various national interests is an essential part of the process of defining the national interest. International human rights law leaves states considerable latitude with respect to the weight they attach to human rights objectives in their foreign policy. There is no requirement that they include international human rights goals. But states are free to use the full range of foreign policy instruments, short of force, on behalf of international human rights objectives.

For those states that have included international human rights in their foreign policies, however, we can reasonably demand that human rights actually enter into calculations balancing competing interests, with a weight that roughly matches their stated place in the hierarchy of national interests. Two tests are particularly appropriate and revealing. If human rights objectives are pursued with friends as well as enemies and particular human rights policies cause problems in other areas of ongoing relations, there is at least prima facie evidence that human rights really are being taken seriously in a country's foreign policy.

People may reasonably disagree over whether a state has appropriately ranked its international human rights objectives or is doing enough on their behalf. At minimum, though, we should insist that pursuing human rights objectives should sometimes be inconvenient, even costly—as the pursuit of security and economic objectives regularly is. Otherwise, human rights are not really a part of foreign policy, but a moral add-on after the "real" foreign policy decisions have been made—which was the typical situation before the transformation of foreign policies, noted above, that took place in the 1970s, 1980s, and 1990s.

There certainly is something morally disquieting about subordinating international human rights objectives to national security objectives, let alone economic objectives of foreign policy. But often this is the right thing to do, all things considered, *as a matter of national foreign policy*. Critics may reasonably argue for moving international human rights objects up on the list of national foreign policy priorities. In the foreseeable future, though, there is no prospect that they will reach the pinnacle, let alone occupy that pinnacle alone. The national interest and the "human interest" represented by universal human rights cannot be expected to coincide, although we can reasonably work to bring them closer together.

B. Inconsistencies in Human Rights Policy

Human rights advocates are also often critical of inconsistent policies that treat comparable human rights violations in different countries differently.

Issues of consistency do have a special force in moral reasoning. In fact, as the Golden Rule suggests, morality in significant measure means not making an exception for oneself (or those one is allied with). From a purely deontological (or duty-based) moral point of view, only comparable human rights violations require comparable responses. However, although human rights may be "interdependent and indivisible," that does not require an identical response to every comparable violation of any particular right.

Considered from a consequentialist moral standpoint, considerations of cost may be relevant. Few would consider the United States to be morally bound, all things considered, to risk nuclear war in order to remedy human rights violations in China simply because we acted strongly to remedy similar violations in, say, Guatemala. Conversely, the fact that no state is willing to threaten the use of force to free Tibet from Chinese domination, and thus risk nuclear war, does not mean that considerations of moral consistency should have precluded the use of force in, say, East Timor. Balancing competing values *requires* taking account of all the values involved. And consistency requires treating like cases alike, *all things considered,* not just looking at human rights violations.

We should thus not bemoan trade-offs of human rights to other foreign policy interests any more than we bemoan the sacrifice of economic interests to human rights interests, *so long as these trade-offs properly reflect reasonable assessments of the value of the interests at stake.* And we should not criticize as inconsistent treating comparable human rights violations differently—any more than we bemoan pursuing comparable international economic interests more aggressively in some countries than in others—so long as the differences reflect a reasonable balancing of the full range of national interests at stake in the particular cases.

Hypocrisy, however, is a completely different matter. When the subordination of international human rights objectives cannot reasonably be justified in terms of previously established foreign policy priorities, we have an unjustifiable sacrifice of human rights interests rather than a defensible foreign policy trade-off. And if human rights almost always lose out in a contest with almost any other foreign policy objective, we have concrete evidence of a very low effective evaluation of the significance of a country's international human rights objectives. (The problem here, though, is not inconsistency. Rather, the complaint is that the state in question consistently gives inadequate weight or attention to international human rights objectives.)

We have drawn the distinction between morality and foreign policy overly sharply. In countries with international human rights policies, human rights are matters of both moral and national interest. Moral inconsistency thus does pose problems for foreign policy—although, again, hypocrisy seems more the problem than inconsistency. And such cases should not be confused with a policy that carefully balances human rights against other national interests. Such a policy is not likely to undermine seriously the moral value of human rights. In fact, by identifying clearly just what place human rights have in a nation's foreign policy, such reasoned trade-offs may provoke discussions that lead to increasing the relative place of human rights in a nation's foreign policy.

C. Blowback

A final concern is when states subject to international human rights pressures push back. This problem is not new. As we noted in Chapters 1 and 4, there has always been some reticence about the West using global norms to infringe upon the sovereignty of states in the global South. As the relative power of these states has grown, though, their ability to more successfully push back against human rights pressures has also grown. For example, as China's power has risen, it has been willing, especially in sub-Saharan Africa, to enter into aid relationships without the human rights conditionalities that often come with Western aid.

Recent events in the Philippines offer an extreme example of blowback against international human rights pressure. Rodrigo Duterte became president in May 2016, vowing to enact a series of radical policies to combat drug-related crime. And he has delivered on this particular campaign promise. National and transnational journalists and human rights groups have documented mass arrests and extrajudicial killings of drug users, petty criminals, and street children by government agents, paramilitaries, and individual vigilantes. Official Philippine police records indicate that by late 2016 the death toll from Duterte's "drug war" was more than 6,000—nearly two-thirds as a result of extrajudicial or vigilante-style killings. The U.N. special rapporteur on summary executions reported that Duterte had given ordinary citizens a "license to kill."

Duterte's threats to withdraw from the United Nations are certainly empty, but they are a striking example of his sense of impunity. Somewhat less incredible have been his taunts and threats in response to pressure from the United States. "Prepare to leave the Philippines," he recently remarked, in reference to the current military basing agreement between the two countries. In one particular anti-American tirade, Duterte taunted, "You know, tit for tat . . . if you can do this, so (can) we. It ain't a one-way traffic. Bye-bye America," while praising China for its promise of a "grant" of $14 million in small arms to assist Duterte's antidrug efforts, as well as a $500 million long-term "soft loan" guarantee for other equipment. "So what do I need America for?"

This may be an extreme example. It is not, however, even close to unique. And it vividly illustrates the limits of standard international human rights pressures. The recalcitrant government of even a not particularly wealthy or powerful country with a reasonably good human rights record, which would ordinarily be a sign of at least some openness to international human rights pressures, may not only successfully resist but actively flout international policies that challenge its human rights violations—especially if that government has considerable popular support for its human rights violations (as in the Philippines or in the persecution of Muslims in Myanmar) or if it can effectively repress popular resistance (as in North Korea and many states in Central Asia). Most human rights violators are able to ignore most international human rights pressures most of the time at only modest cost. And some who thumb their noses at those pressures may even gain some degree of local respect for standing up against challenges to national sovereignty.

5. Political Rhetoric Versus Political Will

For many countries it is quite easy to simply say, "We value human rights in our foreign policy." The important question is what place they have in foreign policy. *How much* are human rights valued, both intrinsically and relative to other national interests? And how seriously are those values in fact taken in the practice of foreign policy?

Many states have made substantial progress toward a more serious incorporation of human rights into their foreign policy. Most, if not all, though, could pretty easily do more. Compared to thirty years ago, most democratic states today have more aggressive and more effective international human rights policies. That, how-ever, is nowhere near enough. The moral demands of human rights continue to push for a deeper penetration of human rights into national foreign policy and a greater willingness to take full advantage of the space available for the pursuit of interna-tional human rights objectives.

As we just noted, successful resistance by recalcitrant governments is the norm. But even moderately more aggressive international human rights policies might significantly increase the costs of such recalcitrance (or even modestly reduce the likelihood of success). And in target countries with a certain degree of openness to international human rights pressures, whether out of a desire to improve or because of limited incentives or capabilities to resist, even relatively modest improvements in the strength, persistence, or consistency of bilateral human rights policies could have a significant impact.

Such modest improvements are well within the reach of almost all countries with active bilateral international human rights policies—if they decide to make the effort. No state is anywhere near to pushing the limits of what inalterable national and international political constraints on their international human rights diplo-macy allow. Any state that really wants to do more can—if it really wants to. In all but the most difficult cases, limited desire is at least as serious a constraint on the success of bilateral international human rights policies as limited capabilities.

Discussion Questions

1. What do you think of the distinction drawn in the chapter between hu-man rights policy consistency and foreign policy consistency? Is it really appropriate to treat similar human rights situations differently because of other foreign policy interests? How does your answer to this question change if you adopt the perspectives of, say, a foreign policy decision maker, a human rights advocate, a concerned citizen of your own coun-try, or someone who sees herself as a citizen of the world?
2. How can one justify trading off human rights? Are human rights really the kind of thing that is appropriately balanced against, say, the economic interests of corporations? What are your criteria for judging whether a trade-off is justified?
3. How do your answers to the preceding question vary when the human rights in question are those of your fellow citizens versus those of foreign citizens?
4. Can a viable international human rights policy be constructed by re-sponding to violations according to the principles of severity, trends, re-sponsibility, and efficacy? Are all of these criteria of equal weight? Are there other principles that are no less important?
5. What *is* the mix between limited desire and limited opportunities in ex-plaining the relatively modest achievements of most human rights for-eign policies? Is the assessment at the end of this chapter too optimistic

in suggesting that there is considerable space available for stronger and more effective policies?

6. Think about your own country's human rights diplomacy. Has it gotten the balance right between human rights and other national interests in general? In specific prominent recent cases?

Suggested Readings

Very little has been written separately on the general question of human rights and foreign policy—although many of the suggested readings in the following chapter address the issue. Perhaps the best general discussion is Peter R. Baehr and Monique Castermans-Holleman, *The Role of Human Rights in Foreign Policy,* 3rd ed. (New York: Palgrave Macmillan, 2004). And two pamphlets from the late 1970s remain well worth reading, even though the examples are dated. Evan Luard, *Human Rights and Foreign Policy* (Oxford: Pergamon Press, 1981), provides a good short introductory discussion, with an especially thorough presentation of the means available for use on behalf of human rights. An abbreviated version of this essay is available in Richard Pierre Claude and Burns H. Weston, eds., *Human Rights in the World Community* (Philadelphia: University of Pennsylvania Press, 1992). And Hans Morgenthau's *Human Rights and Foreign Policy* (New York: Council on Religion and International Affairs, 1979) offers a classic statement of the realist perspective.

8

Human Rights in American Foreign Policy

Building on the general discussion of human rights and foreign policy in the preceding chapter, this chapter looks in some detail at human rights in U.S. foreign policy. We do so both because the United States enjoys a position of leadership in the contemporary world and because of the long American tradition of framing its foreign policy in terms of the dissemination of humane values and principles. And since the mid-1970s, commitment to upholding human rights has been a central feature of the stated foreign policy of the United States.

Following a brief historical overview of American human rights policy, we examine American "exceptionalism" as a guiding thread for understanding American human rights policies and practices. We then consider two Cold War–era case studies (Central America and South Africa) and two post–Cold War cases (Myanmar and Israeli settlements in the West Bank). We then compare U.S. policy to other Western "like-minded countries." The Problem that concludes the chapter looks at another side of American exceptionalism, namely, the reluctance of the United States to ratify international human rights treaties.

1. Historical Overview

As we saw in Chapter 1, concern for the protection of human rights was integral to American postwar policy, especially in the creation of the United Nations. Policy makers in the U.S. State Department had proposed the inclusion of a bill of human rights in an early draft of the U.N. Charter. Although that proposal was not included in the final American draft of the Charter that was adopted at the 1944 Dumbarton Oaks meetings, at the San Francisco Conference, where the United Nations was created, a number of American NGOs successfully lobbied for including language about protecting human rights and creating a Commission on Human Rights in the Charter.

President Harry S. Truman was a very strong supporter of human rights at the United Nations and he named Eleanor Roosevelt as the American representative to the newly formed Commission on Human Rights in 1946. The Commission unanimously elected Roosevelt as chair, and she guided it through its first significant agenda item: the drafting of an international bill of rights, which became the Universal Declaration and the two Covenants (see §§1.2 and 1.3).

In the late 1940s and early 1950s, however, significant opposition to international human rights treaties emerged from conservative lawyers (represented by the American Bar Association) and lawmakers. Fear of "backdoor communism" (through the inclusion of economic and social rights in the Declaration and the draft Covenant) and fear of compromising American sovereignty (along with congressional concerns about an overly active and independent presidency) led to substantial support for the Bricker Amendment proposed by Ohio Republican senator John W. Bricker. Under Article II, Section 2 of the U.S. Constitution, treaties are negotiated and signed by the president and must be ratified by a two-thirds vote of the Senate to become law. Among other things, the Bricker Amendment would have required the president to secure congressional approval prior to entering into any treaty-making negotiations and would have also extended the requirement of Senate approval to executive agreements. Both requirements would have pushed the United States back toward isolationism and seriously undermined the further development of the institutional architecture of postwar international society.

When General Dwight D. Eisenhower, a Republican, assumed office as president in 1953, he announced that the United States would neither continue to participate in negotiating the Covenants nor sign any multilateral human rights treaties. After further discussions, the Bricker Amendment was withdrawn. Mary Lord—a granddaughter of Charles Alfred Pillsbury, the founder of the Pillsbury Company—replaced Eleanor Roosevelt as the American delegate to the Commission on Human Rights and the official American human rights policy at the United Nations emphasized advisory services rather than treaties.

This turn away from the immediate postwar enthusiasm for human rights was rooted in a fundamental change in the priorities of the United States as the Cold War developed between the West (with the United States as its anchor) and the Communist world (the USSR, its Eastern European satellites, and then, after 1949/1950, China and North Korea). American policy came to be oriented around "containment": halting any perceived expansion of Soviet power or influence.

This was seen as requiring that human rights concerns be subordinated to strategic and ideological rivalry with the Soviet Union and the communist bloc and led the self-proclaimed "leader of the free world" to support, repeatedly and enthusiastically, policies and regimes that violently suppressed democracy or human rights in the name of "freedom" (understood as anticommunism). For example, the United States supported coups d'état in Iran (1953), Guatemala (1954), and Chile (1973) to prevent communist takeovers and backed a veritable rogues' gallery of right-wing authoritarian governments, including Ferdinand Marcos in the Philippines, the Somoza family in Nicaragua, the Pahlavi dynasty in Iran, Fulgencio Batista in Cuba, and the avowedly fascist Francisco Franco in Spain. As Franklin Roosevelt supposedly said of Nicaragua's Anastasio Somoza García: "[He] may be a son of a bitch, but he's our son of a bitch."

At the United Nations, the United States continued to keep a fairly low profile during the 1960s and early 1970s. Although the United States did support the Convention on the Elimination of All Forms of Racial Discrimination (CERD) in 1965 (which followed on the heels of the passage of the Civil Rights Act of 1964 and the Voting Rights Act of 1965) and did vote for the adoption of both International Covenants in December 1966, American involvement at the 1968 International Conference on Human Rights in Teheran was mostly concerned with keeping more strident Third World demands regarding anticolonialism in check.

By the mid-1970s, a relaxation of Cold War tensions—the policy of **détente**—began to open up policy space for human rights to return to a more prominent place in U.S. foreign policy, although in a rather unusual way. The leading American architect of détente was Henry Kissinger, who was President Richard Nixon's national security advisor (and later served as secretary of state under President Gerald Ford). Kissinger saw détente as a way for the United States to back down from many of its more ideologically motivated stances toward the Soviet Union in favor of a more stable and less immediately hostile relationship. This, however, angered many in Congress, both for ideological and principled human rights reasons.

Soviet violations of fundamental human rights and, in particular, its refusal to grant rights of emigration to Soviet Jews, emerged as the focal point of controversy—precisely when the Nixon administration was attempting to open up not only diplomatic but trade relations between the United States and the USSR (and the rest of the Eastern bloc). One result was the 1974 Trade Act, signed by Gerald Ford in early 1975, which included a provision introduced by Senator Henry M. "Scoop" Jackson and Representative Charles Vanik that denied special trade preferences to nonmarket (command) economies that restricted freedom of emigration and other human rights.

Furthermore, the détente-inspired 1975 Conference on Security and Cooperation in Europe (the Helsinki Conference), which intended to finally accept the post–World War II East-West divide that had existed since the Yalta Conference in early 1945, included, as a result of Western European pressures, a limited range of human rights issues. Basket III of the Helsinki Accords stipulated that all parties, including the Soviet-bloc countries, respect certain fundamental human rights principles, including freedom of speech, conscience, and religion or belief. In the following years, this provided unprecedented, if limited, protections to Soviet-bloc human rights advocates and dissidents such as Václav Havel in Czechoslovakia, Lech Wałęsa in Poland, and Andrei Sakharov in the Soviet Union, as well as Karol Wojtyła, a Polish cardinal who in 1978 became Pope John Paul II. Basket III, reflecting the American pressure on the plight of Soviet Jews, also included important provisions on freedom of emigration and family reunification.

By the time Jimmy Carter entered the White House in January 1977, the international and internal moral excesses of anticommunism—most immediately, the war in Vietnam and the domestic lawlessness of the Watergate scandal—had, along with the emergence of détente, created space for a renewed commitment to human rights in American foreign policy. In 1976, the Ford administration had created the post of assistant secretary of state for human rights and humanitarian affairs. The Carter administration drafted Presidential Review Memorandum 28 (PRM-28), which outlined reinvigorated American support for human rights and created the Bureau of Democracy, Human Rights and Labor within the State Department. That same year, Carter signed the American Convention on Human Rights and both International Human Rights Covenants.

These changes, however, were more symbolic than practically efficacious. Other international events soon preoccupied the Carter administration, most notably the Iranian revolution in April 1979, the socialist Sandinista victory in the Nicaraguan revolution the following July, and the Soviet invasion of Afghanistan in December. In particular, the Afghan situation and the Iranian hostage crisis (which began on November 4 and lasted until the day Carter left office in January 1981) overwhelmed Carter's State Department for the balance of his only term in office. And, with the Cold War heating up again, the Senate refused to ratify the American Convention and the Covenants.

When Ronald Reagan became president in 1981, U.S. foreign policy shifted strongly and explicitly toward a confrontational stance toward communism in general and the Soviet Union in particular. Although the Reagan administration did not entirely shed the new human rights apparatus that Carter had established, it dramatically downgraded attention to human rights and ostentatiously dropped all attention to economic and social rights (other than the right to private property).

Democracy—or at least elections of pro-American governments—became the centerpiece of Reagan's "human rights" policy. In a speech to the British House of Commons in 1982, Reagan outlined that, by fostering the "infrastructure of democracy," the United States would leave "Marxism-Leninism on the ash-heap of history." In 1983, the United States created the National Endowment for Democracy (NED), a bipartisan nonprofit organization that receives annual appropriations from Congress.

Although these efforts were central rhetorical elements of Reagan's approach to winning the ideological conflict with the Soviet Union (especially with respect to communist Eastern Europe), American foreign policy in other parts of the world, especially in Central America, compromised much of his lofty rhetoric on freedom and self-determination (see the case study on page 130).

There was a modest softening of the Reagan administration's anticommunist stance in its second term. Of perhaps greatest symbolic importance, the United States in 1988 signed the Torture Convention and, after forty years, finally ratified the Genocide Convention. But, throughout the 1980s, an active American international human rights policy was driven largely by a bipartisan coalition in Congress that refused to sacrifice international human rights to ideological and geopolitical struggles against communism.

As we emphasized in Chapter 1, the end of the Cold War opened up new policy opportunities for the administration of Bill Clinton, who took office in January 1993. (The presidency of George H. W. Bush [1989–1993] was a transitional era, both in the world and in American foreign policy.) Clinton's State Department was reorganized again to place development, democracy promotion, and human rights, as well as reinvigorated engagement with the United Nations, at the heart of U.S. foreign policy. With significant support from civil society organizations, the United States actively lobbied for strengthening U.N. human rights mechanisms at the 1993 World Conference on Human Rights. Most notably, it pressed for a U.N. high commissioner for human rights, a position that the United States had long supported in words but now was willing to exercise political resources to help create. The United States also lobbied successfully to ensure that the 1994 Conference on Population and Development (held in Cairo, Egypt) reaffirmed women's reproductive health as a human right, and Hilary Clinton's speech at the 1995 World Conference on Women, held in Beijing popularized the slogan "women's rights are human rights."

Early in Clinton's first term, the Senate finally ratified the Covenant on Civil and Political Rights (but not the Covenant on Economic, Social and Cultural Rights and only with a reservation that claimed that ratification would have no effect in American law). The following year, the Senate ratified the Convention on Racial Discrimination and the Torture Convention. But although Clinton signed the Convention on the Rights of the Child in 1994, the Senate has (for petty partisan political reasons) refused to ratify it, leaving the United States the *only* country in the world that is not a party. And, before leaving office in January 2001, President Clinton signed the Statute of the International Criminal Court (although he did not bother to submit it to the Senate, where bipartisan fears over "the loss of American sovereignty" would have precluded even a serious discussion of ratification).

The administration of George W. Bush was initially hostile to international multilateral institutions—for example, "unsigning" the ICC Statute and withdrawing U.S. support for the Kyoto Protocol to the Framework Convention on Climate Change. And after the terrorist attacks of September 11, 2001, the administration turned decidedly unilateralist. The Bush administration did not eliminate talk of and even action on international human rights. It did, however, focus on a narrow range of rights, especially freedom of religion, the right to private property, and modern slavery. In addition, as we will see in Chapter 12, antiterrorism significantly intruded into the pursuit of international human rights objectives in American foreign policy.

Particularly remarkable was the decision of the Bush administration, when the United Nations voted in 2006 to replace the Commission on Human Rights with a new, more effective and smaller Human Rights Council, not to seek membership (which would have been effectively automatic). And the following year, citing what it viewed as the Council's continuing "harassment" of Israel (and its failure to condemn human rights violations in Iran, Cuba, and North Korea, targets of American ire), the U.S. Senate voted to cut off American funding to the Council.

Barack Obama, however, rejoined the Council in 2009 and redeployed resources within the State Department largely as they had been during the Clinton years. And although Obama did not take any formal steps toward becoming a party to the Rome Statute, engagement with the ICC as an observer to its annual meeting of the Assembly of States-Parties was included in Obama's first National Security Strategy (NSS) document. Obama's State Department (under Secretaries of State Hillary Clinton and John Kerry, and U.N. ambassadors Susan Rice and Samantha Power) strongly supported the work of the Court, especially with respect to sharing information needed to indict suspected humanitarian criminals. The Obama administration returned to a broad conception of human rights at the same time that it gave special attention to the human rights of women and girls and strongly supported the Council's efforts to address discrimination based on sexual orientation and gender identity.

As we are at the beginning of the Trump administration (2017–), it is not at all clear what its human rights policy will look like. International human rights policy was not mentioned either in the campaign or in public planning for the transition. However, given the general tenor of Trump's public pronouncements and the character of his cabinet appointments, it seems reasonable to expect a partial resubordination of human rights to other foreign policy concerns. While we would expect public human rights diplomacy to remain part of American foreign policy—because this is generally expected, pretty much across the political spectrum, and because there are many in Congress, supported by a sophisticated human rights lobby, who will insist on raising human rights issues even where the administration may prefer not to—the early actions of the Trump administration are very troubling.

First among these was the haphazard and highly controversial executive order that halted the entire American refugee admissions program for 120 days and placed on hold *all travel* to the United States of persons from seven "Muslim-majority" countries, pending further review of admissions procedures. Future refugee admission from those countries would give priority to persons belonging to "minority religions" (read: Christians), which some maintain would be a violation of the U.S. Constitution. Although these policies were immediately put on ice by a challenge in the federal court, a somewhat more modest version was announced in early March 2017.

Second, and just as alarming, the administration appears to be considering abandoning the seat the United States currently holds on the Human Rights Council (through 2019), in protest of the Council's "harassment" of Israel. No member of the Council has ever before resigned. Such a move will certainly be seen by the international community as a significant vote of no confidence in the most important institution in the U.N.'s human rights machinery—which will most likely give aid and comfort to regimes that are already hostile to that system.

2. Human Rights and American Exceptionalism

Although American foreign policy since World War II has always advocated freedom, democracy, and human rights, there are many ways to achieve these goals—which, as we have seen, often compete not only with other foreign policy objectives but also with one another. As the world's most powerful state, the United States has both a considerable interest in and broad responsibilities toward a stable international society and the protection and provision of "global common goods," including human rights. And, as the historical overview in the preceding section has suggested, over the past seventy years there has been an often-fluctuating but ultimately steady evolution toward an increasingly deep engagement with international human rights.

At the same time, the United States has always done human rights its way. This is usually discussed as a matter of **American exceptionalism,** the belief that the United

States is different from (and generally superior to) most other countries, in large part because of its domestic commitment to individual rights. The isolationist variant of American exceptionalism, expressed with particular clarity in George Washington's Farewell Address, portrays the United States as a beacon of hope for an oppressed world—but only an example, not an active participant in the struggle for freedom overseas. No less powerful, however, has been interventionist exceptionalism, which stresses an active American mission to spread its values through direct foreign policy action, sometimes even through the use of military force.

This interventionist strand, however, has often too easily equated the strategic, political, and economic international interests of the United States with the promotion of democracy and human rights. During the Cold War, the logic was roughly: Communism is opposed to human rights. The United States favors human rights. Therefore, (any) American action against communism is action on behalf of human rights.

In addition, there has been a strong tendency to emphasize civil and political rights and the right to private property, sometimes even to the exclusion of (other) economic and social rights—particularly in light of the communist (and especially Soviet-bloc) emphasis on state control over economic activity as the fulfillment of economic and social rights. This contributed to an American tendency to react suspiciously to regimes, opposition groups, and "revolutionaries" that prioritized economic redistribution. By labeling economic and social reformers "communists" and "subversives," right-wing rulers during the Cold War could generally retain U.S. support for systematic repression to protect their own wealth, power, and privilege, often under a banner of democracy (or at least freedom). But beyond their devastating human rights consequences, such policies frequently prevented the achievement of professed American goals. For example, repressive dictatorships of the Right often eliminated not only the Far Left but also the political moderates that the United States claimed to support.

Anticommunism was also at the heart of a striking American inconsistency toward elections. The United States regularly, and rightly, criticized one-party elections in communist countries. But the mere existence of elections in anticommunist countries, even in the face of clear evidence of restrictions on political participation, corruption, intimidation of voters, or outright fraud, was usually accepted as evidence of the ruling regime's democratic character. And when the United States disapproved of left-leaning governments that came to power through free and fair elections, it was not above using force to remove them. Striking examples include sponsorship of the 1954 military coup in Guatemala, subversion in Chile in the early 1970s, and continuation of American support for the Nicaraguan "contras" (violent anticommunist revolutionaries) after the unquestionably fair 1984 election.

Elections that brought (alleged) communists to power were bad and had to be overturned. When force or fraud brought anticommunists to power, that was an acceptable price to pay to keep communists out of power and on the run. And the United States, the leader of the "free world," was the self-appointed judge of democratic credentials.

Other strands or elements of American exceptionalism are less controversial but still important to consider—what some observers call "exemptionalism": the idea that American domestic institutions and indeed the U.S. Constitution itself necessitates exemptions from the human rights rules that other countries must follow. Human rights are seen as for "them" but not for "us," because we already have constitutional rights, and, in any case, we really "invented" human rights. In addition, American power has for a good century now given the United States the "right"—as in "might makes right"—to define for itself and its foreign policy what human rights are and how they ought to be pursued.

Such exemptionalism has unfortunate international *and* domestic implications. For example, the United States regularly arrogates to itself the power to refuse to participate in global mechanisms (like the ICC), to bend the rules, or worse, to claim exemptions from the rules all together. Most dramatically, the United States declared that combatants captured in Afghanistan after the November 2001 invasion (which was authorized by the U.N. Security Council) were not proper combatants and therefore could be legally denied the protections of the Fourth **Geneva Convention**—and then moved many of them to the American military base in Guantanamo Bay, Cuba (held under the terms of a disputed lease with Cuba), where the United States has maintained that neither international law nor most U.S. law applies. More generally, the United States strongly supports prosecuting others in the International Criminal Court but has aggressively negotiated exemptions for Americans from states that have accepted the jurisdiction of the ICC (and thus might be called on to turn over indicted Americans to the Court).

Domestically, exemptionalism is evident in the continuing American refusal to provide basic economic and social rights such as access to health care, housing, and parental leave and by the refusal to be legally bound even by most of the international human rights treaties that it has ratified, an issue to which we will return at the end of the chapter.

In the case studies that follow, we will explore these tensions and contradictions in some detail. We hope that these will give students some tangible cases to ponder as they consider the complexities of integrating and balancing human rights concerns with other foreign policy priorities. The result, however, is a very long chapter. The remainder of the chapter thus has been written to allow readers to skip individual case studies as their interests or available time indicate.

We would suggest, though, that every reader review at least one of the Cold War cases, where the broad parameters of American international human rights policy were forged. And we strongly encourage all readers to look at §§7 and 8, which compare American international human rights policies with those of countries such as Norway, the Netherlands, and Canada. We also encourage all readers to consider Problem 5, at the end of the chapter, which addresses American ratification of international human rights treaties.

3. Case Study: U.S. Policy in Central America

Central America, the geographical area that lies between North America (Canada, the United States, and Mexico) and South America, became a major international human rights concern in the 1980s largely because of U.S. support for the right-wing government of El Salvador and parallel U.S. efforts to overthrow the elected leftist government of Nicaragua. These countries will be our focus here.

A. Human Rights in El Salvador

Salvadoran independence from Spain in the 1820s was in many ways less significant than the economic reforms in the second half of the nineteenth century that transferred one-third of the country's land to a small coffee oligarchy. For the following half century, protests by dispossessed peasants were ruthlessly suppressed, culminating in the systematic killing of at least 10,000 people and as many as 30,000 in the *matanza* (massacre) of 1932.

Elections were held regularly, but the official military-backed party used patronage, threats, and, when necessary, blatant fraud to ensure victory for its candidates. And the ruling oligarchy regularly used force against those seeking a more egalitarian society. In the mid-1970s, more than two-thirds of children under age five suffered from malnutrition.

The government of General Carlos Humberto Romero, installed after the fraudulent elections of 1977, imposed total press censorship, outlawed not only strikes but also public meetings of all sorts, and suspended judicial due process. Death squads, which worked closely with both the party and the Salvadoran security forces, became a regular part of the Romero regime's repressive apparatus. A succession of military juntas between 1979 and 1983 supervised an effective reign of terror that in response provoked an armed civil war. Americas Watch, a human rights NGO, estimated that out of a total population of fewer than 5 million, there were more than 30,000 government-sponsored murders in 1980–1983 alone (roughly equivalent to killing 1.25 million Americans).

The election of José Napoleón Duarte as president in 1984 (largely as a result of U.S. pressure) helped to reduce the level of violence. The human rights situation, however, remained dismal. The government estimated that death squads were killing "only" about thirty people a month in 1985, although most independent observers put the number substantially higher. Torture continued. The number of political prisoners even increased, apparently because of the decline in political murders.

A U.N. mediated end to the civil war was finally agreed to at the end of 1991. The arrival of U.N. monitors in 1992 stopped the fighting and initiated efforts at structural political reform (especially greater civilian control over the armed forces). And, by 1997, in the annual Freedom House ratings of political rights and civil liberties, El Salvador had returned to the level it held in the early 1970s (just barely "free" in the human rights NGOs' categorization) and has maintained this ranking consistently since then.

B. Human Rights in Nicaragua

Nicaragua's early political history was not much different from that of El Salvador. In 1936, however, Anastasio Somoza García seized power and initiated what would be more than forty years of authoritarian family rule. When Somoza was assassinated in 1956, power passed first to his son Luis Somoza Debayle and then to his younger son, Anastasio Somoza Debayle, who ruled until overthrown in 1979.

Although the Somozas retained the forms of democracy, elections were rigged and civil and political rights regularly violated. (Large-scale systematic killings, though, were not part of their repertoire.) Economic and social rights were also systematically infringed, both through the predatory accumulation of immense personal wealth by the Somozas and their cronies and through disregard of social services. For example, in the early 1970s, the Nicaraguan government spent three times as much on defense as on health care.

Massive corruption in the cleanup and recovery effort following the 1972 earthquake in the capital city of Managua, which left perhaps 10,000 dead and hundreds of thousands homeless, exacerbated and highlighted the endemic problems of inequality. Two years later, Somoza was reelected in a contest that even by Nicaraguan standards was farcical. In January 1978, the pace of disaffection accelerated after the assassination of Pedro Joaquín Chamorro, the leader of the moderate opposition. Even the business community turned against Somoza, under whom it had profited, organizing a general strike to protest Chamorro's death. Eighteen months later, Somoza was forced into exile.

Somoza was swept from power by a mass popular revolt incorporating many different social and political groups. Although its military forces were led by the Sandinista National Liberation Front (FSLN), established in 1961 as a radical breakaway from the Soviet-oriented Nicaraguan Socialist Party, during his final two years in power Somoza was opposed even by Nicaragua's conservative Catholic Church and by the United States, the Somozas' traditional patron.

The revolution, although widely supported, had immense human and economic costs. About one-fifth of Nicaragua's population of roughly 2.5 million became refugees. Casualties included 40,000–50,000 people killed, 150,000 wounded, and perhaps 40,000 orphaned. The war also disrupted agricultural production and most other sectors of the economy. The nation's gross domestic product fell by one-fourth in 1979 and by another one-fifth in 1980. Direct economic losses from the revolution were about $2 billion, or roughly Nicaragua's entire annual GDP.

Human rights conditions generally improved in revolutionary Nicaragua. The Sandinista government increased spending on social programs, especially health care, and redirected spending for education toward mass literacy. Personal and legal rights were fairly widely respected. Internationally recognized civil liberties were extensively implemented for the first time in Nicaraguan history. Mass political participation was actively fostered, and the 1984 election was generally considered by outside observers to have been relatively open and fairly run.

Nevertheless, the government itself admitted serious human rights violations during the forced relocation of Indian populations on the Atlantic Coast. Restrictions on freedom of the press, freedom of association, and due process were imposed. Sandinista mass popular organizations and the government-controlled media received preferential treatment. Nonetheless, political opponents operated under fewer constraints, and with far less fear of retaliation, than Somoza's opponents had. Human rights NGOs such as Americas Watch consistently judged the human rights situation to be significantly better than those in neighboring El Salvador and Guatemala.

This record, although acceptable only in relative terms, was noteworthy because the Sandinista government was under intense attack from U.S.-financed "contras" (a shortened form of the Spanish word for counterrevolutionaries). Contra strategy emphasized terrorism, including kidnappings; assassinations; and attacks on farms, schools, health clinics, and civilian economic targets. These tactics mirrored U.S.-supported governments in neighboring Guatemala and El Salvador, which typically justified state terrorism by the need to combat guerrilla violence.

With the winding down of the contra war in 1988 and 1989, respect for civil and political rights again improved. In national elections in February 1990, the Sandinistas were voted out of power, initiating two decades of lively contestation between the Left and Right. But, in November 2016, in elections that the head of the Organization of American States (OAS) observer mission described as "worrying," Ortega was reelected to a third term, after the Sandinista-dominated Supreme Court overturned term limits and excluded the leader of the opposition from the contest, reflecting a general decline in respect for civil and political rights.

C. U.S. Policy in Central America

In the early twentieth century, U.S. policy in Central America was directed toward establishing military, economic, and political hegemony. Central America was strategically significant for its proximity to the United States, the Panama Canal, and Caribbean sea-lanes. U.S. pressure and intervention were also regularly used to further the interests of U.S. banks and corporations. By the 1920s, Central America had become a special U.S. sphere of influence, "our backyard," as it was still often put in the 1980s.

After World War II, however, anticommunism became an increasingly important motivating force. By the 1980s, when Central America reemerged as a focal issue in U.S. foreign policy, economic interests were largely irrelevant. For example, U.S. exports to Nicaragua averaged just under $200 million per year from 1976 to 1978, and total U.S. direct foreign investment was a meager $60 million. U.S. policy was driven principally by the fear that domestic instability might increase support for local communists and their Soviet (and Cuban) backers. U.S. policy thus usually supported the military and traditional civilian elites, to the detriment of the rights of most Central Americans.

Consider Nicaragua. In 1912, U.S. troops prevented a liberal political revolution and then remained until 1933, except for eighteen months between 1925 and 1927. Furthermore, the United States was the leading force behind the creation of the National Guard, the principal base of Somoza power. Economic interests and strategic concerns over a potential second canal through Nicaragua explain the initial U.S. involvement. But, after World War II, the Somozas' support of U.S. Cold War policies became their major asset. U.S. policy in Guatemala and El Salvador was similar.

The postwar U.S. record on economic and social rights in Central America was more mixed. The Alliance for Progress, a major foreign aid initiative for Latin

America launched in 1961, brought substantial increases in U.S. aid to Central America. This seems to have contributed to rapid economic growth in the 1960s and early 1970s. U.S. aid also helped to improve life expectancy and literacy. The benefits of growth, however, were distributed so unequally that the gap between rich and poor widened in the 1960s and 1970s. And in El Salvador, Guatemala, and Nicaragua alike, U.S.-backed governments regularly used their power against political parties, trade unions, peasant organizations, and most other groups that tried to foster more rapid reforms or structural changes in society or the economy.

The Carter administration entered office in 1977 intent on giving human rights at least equal place in its policy. In Central America, the administration took both concrete and symbolic action. Most dramatically, Carter, with congressional support, cut aid to Guatemala. But although new military aid to Guatemala was cut off, already committed (pipeline) aid was continued. And Carter never seriously pressed for major structural reforms.

When Nicaragua emerged as a major concern of U.S. foreign policy in the fall of 1978, internal turmoil rather than human rights was the major American concern. Carter's goal was to remove Somoza without yielding power to the Sandinistas, who were seen as too closely tied to Cuba and the Soviet Union. The desire to avoid "another Cuba" dominated policy.

The United States tried to strengthen Nicaragua's political center, but it was suffering under political and financial retaliation by Somoza, and the assassination of Pedro Joaquín Chamorro had deprived it of its most respected and effective leader. After four frustrating months of U.S. mediation, Somoza simply refused to leave. Carter responded by terminating military and economic aid, withdrawing the Peace Corps, and halving the size of the U.S. Embassy in Managua. But when these sanctions failed to convince Somoza to step down, there was little that could be done short of the use of force—which Carter refused to consider, for reasons of principle and policy alike.

In June 1979, when the Sandinistas (FSLN) launched their "final offensive," the United States again tried to promote a centrist "third force." The pace of events, however, combined with the moderate opposition's lack of organization and foresight, proved fatal. When Somoza left in July, power passed to a provisional coalition government dominated by its most astute and best-organized faction, the FSLN.

The Carter administration attempted to set aside its suspicions. Food and medical supplies were sent almost immediately. When Carter left office in January 1981, eighteen months after Somoza's fall, the United States had provided $118 million in aid to Nicaragua. This was more than the United States gave to any other Central American country in the same period and was the largest amount provided to Nicaragua by any Western government.

In El Salvador, however, the United States continued to describe the repressive military governments as reformist—despite massive and mounting violations of civil and political rights and lack of progress on land reform and economic and social rights. And even such limited efforts met with substantial domestic opposition. Furthermore, the Carter administration also included skeptics among its high officials, most prominently the national security adviser, Zbigniew Brzezinski. As these elements increasingly came to dominate policy making, the Carter administration began moving the United States toward what would become President Ronald Reagan's new approach.

Central America (along with Afghanistan) became a test case for the Reagan administration's new global political strategy. By summer 1981, the Central Intelligence Agency (CIA) was working with the military opposition in Nicaragua. On March 14, 1982, the war began when two bridges were destroyed by former members of the National Guard who had been trained by the CIA.

The Kirkpatrick Doctrine provided a rationale for this new approach. In an influential article that helped to earn her the position of U.S. ambassador to the United Nations, Jeane Kirkpatrick argued that Carter had failed to understand that the most serious threats to human rights were posed not by authoritarian dictatorships but by totalitarian communists. For the Reagan administration, global strategic rivalry with the Soviet Union *was* a struggle for human rights, regardless of the actual human rights practices of the governments in question. In contrast, many in Congress, supported by a wide range of liberal interest groups, were more cautious about backing the contras but acquiesced for a time.

The American-backed campaign of military and economic aggression against Nicaragua had devastating consequences. As many as 40,000 people were killed and at least a quarter million displaced. Food production declined by at least one-fourth. Advances in health care and social services were reversed by terrorist attacks on clinics, schools, and social service offices. By 1988, Nicaragua's economy had been destroyed, with hyperinflation raging at 31,000 percent per year.

The intense U.S. opposition to the government of Nicaragua contrasted sharply with the strong U.S. support for the government of El Salvador. The human rights situation in El Salvador in the late 1970s and early 1980s was far worse than that in Nicaragua under either Somoza or the Sandinistas. And in addition to the tens of thousands of Salvadorans killed, Americans were also victims. In December 1980, four American churchwomen were abducted, raped, and murdered. In March 1981, two officials of the American Institute for Free Labor Development were assassinated in the San Salvador Sheraton Hotel. Yet massive aid continued—about $500 million a year in 1984 and 1985 (compared to less than $100 million in 1979 and 1980 combined), totaling almost $4 billion for the decade.

As Americas Watch put it, "So consistent is this [American] double standard that it can be fairly said [that] the Reagan administration has no true human rights policy."[1] Criticisms of the human rights practices of leftist regimes and the defense of the human rights practices of friendly governments were simply a continuation of the struggle with the Soviet Union by other means.

Rhetoric, however, exaggerates the differences in American policy under Carter and Reagan. Carter spoke of human rights as the heart of U.S. foreign policy, but in practice they were only a secondary goal. And Reagan's attempts to relegate human rights to the bottom of the list of U.S. foreign policy objectives were at least partially defeated by Congress. Carter did significantly elevate the place of human rights in U.S. policy toward Central America, but they never reached the top. Reagan did force human rights back down the list, but they never reached the bottom.

The first Bush administration's Central America policy, both in word and in deed, lay between those of its predecessors. Bush generally supported the Salvadoran and Guatemalan governments, despite their lack of control over the military. He did, however, act to prevent further deterioration. And in Nicaragua he pursued a somewhat less belligerent strategy of opposition to the Sandinistas.

The end of the Cold War led to a decline in Central America's geopolitical significance, and thus U.S. attention. But human rights concerns have over the past twenty years been an important—and nonpartisan—part of U.S. foreign policy in the region. And improvements in national human rights practices across the region have meant that U.S. initiatives have often been met with less resistance, although with continued concern for national sovereignty and fear of U.S. regional hegemony.

4. Case Study: U.S. Policy Toward South Africa

For nearly a half century, South Africa was synonymous with **apartheid,** a distinctive style of unusually deep and wide-ranging systematic legalized racial domination. Officially abolished in 1992, apartheid was a major international human rights issue for thirty years.

A. A System of Racial Domination

Racial discrimination in South Africa goes back to the initial Dutch colonization in 1652. Indigenous hunter-gatherers (San, or "Bushmen") were largely killed off or pushed out, and local herding peoples (Khoikhoi, or "Hottentots") were forced off their lands. Slaves began to be imported in 1658. Blacks, discriminated against in voting from the very beginning, lost the formal right to vote in 1936. They were legally excluded from many jobs after 1911.

With the electoral victory of the conservative Nationalist Party in 1948, race became the basis for regulating all aspects of life in South Africa. The Nationalist government created a totalitarian bureaucracy to enforce racism throughout South African society.

The Population Registration Act of 1950, the cornerstone of apartheid, required racial registration of each person at birth. The Group Areas Act of 1950 (amended in 1957) consolidated and extended earlier laws designating land by race. The 1954 Natives Resettlement Act provided for forced removals of blacks from white-designated land. These racial designations, however, did not necessarily have any connection to previously existing facts. More than 3.5 million blacks were removed from white areas, and more than 1 million were forced to relocate within designated black areas, often great distances away from their actual homes.

Controls on the movement of nonwhites resulted in a series of "pass laws" and regulations that made it illegal for most blacks to be in urban areas for more than seventy-two hours without special permission. The result was the creation of black townships, with inferior housing, education, and social services, on the outskirts of (white) cities, often two hours away from where residents worked. Because of the absurdities of the system of restrictions on movement, the ordinary nonwhite was subject to the constant threat of prosecution. More than one-fifth of the nonwhite population could expect to be prosecuted for pass-law violations within a ten-year period, a staggering level of legal intrusion on the basis of just one set of rules. And because prosecutions often led to expulsion from the area and the loss of a person's only source of income, the pass laws were an extraordinarily powerful instrument of social control.

Increasingly repressive internal-security laws were passed to prevent political opposition. By 1967, few legal safeguards remained for those suspected of political offenses. Over the next decade, at least one hundred people died while being detained by the police or security forces, usually after having been tortured. The best-known victim was black-consciousness activist Steve Biko.

Many who were not formally detained were brought in by the authorities for questioning, often as a not-so-subtle warning. Most nonparliamentary opposition was forced underground. This does not mean that there was no resistance. The African National Congress (ANC), the leading political group in contemporary South Africa, was founded in 1912. The 1952–1953 pass-law demonstrations marked the beginning of organized resistance to apartheid. Resistance took new forms, however, after the police fired on a group of peaceful demonstrators on March 21, 1960, killing sixty-nine people and wounding about two hundred others in what quickly came to be known as the Sharpeville Massacre.

When the ANC and several other groups were banned, a number of leading activists of the 1950s, including Nelson Mandela, concluded that peaceful protest alone could not be successful and launched a (quite ineffective) sabotage campaign. When Mandela and several other leaders were convicted in 1964 and sentenced to life imprisonment, the ANC was forced into exile. The government weathered mass protests and riots in 1976 and 1977 through a combination of force, new restrictions, and minor concessions.

Peaceful opposition also continued, despite government efforts to make it illegal. South African churches became particularly important, because almost all overtly political opposition organizations were banned. The award of the Nobel Peace Prize in 1984 to Bishop Desmond Tutu symbolized this struggle. Black trade-union activity also increased and became politically important in the mid-1980s.

New and unusually violent uprisings in the townships broke out in the fall of 1984 and lasted for nearly two years. Torture and abuse of those detained increased dramatically. Official violence against those not detained also increased. Symbolic of all this was the widely seen footage of armed security-force personnel popping up from their hiding place inside a passing vehicle and opening fire on unarmed children. Even more ominous was the dramatic increase in violence by police-sponsored vigilante groups.

Direct repression was accompanied by no less severe social and economic exploitation and degradation. For example, the average white under apartheid had an income more than twelve times that of the average black. A black child was almost ten times more likely to die before the age of one than a white child. Other standard statistical measures revealed a similar picture.

B. U.S. Policy on Apartheid

Before the Sharpeville Massacre in 1960, the United States treated apartheid as an internal South African matter. The turmoil following Sharpeville, however, raised the specter of revolution and mobilized American fear of communism. The United States thus began to treat apartheid as a matter of international concern. The Eisenhower administration even agreed to put apartheid permanently on the agenda of the U.N. Security Council. And the Kennedy administration imposed a selective arms embargo even before the Security Council called for a voluntary embargo at the end of 1963.

As the crisis receded, however, so too did U.S. attention. Sanctions remained in effect, but they were modest and had no discernible impact.

The Nixon administration changed course, believing that a closer association with South Africa would put the United States in a better position to press for reform. This approach, however, had no more impact than the Kennedy-Johnson strategy of dissociation. Part of the problem was weak and inconsistent implementation: U.S. concessions were tied to no particular demands on South Africa. In other words, there was no real policy on South Africa.

There were also major conceptual flaws in both American approaches. Although willing to ease some elements of "petty apartheid" (for example, by desegregating some public facilities in large cities), the South African government was unwilling to end racial separation. Democratic majority rule was not even open for discussion. The negative sanctions and positive inducements the United States were willing to use fell far short of what would have been necessary to make the white government change its policies.

The other conceptual error in U.S. policy was an excessive reliance on economic change and private enterprise. Liberals and conservatives alike believed that South Africa's atavistic racial policies would inevitably be eroded by the modernization that accompanied economic development. In practice, however, South Africa's immense bureaucracy, which intervened with totalitarian thoroughness in all aspects of life, largely prevented changes in the fundamental character of apartheid.

After the Portuguese coup in April 1974, which led to the rapid decolonization of Angola and Mozambique, even these modest U.S. efforts were largely abandoned in favor of a focus on regional security—that is, containing expanding Soviet influence. South Africa now appeared as a pro-Western regional power.

The Soweto riots of 1976 returned apartheid to the center of international attention. Soon afterward, Jimmy Carter changed the U.S. approach, although actions such as U.S. support in the Security Council for a mandatory arms embargo were largely symbolic. Furthermore, there were tensions within the Carter administration. Zbigniew Brzezinski, Carter's national security adviser, favored a policy that, like Kissinger's, emphasized regional security. As Brzezinski's influence grew in the second half of Carter's term, U.S. policy took on an increasingly Cold War tone, stressing the Cuban presence in Angola and the Soviet naval threat in the South Atlantic and Indian Oceans. Even more than in Central America, the end of the Carter administration is best seen as preparing the way for Reagan's policies.

Reagan's policy of constructive engagement returned to the Nixon-era strategy of pursuing closer relations to increase U.S. leverage. Despite international calls for new sanctions, the United States eased many that were already in place. Restrictions on the sale of aircraft, computers, and nuclear-related equipment with dual military and civilian uses were eased. In fact, the United States became South Africa's largest trading partner. Total private investment and loans rose to $10 billion. And, as in the early 1970s, the United States did not insist on any concrete human rights improvements in return for closer relations.

Events in South Africa, however, again forced a reevaluation of U.S. policy. Violence erupted in August 1984 in protest over elections held under the new constitution of 1983, which completely excluded blacks from direct political participation. When repression once more tightened rather than eased, constructive engagement lost any remaining credibility. But, as late as July 1986, Reagan still argued that "we and our allies cannot dictate to the government of a sovereign nation—nor should we try"—despite supporting a terrorist war against the freely elected government of Nicaragua and the decades-old policy of comprehensive sanctions against Cuba.

Change in U.S. policy came from a bipartisan congressional coalition that in 1986 overrode a presidential veto of a new sanctions bill. This reflected the culmination of the mobilization of antiapartheid NGOs over many decades.

Activity on South Africa by U.S. NGOs goes back to at least 1912, when the National Association for the Advancement of Colored People was involved in the initial formation of South Africa's African National Congress. In the late 1970s and 1980s, groups like TransAfrica focused their efforts on apartheid. Other NGOs, such as the American Friends Service Committee, the Interfaith Council on Corporate Responsibility, and the Lawyers' Committee for Civil Rights Under Law, made South Africa a major priority. In addition, churches, state and local governments, colleges and universities, student organizations, unions, and black organizations divested assets in corporations that did business in South Africa. Many of these actions were coordinated with divestment campaigns in other countries, with international antiapartheid groups such as the International Defense and Aid Fund and with other international NGOs such as the World Council of Churches and the Lutheran World Fund. They were also facilitated by Bishop Desmond Tutu's Nobel Peace Prize and his well-publicized visit to the United States at the end of 1984.

It is important not to overestimate U.S. efforts. American sanctions were limited and quite incomplete. Nonetheless, South Africa was losing access to international capital (although in the short run more from lender fear caused by the 1984–1986 township riots than from sanctions). And the loss of U.S. support, even if the Reagan administration never actively opposed the white government, created concern among many of South Africa's less conservative leaders and citizens, particularly in light of the growing internal crisis.

Apartheid ultimately collapsed because of the inability of the white government to keep opposition repressed. Nonetheless, changes in U.S. policy, particularly in the context of the global antiapartheid campaign, made a small contribution to the final demise of apartheid. And even though American sanctions were largely symbolic, it was a very different sort of symbolism than had been typical of U.S. policy in the preceding years.

5. Case Study: American Policy
Toward Myanmar (Burma)

The United States recognized Burmese independence from Britain in late 1947 even before Burma's formal independence early the next year. The United States both extended an economic support package to the newly independent state and provided covert support to Chinese Nationalist (Kuomintang) forces in Burma fighting in the Chinese Civil War again the communists under the leadership of Mao Zedong (who declared victory in October 1949).

Twelve years of multiparty elections came to an end in 1962 when the military under General Ne Win staged a coup d'état and established a "socialist" regime under the direction of a Revolutionary Council. A constitution was adopted in 1977, but it did little more than entrench the generals under the guise of constitutional legitimacy.

Growing unrest with one-party rule resulted in widespread prodemocracy demonstrations in 1988. Security forces killed thousands of demonstrators. Eventually, the military staged a restoration coup under the direction of General Saw Maung, who established the State Law and Order Restoration Council (SLORC). The SLORC declared martial law the following year, and changed the country's official name from the Socialist Republic of the Union of Burma (which had been adopted in 1974, replacing Union of Burma)—Burman or Burmese being the name of the predominant ethnic group in the country—to the Republic of the Union of Myanmar.

In free elections in 1990, the National League of Democracy (NLD, the party of Aung San Suu Kyi) won an 80 percent majority in Parliament. The generals, however, refused to cede power, placed Suu Kyi under house arrest, and continued to rule until reforms began in 2011. From 2011 through 2015, negotiations with the democratic opposition eventually led to the release of Suu Kyi from house arrest, creation of a National Human Rights Commission, amnesty for political prisoners, an end to overt censorship of the media, and the legalization of labor unions (which also obtained the right to strike).

Before 1988, American support to Burma was mostly in the form of on-again, off-again economic assistance and aid programs, supplemented in the 1970s by military training to curb the production of opium. After the military failed to recognize the results of the 1990 elections, however, the United States cut off military and economic assistance to Myanmar and recalled its ambassador. In 1997, the United States prohibited American investments in Myanmar and imposed a number of other (minor) sanctions. In 2003, after a government attack on members of the NLD, Congress passed the Burmese Freedom and Democracy Act, which imposed harsher sanctions, including import restrictions and asset freezes targeted at members of the ruling regime. These sanctions were expanded again in 2007 and 2008. And, in 2008, George W. Bush nominated Suu Kyi to receive a congressional gold medal "in recognition of her courageous and unwavering commitment to peace, nonviolence, human rights and democracy in Burma." Congress unanimously agreed.

Immediately after taking office, the Obama administration adjusted American policy, attempting to balance economic sanctions with pragmatic engagement with Myanmar's military leaders. (Carrots were added to the sticks that were still being wielded.) High-level visits ensued. In 2011 Secretary of State Hillary Clinton visited the country and promised humanitarian aid from the United States and economic assistance through the International Monetary Fund (IMF) and the World Bank (which the United States had previously blocked). In 2012, full diplomatic relations were restored: the first American ambassador in twenty-one years was posted, a U.S. Agency for International Development (USAID) mission was created, and economic sanctions were formally eased.

In the United States, a standard reading of this case is that American sanctions work: after having been punished for their bad behavior, the military leaders in Myanmar made the right choice, and the United States is now rewarding them for seeing the light. But the elections were far from free and fair, and many of the new governmental positions are held by former military officers. And the broad human rights picture, although substantially improved, is far from excellent and shows little sign of continued, let alone rapid, improvement. In fact, there has been a recent increase in discrimination against minorities, especially the Rohingya, and an uptick in political imprisonments.[2] There also are reasonable fears that, having lifted sanctions, the United States has lost much of its influence with Myanmar's military.[3]

Furthermore, all of these human rights changes are consistent with, and actually support, American interests in responding strategically to the rise of China's regional power. In fact, it is just as likely that Myanmar's leaders, dissatisfied with the results of its previous tilt toward China, moved in this more rights-amenable direction to engage the United States as a strategic partner. In other words, both the Obama administration and Myanmar's military rulers may have had much more material motives behind their policies of democracy promotion. To the extent that this is true, Myanmar was an easy case; human rights improvements did not conflict with interests of equal or higher value. And some cynics have suggested that even this overstates the relative importance of genuine human rights considerations in American policy.

6. Case Study: Israeli Settlements in West Bank Palestine

Perhaps no other American foreign policy relationship is at once as central and as contentious as its very special relationship with Israel. Since being one of the first countries to recognize Israeli independence in 1948, the United States has remained a stalwart political, economic, and military ally of Israel. However, the United States, cognizant of its broader geopolitical interests, has always sought friendly relations with Arab states as well. It has also seen itself (although has not always been seen by others) as an honest broker for peace in the region.

We look here narrowly at Israeli settlement policy in the occupied West Bank (the Israeli government unilaterally evacuated and dismantled its settlements in the Gaza Strip in 2005). This not only provides an excellent example of the complexities of U.S.-Israeli international human rights relations; it also allows us to look at American policy with respect to an ally that in many areas has an excellent human rights record but in other ways is a systematic violator of international human rights law. In addition, by focusing on settlement policy, rather than Israeli violations of human rights such as arbitrary arrest and detention, torture, denials of freedom of movement, the use of collective punishments, and a general practice of **impunity** (see under **amnesty**) for security forces,[4] this case also illustrates the increasingly important interaction of human rights law with international humanitarian law (the law of armed conflict), to which we will return in some detail in Chapter 10.

During the Six-Day War in June 1967, Israel captured and occupied the West Bank of the Jordan River (which had been under the administration of Jordan), the Golan Heights (territorially part of Syria), and Egypt's Gaza Strip and Sinai Peninsula. To this day, the West Bank, which is our focus here, has not been recognized internationally as Israel's. In fact, Israel agrees that nearly all of this land is Israeli-occupied territory, not part of the state of Israel, and it has accepted the Palestinian Authority as a legitimate administrative government in the West Bank.

As a matter of both international and Israeli law, the West Bank remains a territory under the military occupation of Israel. Therefore, the laws of war govern Israel's actions there.

An occupying authority, according to the Geneva Conventions, is prohibited from taking measures that might lead to a de facto annexation of the territory, such as forcibly altering the demographic structure of the territory (for example, through population transfers). This, however, is precisely what successive Israeli governments have promoted though their settlement-building policies in the West Bank. Not only has this displaced Palestinians and brought nearly 400,000 Israelis to live, ostensibly permanently, on Palestinian territory, but these settlements have been crafted into a coherent network secured by the Israeli Defense Forces (IDF). (In this case study we do not address the more than 300,000 Israeli settlers in East Jerusalem, whom Israel—with almost no international support—claims have a different legal status than do the settlers in the West Bank and some 20,000 settlers in the Golan Heights.)

Settlement policy has always been controversial in Israel's internally vibrant multiparty democracy, leading to recurrent freezes on new settlements and occasionally even minor withdrawals from particular settlements. Since the early 2000s, though, Israeli governments have been generally steadfast and often quite enthusiastic in their support of not merely maintaining but steadily expanding Israeli settlements in the Palestinian territory.

This has created immense problems for American policy, the primary stated goal of which has always been a final settlement to the Israeli-Palestinian conflict in the form of a "two-state solution." Even setting aside the political problems caused by its flagrant illegality, Israeli settlement policy, by changing facts on the ground, has made it more difficult to imagine a final territorial settlement acceptable to both Israel and Palestine. Every American presidential administration since 1967 thus has, with varying degrees of intensity, condemned Israeli settlements.

Despite the fact that settlement activity has expanded under every American president since Lyndon Johnson, American action has been weak and inconsistent. For example, although U.S. law provides that aid to Israel (which until very recently was $3 billion annually) be reduced dollar for dollar by what Israel spends on settlement activity, the last such reduction was in 2005. And a 2004 letter to Israeli prime minister Ariel Sharon conceded that, given the expansion of settlement activity, it was unrealistic to expect that the outcome of final status negotiations would be based on the original armistice lines following the Arab-Israel War of 1948–1949 (this position has since changed to the armistice lines of 1967).[5] This statement was interpreted by Palestinian leaders as an implicit American support for Israeli settlement construction.[6]

Upon assuming office, Barack Obama urged Israeli leaders to freeze settlement activity in the West Bank. In his 2009 Cairo speech, Obama forcefully repeated the long-established policy that the United States "does not accept the legitimacy of continued Israeli settlements. This construction violates previous agreements and undermines efforts to achieve peace. It is time for these settlements to stop." Although this did result in a ten-month settlement freeze, new settlements resumed, and the prospects for peace remained dismal. The United States not only has failed to institute diplomatic sanctions; in 2011 it even vetoed a draft resolution in the Security Council condemning the Israeli settlements as illegal—despite continued American insistence that the settlements are illegitimate and undermine peace efforts. And not only does the United States continue to refuse to link military aid to settlement drawdowns, a ten-year, $38 billion dollar arms deal confirmed in September 2016 is the largest ever American aid package of its kind.

This policy of largely verbal opposition reflects the priority given to a long-standing special relationship, the central place of Israel in America's established geopolitical orientation to the region, the historical memory of the Holocaust, and American domestic politics—involving not only ethnic electoral mobilization in large and politically important states such as New York and Florida but an extremely active and effective pro-Israel lobby that extends far beyond Jewish groups and their supporters.[7] These factors, plus a general inclination in post-9/11 American foreign policy (which we discuss in some detail in Chapter 12) to tolerate human rights violations of friends undertaken in the name of antiterrorism, have made supporting Israel quite popular with both the American public and American legislators. Israel's human rights violations and flouting of international humanitarian law in the Occupied Territories thus have been kept on the back burner, even by a president such as Obama who seemed inclined to want to do more. And the early signs from the Trump administration, both in campaign speeches and in the nomination of David Friedman—a strong and intemperate supporter of Israeli settlements—as the American ambassador to Israel, may suggest an effort even to take settlements off that back burner. (Such an outcome now seems more likely, in the aftermath of the Obama administration's decision to abstain on a U.N. Security Council resolution condemning the settlement policy, which was adopted by the Council by a vote of 14–0–1 in late December 2016.)

7. Other Western Approaches to International Human Rights

Although the United States led the way in the 1970s in introducing human rights into bilateral diplomacy, other countries also incorporated human rights into their foreign policies. Particularly notable were the efforts of the **like-minded countries,** a dozen smaller Western countries that since the mid-1970s have attempted to act together in international diplomacy as intermediaries between the larger Western countries, with which they are formally or informally aligned, and the countries of the Third World, for whose aspirations they have considerable sympathy. Norway and the Netherlands, in particular, have emphasized human rights in their foreign policies, signaled by white papers on the subject in 1977 and 1979.

Even more than in U.S. policy, foreign aid has been a central instrument in the international human rights policies of the like-minded countries. Development assistance tends to be not only an important element of their foreign policies but a matter of consensus among the major political parties. In the Netherlands, there is even a separate minister for development cooperation within the foreign ministry. By contrast, in the United States, foreign aid is a relatively peripheral part of foreign policy yet, during the 1970s and 1980s, a subject of considerable partisan political controversy.

Furthermore, the United States tends to base initial foreign aid decisions on political and humanitarian factors, modifying allocations at a later stage in light of human rights concerns. The like-minded countries, which lack the resources to engage in a massive, global foreign aid program, target their development assistance at a small set of countries—variously called "core," "program," or "priority" countries— with which they seek to develop relatively intensive, long-term aid relations. The Dutch and Norwegians, in particular, have emphasized both civil and political rights and economic, social, and cultural rights in selecting program countries. In Norway, selection criteria since 1972 have included a strong preference for countries in which "the authorities of the country concerned [are] following a development-oriented and socially just policy in the best interests of all sections of the community," reflecting the fact that social justice is given roughly equal priority to civil and political rights largely across the Norwegian political spectrum. And as early as 1973, the Dutch officially emphasized a "close relationship between peace, a just distribution of wealth, international legal order and respect for human rights."[8]

Even more striking than the selection of priority countries has been the relatively rapid response of the like-minded countries to changes in human rights conditions. For example, Norway broke its aid relationship with Uganda in 1972, the year that Idi Amin overthrew the government of Milton Obote and embarked on a dictatorial career that made him one of the most notorious human rights violators of the decade. The Netherlands dropped Uganda from its list of program countries in 1974. The United States, by contrast, was Uganda's largest trading partner until October 1978, less than a year before Amin was overthrown.

Sweden stopped all assistance to Chile shortly after Pinochet's coup and was a significant international supporter of the work of the Vicaría, a Catholic human rights organization in Chile. Canada was also a vocal critic of military rule in the Southern Cone. In the 1980s, as ethnic violence escalated in Sri Lanka, a country with which Norway had developed close ties in the 1970s, the Norwegians dramatically downgraded their relationship. Canada, the Netherlands, and the Nordic countries all increased their aid to Nicaragua in the 1980s, reflecting a radically different understanding of human rights than that held by the Reagan administration.

The Dutch response to the deteriorating human rights situation in its former colony of Suriname is especially revealing. It strongly condemned the 1980 military coup. Following the execution of fifteen opposition figures in 1982, the Netherlands not only suspended all aid but refused to provide new aid for the remainder of the decade. The Dutch also led the effort to apply international pressure on Suriname. The contrast to U.S. behavior toward its Caribbean Basin clients in Guatemala and El Salvador, who were guilty of much more severe human rights violations, is striking. The Dutch even carried human rights into relations with Indonesia, a country of far greater importance, and accepted some real economic and political costs as a result.

The like-minded countries also adopted an approach to South Africa very different from that of the United States in the 1970s and 1980s. Starting in 1969, Sweden and Norway provided both political support and development assistance funds to the ANC during its exile from South Africa. The Dutch adopted a similar policy in 1973. And in the 1980s, these efforts were expanded into broad, high-priority programs for the whole region of Southern Africa and a leading role in the international movement for sanctions against South Africa.

Since the end of the Cold War, these countries have continued to pursue their human rights policies in such distinctive ways. And they have been joined by countries from the global South such as Costa Rica and South Africa, which have also put human rights at the forefront of their foreign policies.

We should be careful not to romanticize the policies of the like-minded countries. Considerations other than human rights are central, sometimes even overriding, in their foreign policies. For example, Dutch aid sanctions against Indonesia did not extend to trade or other economic relations. Canada also pursued close relations with Indonesia for commercial reasons. Economic interests in South Africa seriously delayed Canada's decision to adopt sanctions and led Norway to exclude shipping from its initial sanctions. Nonetheless, the overall international human rights record of the like-minded countries is clearly superior to that of the United States, both in avoiding associations with severe violators and in responding to abuses in countries with which they have special relations. The like-minded countries have also given human rights a much higher priority in their multilateral foreign policies.

8. Explaining Differences in Human Rights Policies

Jan Egeland, in comparing Norwegian and U.S. international human rights policies, argued that "small and big nations are differently disposed to undertaking coherent rights-oriented foreign policies." In fact, Egeland asserted that the relatively meager international human rights accomplishments of the United States are "because of, rather than in spite of, her superpower status."[9] Small countries are not so much better, in this analysis, as less constrained than large states. "The frequency and intensity of the conflict between self-interest and [international human rights] norms seems, in short, proportional to a nation's economic and military power, as well as to its foreign policy ambitions."[10] Large states have multiple interests and responsibilities that preclude the consistent pursuit of human rights objectives. Small states rarely have to choose between human rights and other foreign policy goals.

This explanation focuses on the structure of the international system. Large states are also more likely to pursue bilateral policies because they are more likely to have the power to achieve their aims without multilateral support. Small states, by contrast, tend to prefer international organizations because multilateral processes increase their opportunities for influence. Such structural explanations would also seem to be supported by the fact that larger powers, such as Britain, France, Japan, and to a lesser extent Germany, have international human rights policies closer to those of the United States than to those of Norway or the Netherlands.

Size alone, however, cannot explain even the differences that are influenced by relative power. For example, despite declining American power, the United States remains reluctant to operate through multilateral channels (unless it can control the organization). As Germany's power grows, it continues to rely heavily on multilateral organizations. Britain has tended to pursue a much more unilateral foreign policy than has France, Germany, or Japan. Among small states, Sweden, Austria, and especially Switzerland have emphasized a neutral foreign policy. Canada, Belgium, and the Netherlands have had a strong Western orientation in their foreign policies. Size or power at most inclines states in certain directions.

Furthermore, numerous factors unconnected with size are also important. Why did the United States emphasize international human rights in the 1970s while other large powers did not, and Japan still does not? Why did Britain intervene in its sphere of influence so much less frequently than did the United States? Why are human rights as a foreign policy issue so much more controversial in the United States than in most other Western countries? Why does Belgium have a much less active international human rights policy than does the Netherlands? Such questions can be answered only if we take history, political culture, and institutions into account.

Throughout the cold war era, the United States viewed the world in East-West terms, reducing all foreign policy issues to U.S.-Soviet rivalry. But the Cold War was not simply a bipolar political rivalry between hegemonic states; it involved a heavy emphasis on ideology. As a result, Americans generally assumed that radical reformers and their programs were Soviet backed, inspired, or influenced. And without the ideological element, many actual or attempted political changes in the Third World would not have been deemed such a threat to the United States. Ideology, however, has nothing to do with size. Many small states, especially in Latin America, were at least as anticommunist as the United States. Conversely, it is historically rare for a large state to define its interests in ideological terms.

Consider also the tendency of the like-minded states to view international conflicts more in North-South than East-West terms. During the Cold War, these countries saw the principal lines of international cleavage as dividing rich and poor, not capitalist (or liberal-democratic) and communist. For example, in 1982, Mark Mac-Guigan, the Canadian secretary of state for external affairs, argued, "Instability in Central America . . . is not a product of East-West rivalry. It is a product of poverty, the unfair distribution of wealth, and social injustice. Instability feeds poverty and injustice. East-West rivalries flow in its wake."[11] The Dutch and the Nordic countries shared this view.

Some part of this might be related to size. For example, it is not surprising that a country like Canada, which fears being overwhelmed by the United States, or the Netherlands, which borders on powerful Germany and is not far from France and Britain, is more sympathetic to a perspective that sees differences in power as no less important than differences in ideology. But size alone cannot explain the difference in ideological perspective.

We can see this even in Egeland's own analysis. In explaining the "strong moral impact" on Norwegian policy, he stressed four factors: (1) no legacy of imperialism and intervention, (2) a good domestic human rights record, (3) a high level of foreign aid and support for changes in the world economy to favor Third World countries, and (4) consistent support for decolonization and national liberation movements.[12] The first of these factors is perhaps related to size—although Belgium, Portugal, and the Netherlands had significant colonial holdings, German, Austrian, Russian, and American colonial holdings were small, and the Netherlands rapidly overcame its imperial legacy. The other three factors, however, have little or nothing to do with size.

Size explains almost nothing about internal human rights records, as a comparison of pairs of similarly sized countries such as the United States and the Soviet Union, China and India, Japan and Indonesia, and Costa Rica and Guatemala vividly illustrates. Nor does size have much to do with levels of foreign aid. The United States chooses to be niggardly, whereas Norway and the Netherlands (and Japan) choose to be generous.[13] And the United States has had a better record on supporting decolonization than small states such as Portugal and Spain or second-tier powers such as Britain and France.

Much the same can be said of the role of consensus in Norwegian international human rights and foreign policy, another factor Egeland emphasized. Foreign policy consensus is hardly characteristic of small states, as the varying policies of dozens of Third World countries indicate. In the Nordic countries, foreign policy consensus is a function of a parliamentary system, in which there is no sharp division between executive and legislative branches, a strong reliance on a professional foreign and civil service (in contrast to the extensive use of political appointees in the U.S. bureaucracy), and a political tradition that ensures direct representation and special consideration for all major social groups.

Size does not explain why Norway and the Netherlands in the 1970s embarked on unusually active international human rights policies but Austria, Belgium, and Greece did not. Likewise, size cannot explain either the active (if inconsistent) international human rights policy of the United States or the lack of an active international human rights policy in Japan, let alone China.

How a country defines its interests certainly is constrained, and often shaped, by its power and its position in the international system. But power and position do not come even close to determining interests. Most impediments to strong international human rights policies lie in the relatively free decisions of states to give greater weight to other foreign policy objectives. Most of the factors that contribute to aggressive efforts to pursue international human rights in a country's foreign policy have much more to do with its national political culture and contingent political facts (for example, the election of Jimmy Carter) than with its international political position. For example, Dutch membership in Amnesty International, on a per capita basis, exceeds American membership in the National Rifle Association, one of the largest and most powerful interest groups in the United States.

National political culture is especially important in explaining the striking differences between the attitudes of the United States and the like-minded countries toward economic and social rights. American foreign aid has been used almost exclusively in the pursuit of civil and political rights objectives. Humanitarian objectives such as nutrition, literacy, and health care have been pursued, but in the United States these objectives simply are not perceived in terms of human rights. U.S. foreign aid and human rights policy are seen as two fundamentally separate issues that are tactically linked. The like-minded countries, by contrast, see development assistance as central to their international human rights policies. They also emphasize the intrinsic importance of economic, social, and cultural rights and their interdependence with civil and political rights.

Differences between the United States and the like-minded countries are largely matters of choice. Norway and the Netherlands place a relatively high value on international human rights not because they are small and weak but because of how their citizens understand themselves, their place in the world, and the obligations associated with their identity.

Problem 5: U.S. Ratification of Human Rights Treaties

The Problem

The United States is a leading global advocate of human rights. It regularly makes use of the body of international human rights law to criticize other states. But the United States is a party to only three of the seven core treaties: the Covenant on Civil and Political Rights, the Convention on Racial Discrimination, and the Torture Convention. The United States has failed to ratify the Covenant on Economic, Social, and Cultural Rights; the Women's Convention; the Convention on the Rights of the Child (the only state in the world that has failed to ratify); and the Convention on the Rights of Persons with Disabilities (which it played an outsized role in drafting). It does not permit individual communications under the treaties to which it is a party. And the United States is not a party to the regional American Convention.

This is widely seen by other countries as hypocrisy. (We see a similar, perhaps even more striking, hypocrisy in U.S. support of the ICC and the tribunals for the former Yugoslavia and Rwanda but its refusal to include itself under the jurisdiction of the ICC.) This hypocrisy hinders American international action. And it undermines what we have argued is the most important contribution of the global human rights regime, namely, an agreed-upon set of comprehensive global standards.

A Solution

The obvious solution is for the United States to ratify these treaties. But this is almost certainly not going to happen in the foreseeable future. In other words, there is no practical solution. The best we can do is understand what is behind this problem and why it persists.

Opposition to human rights treaties in the U.S. Senate has historically been concentrated among (although by no means excusive to) Republicans, going back to the Bricker Amendment controversy (see §8.1 above). As the Republican Party has moved further and further to the right and toward unilateralism and nationalism, its objections are based ostensibly on fear of infringements on American sovereignty and a challenge to the supremacy of American courts. There is simply no rational legal basis to such fears—although they have considerable emotional appeal to a growing and increasingly fearful and willfully ignorant segment of the American electorate.

There is a limited basis for concerns that some treaties may be inconsistent with the U.S. Constitution. Such concerns, however, can easily be handled by attaching reservations, understandings, or declarations to American ratification that exempt the United States from those provisions. In fact, this is precisely what the United States did with perhaps the most blatant conflict between international human rights law and American constitutional law, namely, the provision of Article 4 of the Racial Discrimination Convention that requires legally prohibiting "all dissemination of ideas based on racial superiority or hatred." This clear conflict with the deeply embedded American constitutional law that protects hate speech was easily handled by a declaration that rejected any infringement of free speech that does not incite violence. In ratifying a treaty, one *may* (within certain broad limits) pick and choose among the obligations a state undertakes, especially when the reservations include only a few particular provisions of a treaty.

It has also been claimed that some international human rights treaties threaten "American values." This has been at the heart of opposition to the Convention on the Rights of the Child (CRC). In fact, however, such arguments have little or nothing to do with the substance of the CRC. They simply give vent to a highly politicized vision of "family values," a minority view that is as inconsistent with existing American law as it is with the CRC. And if there are any real problems, reservations, as we just saw, provide a ready and effective remedy.

American values, law, and sovereignty have been in no way harmed or infringed upon by the human rights treaties that the United States has ratified. Nor would they be harmed by ratification of any of the other treaties. What we see here is a particularly striking example of American exceptionalism and exemptionalism. Any legitimate worries about ratification largely involve a desire to continue to sweep under the rug parts of American law and practice that fall short of international human rights norms—especially with respect to many economic and social rights.

This situation can only be expected to continue. No president has been willing to even try to expend the amount of political capital that would be needed to overcome Senate opposition (which requires only one-third of the Senate to block ratification). Only a small segment of the American population attaches positive significance to U.S. ratification of international human rights treaties. And almost no one would vote on that basis. But an important part of the Republican electorate can be mobilized against ratification—and the charge of sacrificing American sovereignty has considerable resonance in the political center. The electoral calculus is thus clear: nothing is to be gained from supporting ratification, but something may be lost. Thus, international human rights treaties continue to sit on the shelf—even though the Conventions on Discrimination Against Women and the Rights of the Child actually have considerable substantive attraction to the majority of the American population.

Further Problems

International scrutiny is a mechanism to help states hold themselves to the highest standards. And they provide citizens of participating states with supplemental mechanisms that in some cases can help them to achieve effective enjoyment of their rights. This is particularly true in countries with relatively good human rights records and active civil societies—that is, countries such as the United States. The United States is thus depriving its citizens of a limited but not insignificant mechanism to guarantee their rights.

Americans are also becoming increasingly isolated from the rest of the Western world, where the language of human rights is being incorporated into national law and politics. This too is likely to lead to slower human rights improvements, both absolutely and relatively, in the United States.

If this continues, America's leadership role may be challenged. People across the globe have for two centuries looked to the United States as a human rights inspiration. The refusal of the United States to participate fully in the body of international human rights law and practice may ultimately lead to that leadership passing to Europe.

Discussion Questions

1. Should we accept the description of post–World War II U.S. foreign policy as dominated by anticommunism? Suppose that we do. Was it a poor policy decision? Should anticommunism have been assigned a less overriding priority? Or was the problem that anticommunism was pursued with unreasonable zeal? Is there an important lesson here about an ideological (or moralistic) foreign policy that leads to such excess? If so, should we reconsider the arguments of the realists?

2. Should the United States be able to define for itself which internationally recognized human rights it wishes to recognize or pursue? If so, why? How can we sustain and enforce an international human rights policy if states can pick and choose the parts they want to comply with? Why should the United States (or any other sovereign state) have to comply with international human rights norms, no matter how widely accepted they are?

3. The United States has a relatively active and aggressive bilateral international human rights policy but has been reluctant to participate in most multilateral international human rights regimes. (The United States did not ratify the International Covenant on Civil and Political Rights until

April 1992, and even then it did not ratify the optional protocol.) Isn't this a double standard? Can it be justified? Why should other countries take U.S. international human rights policy seriously when the United States is so reluctant to open itself to international human rights scrutiny?

4. In reviewing the evidence of U.S. policy toward Central America, South Africa, Myanmar, and Israel, what strikes you more: the continuities or the changes between different U.S. administrations? Were the differences largely symbolic? If they were, how serious a criticism is that? How large a role does symbolic rhetoric play in foreign policy? In international human rights policy?

5. Looking at these cases, which is more striking to you: the weight given to human rights or the weight given to other concerns? Is it fair to say that the United States strongly supports international human rights only when the costs to the United States of doing so are low? Assume that the answer to that question is yes. Is that inappropriate? *Should* human rights have a lower priority? Is there a general answer to that question? Should it be a matter of case-by-case balancing? If so, in which of these cases do you think the United States has gotten the balance right?

6. The same question might be asked about the differences between the international human rights policies of the United States and the policies of the like-minded countries. When it comes to making difficult choices, when it comes to sacrificing their own interests, just how different are Canada, Norway, and the Netherlands from the United States? Compare, for example, the Netherlands' policy toward Indonesia and its policy toward Suriname. Is the difference a matter of kind or merely a matter of degree?

7. Consider the emphasis of the like-minded countries on economic, social, and cultural rights. Is their approach better than or just different from that of the United States? Why? Does your answer change if you look at the issue from the perspectives of foreign policy, foreign aid policy, and international human rights policy?

8. Why do you think that international human rights policies were a matter of intense partisan controversy in the United States in the 1970s and 1980s but not in Norway and the Netherlands? What explains the fact that since the early 1990s there has been a nonpartisan consensus on the importance of international human rights policies in the United States as well?

Suggested Readings

Debra Liang-Fenton, ed., *Implementing U.S. Human Rights Policy* (Washington, DC: U.S. Institute of Peace Press, 2004), provides more than a dozen superb case studies of U.S. human rights policy toward a wide range of prominent countries, focusing on the post–Cold War era. It is the single best source to get some sense of the texture and range of American international human rights policy in recent years. Kathryn

Sikkink, *Mixed Signals: U.S. Human Rights Policy and Latin America* (Ithaca, NY: Cornell University Press, 2005), provides a comprehensive overview of U.S. human rights policy toward Latin America, covering the entire post–World War II era. Michael Ignatieff, ed., *American Exceptionalism and Human Rights* (Princeton, NJ: Princeton University Press, 2005), is an excellent collection of essays covering a wide range of both domestic and international human rights issues. Harold Koh, "America's Jekyll-and-Hyde Exceptionalism," 111–144, and John Ruggie, "American, Exceptionalism, Exemptionalism, and Global Governance," 304–338, are particularly good and especially relevant to the issues covered in this chapter. Taken together, these three books provide an excellent overview of the topic of human rights in American foreign policy. For a more critical assessment, see Julie Mertus, *Bait and Switch? Human Rights and U.S. Foreign Policy*, 2nd ed. (New York: Routledge, 2008). Harold Hongju Koh, "A United States Human Rights Policy for the 21st Century," *Saint Louis University Law Journal* 46 (Spring 2002): 293–344, is a powerful programmatic statement by Clinton's former assistant secretary of state. In our view, there is no single piece that does a better job of provoking serious thought about the appropriate contours of American international human rights policy.

For good illustrations of competing views on human rights and American foreign policy in the late 1970s and early 1980s, see (on the liberal side) Arthur Schlesinger Jr., "Human Rights and the American Tradition," *Foreign Affairs* 57, no. 3 (1979): 503–526; and Stanley Hoffmann, "Reaching for the Most Difficult: Human Rights as a Foreign Policy Goal," *Daedalus* 112 (Fall 1983): 19–49; and (on the conservative side) Jeane J. Kirkpatrick, "Dictatorships and Double Standards," *Commentary* 68 (November 1979): 34–45; and Henry A. Kissinger, "Continuity and Change in American Foreign Policy," in *Human Rights and World Order*, edited by Abdul Aziz Said (New York: Praeger, 1978).

On human rights in the foreign policies of other countries, Alison Brysk, *Global Good Samaritans: Human Rights as Foreign Policy* (Oxford: Oxford University Press, 2009), is the place to begin. (Brysk looks at Sweden, Canada, Costa Rica, Japan, and South Africa.) Older but still useful is David P. Forsythe, ed., *Human Rights and Comparative Foreign Policy* (Tokyo: United Nations University Press, 2000).

9

◄◦►

Transnational Human Rights
Advocacy

We now turn to the final major type of international human rights actor: transnational actors, understood as "private" actors (that is, not states or multilateral organizations) that operate across state borders. Among the diverse array of private actors, we will be concerned with nongovernmental organizations (NGOs), that is, private, noncommercial groups with an issue-specific mandate. More precisely, we will be concerned with transnational or international nongovernmental organizations (INGOs)—NGOs that operate internationally. The "Problem" for this chapter will explore the human rights responsibilities of businesses in some detail.

NGO is a catchall term that describes a variety of groups and organizations that conduct many different types of activities. They are generally thought of as a species of civil society organization (CSO), which includes any group organized for any civic (noncommercial) purpose, which may or may not include a charitable element. In the United States, such groups are typically called "nonprofit" or "charitable" organizations. Internationally, the focus tends to be on the NG in NGO—that is, that they are independent of the state and, as such, sometimes are opposed to or critical of the state.

But not always. In particular, development NGOs, especially in poorer countries, may be engaged in service provision, outreach and education, and implementation of development programs, giving their activities a quasi-governmental character. More generally, NGOs that engage in policy advocacy, monitoring and evaluation, or research in support of programs regularly collaborate with governments and intergovernmental organizations.

In the world of human rights, however, the principal focus of NGO activity is the state itself. Most human rights NGOs spend their time conducting fact finding about human rights violations, assisting victims of violations, and trying to use their resources to change state policies and practices. This does not always pit human rights NGOs against the state, though, especially in countries open to improving their

153

human rights practices. In fact, NGOs often play a vital role in ensuring the democratic accountability of governments. Many governments thus have come to accept, and sometimes even appreciate, the place of national and international human rights NGOs in monitoring and improving compliance with national and international human rights law (see also §5.1.A on the role of NGOs in the Universal Periodic Review process).

About three hundred transnational NGOs define themselves as human rights organizations. These will be our principal focus here. There are also, however, thousands of INGOs that define themselves in other terms but engage centrally in human rights programming and advocacy. For example, most of the large development-assistance and disaster-relief organizations today explicitly use the language of human rights to describe key aspects of their missions. In addition, tens of thousands of national NGOs deal centrally with human rights.

There are two principal types of self-identified human rights INGOs. Some, like Amnesty International, Human Rights Watch, and the International Federation for Human Rights, address human rights generally (although, as a practical matter, they tend to have specific areas of special concern). Others focus explicitly on a subset of internationally recognized human rights or even a single right. Prominent examples include Minority Rights Group, Anti-Slavery International (the world's oldest human rights NGO, founded in 1839), and Article 19 (which addresses freedom of expression, taking its name from the provision in the Universal Declaration).

Rather than discuss transnational human rights advocacy generally, though, the first half of the chapter presents two brief case studies of Amnesty International and Human Rights Watch. This focus on two particularly influential organizations arises in part from the great diversity of transnational human rights NGOs, which makes it difficult to talk about transnational action in general and almost impossible to provide anything even close to a comprehensive survey. The sections following the case studies, however, discuss the expansion of NGO activities on human rights in general, as a reflection of growing civil society involvement in and engagement with a system that remains largely driven by states, which remain the decisive actors in both the national and the international politics of human rights.

1. Case Study: Amnesty International

Amnesty International is in many ways *the* emblematic transnational human rights NGO.[1] To many people, especially in the West, human rights advocacy means the kinds of things that Amnesty does: research on human rights abuses and violations and direct-appeal campaigns through letters, petitions, and protests directed at governments, corporations, and other leaders and decision makers to stop abuses and act to remediate human rights violations. In this respect, Amnesty is an exemplar of human rights advocacy. But it is important to recognize that, like all NGOs, Amnesty is guided by a mission that includes a limited range of actionable goals—it does not address everything. Although Amnesty has in recent years transformed its original mission (discussed below) to address a much wider array of human rights challenges, there are many issues and forms of action, including direct advocacy in foreign countries, that are not part of AI's repertoire. Nonetheless, Amnesty International is indeed one of the most important actors in the global human rights regime.

AI was founded in 1961 by British lawyer Peter Berenson, to draw attention to the plight of prisoners of conscience—individuals detained because of their political, religious, or other beliefs—across the globe. Individual prisoners were identified and verified by the organization, which both publicized their plight centrally and organized local chapters to "adopt" them—typically in clusters of three, one each from the capitalist, socialist, and nonaligned worlds—and advocate on their behalf, usually through letter-writing campaigns addressed to officials of the government holding the prisoner.

In the 1970s, Amnesty refined its strategy of aggressive but nonpartisan public advocacy with effective behind-the-scenes lobbying, both nationally and internationally. In 1973, it began its campaign of Urgent Action appeals. Torture (and later abolition of the death penalty) became a special focus. AI played a major role in securing the adoption of the 1975 Declaration on the Protection of All Persons from Being Subjected to Torture and Other Cruel, Inhuman, or Degrading Treatment or Punishment, a decisive step on the way to the 1984 Convention Against Torture. In 1977, it was awarded the Nobel Peace Prize (following the award in 1974 to Sean McBride, the chair of AI's International Executive Committee from 1961 to 1975, for his lifetime of work on behalf of human rights), and, in 1978, the organization was awarded the United Nations Prize in the Field of Human Rights. By 1979, Amnesty International had a global membership of 200,000—up from 15,000 a decade earlier.

In the 1980s, Amnesty continued to grow and to penetrate the public consciousness. Emblematic were the series of high-profile fund-raising events that began in 1976 and took their title from the 1979 Secret Policeman's Ball. Begun by Monty Python member John Cleese and involving major stars such as Sting and Eric Clapton, the events generated publicity for human rights advocacy among individuals who previously might not have had much interest in the topic. (Bono, the current king of celebrity campaigning for social justice, was in the audience at an early show, which he has identified as a major formative influence.)

The 1986 Conspiracy of Hope tour included five shows in the United States. It was hugely successful in raising awareness of AI among young Americans and increasing their membership. The 1988 Human Rights Now! international tour featured famous artists such as Bruce Springsteen and the E Street Band, Peter Gabriel, Sting, and others. The tour was incredibly complicated to organize, as it traveled to a number of countries, such as Hungary, Costa Rica, Zimbabwe, and India, countries that rarely see such large-scale shows.

With the end of the Cold War, Amnesty continued to grow, evolving into an organization with a broader focus. Today, in addition to the older work on prisoners of conscience, torture, and the death penalty, the organization works on the rights of disadvantaged groups, especially women, children, minorities, indigenous peoples, and refugees, and on eradicating poverty. AI has also devoted considerable attention and resources to expanding membership outside the Western world, symbolized by the fact that since 1992 its secretary-general, the chief executive officer of the organization, has been from the global South—Pierre Sané of Senegal, 1992–2001; Irene Khan of Bangladesh, 2001–2010; and since 2010, Salil Shetty of India.

In addition, AI has shifted from a large London base to opening offices in Africa, the Asia-Pacific, Central and Eastern Europe, Latin America, and the Middle East. The purpose is to allow AI to respond more quickly to human rights abuses and important events around the globe. AI has even developed a mobile app that works like a panic button for activists who are at risk of being arrested or detained. These examples show that Amnesty International is attempting to aid activists and dissenters across the globe in relevant and meaningful ways.

In 2016, AI had 7 million members worldwide, organized into more than fifty country "sections" and a number of "structures" (which are essentially aspiring sections). The highest authority of the organization is the International Council, which meets every two years. Its equivalent of a board of directors is the International Executive Committee, which meets twice a year. An International Secretariat of more than five hundred professionals carries out work in several areas, focused on research, campaigning, communications, and international law and organization. In 2015, AI spent approximately €260 million on its various activities.

AI maintains a presence in seventy countries. In 2016, it was in the midst of six major global campaigns: Demand Dignity (focusing on poverty rooted in injustice and exclusion), Abolish the Death Penalty, Individuals at Risk (focusing on mobilizing protection of individuals at risk of human rights violations around the world), Security with Human Rights (focused on breaking the cycle of violence between armed groups and states), Immigrant Rights Are Human Rights (working at changing immigration laws in the United States on both the national and state levels), and My Body, My Rights (working on ensuring access to sexual and reproductive rights). In 2014–2015, AI issued appeals for urgent action on behalf of individuals in Bahrain, China, Gambia, Guatemala, Honduras, Indonesia, Iran, Iraq, Mexico, Romania, Russia, Turkmenistan, the United States, Uzbekistan, Zimbabwe, and Saudi Arabia. These kinds of urgent appeals often lead to results. In 2012, for example, Tural Abbalsi, a blogger for one of the main opposition parties in Azerbaijan, was beaten and imprisoned along with thirteen other activists for taking part in an antigovernment protest. AI issued an urgent appeal and Abbalsi and his colleagues were later released.

2. Case Study: Human Rights Watch

Human Rights Watch (HRW) is more than a decade younger than Amnesty International and is not a mass-membership organization. Based in New York, its roots are in Helsinki Watch, a group formed in the United States in 1978 to monitor compliance with the 1975 Helsinki Final Act (see §8.1), which included human rights commitments by the countries of Europe on both sides of the Iron Curtain (plus the United States and Canada). Helsinki Watch pioneered the "naming and shaming" tactic of publicly shaming abusive governments' practices through reports, media coverage, and direct exchange with policy makers, which contributed to the dramatic democratic transformations in the late 1980s. The Helsinki model was replicated in other regional watch groups—Americas Watch, founded in 1981; Asia Watch, 1985;

Africa Watch, 1988; and Middle East Watch, 1989—which were united under the umbrella of Human Rights Watch in 1988.

Human Rights Watch constantly monitors human rights conditions in more than ninety countries and it publishes reports on violations of international human rights norms set out by the Universal Declaration and human rights treaties. HRW works by talking with people who were abused or have witnessed abuses. They reach out to journalists, human rights advocates, country experts, and government officials. They publish their findings in approximately one hundred official reports and hundreds of news releases each year.

HRW carries out research, issues reports (on particular countries and particular topics as well as a respected annual report), and engages in public campaigning and political lobbying. HRW has always had a broader focus than Amnesty International—although traditionally with *much* greater attention to civil and political rights than economic, social, and cultural rights. This began to change in the 2000s. HRW reports that it now places a much greater emphasis on economic and social rights than do other human rights organizations. However, HRW will address human rights abuses only where there is credible, reliable evidence of violations and where a perpetrator of violations can be clearly identified. (These are requirements of successful naming and shaming.) Nearly all of its work involving economic and social rights thus addresses officially sanctioned or condoned discrimination (especially discrimination and violence against women) or direct violations of economic and social rights by the state (for example, a forced eviction policy).

In the 1990s, HRW also significantly expanded its scope to include violations of the laws of war and individual criminal responsibility for war crimes and genocide. (In 1997 it shared the Nobel Peace Prize as a founding member of the Campaign to Ban Landmines.) Over the past decade and a half, it has also focused considerable attention on human rights violations associated with antiterrorism policies and practices, and it has begun to supplement its traditional on-the-ground fact finding with statistical research, satellite photography, bomb-data analysis, and other new methods and technologies.

In 2014, HRW raised $130 million from contributions from private individuals and foundations worldwide—in order to maintain an unbiased approach to research and advocacy, HRW does not accept money from governments, either directly or indirectly. In financial terms, its ten principal programs focus on Africa ($6.2 million), Asia ($5.8 million), the Americas ($2.4 million), Europe and Central Asia ($4.6 million), the Middle East and North Africa ($4.3 million), the United States ($3.2 million), Women's Rights ($2.8 million), Health and Human Rights ($1.4 million), Children's Rights ($2.4 million), and International Justice ($1.6 million). Expenditures on other programs total $17 million. These figures represent a major increase over earlier years, in large part as a result of George Soros's $100 million donation to HRW in 2010 (to be disbursed over ten years).

Human Rights Watch's research and advocacy reporting output is formidable. In the first nine months of 2016 alone, HRW issued fifty-five separate reports (in additional to its annual report), covering topics as diverse as the human rights of miners in Malawi, Europe's refugee crisis, sexual discrimination in Sri Lanka, threats to

Indonesia's LGBT community, abuses against children detained as "national security threats," arbitrary detentions and torture in Ukraine, child labor in Afghanistan, and predatory debt-buying and collection operations in the United States.[2]

As this list suggests, Human Rights Watch understands human rights rather broadly, including not only the established body of international human rights law but also additional rights (particularly protection against discrimination on the basis of sexual orientation or gender identity) and violations of the laws of war and other harm to civilians in armed conflicts. HRW is effective because governments and human rights activists have confidence in the high quality of the sourcing and fact checking that goes into its research. These foundations are critically necessary for putting pressure on governments to change their behaviors, establishing the legal and moral groundwork for meaningful change.

3. Nonpartisan Action

Human Rights Watch is unusually independent and aggressive in its actions. It thus provides a focus for a broader discussion of bias and legitimacy in the actions of human rights NGOs.

Like other transnational human rights NGOs, the work of HRW is dependent on its ability to obtain and verify reliable information about violations. Its reporting and advocacy thus are shaped not simply by the severity of violations in a country but by its ability to work in that country (or to obtain reliable information from individuals with recent firsthand local knowledge). In addition, as an advocacy organization, it has a special interest in addressing situations where its work may bring concrete results—not to the exclusion of countries where short-term changes are unlikely or even inconceivable but with special attention to countries that are open or vulnerable to the pressures of publicity. And HRW, like all human rights NGOs, has issues of special organizational concern.

As a result of these political realities, HRW, like all other advocacy groups, has been accused of bias. But rather than factual errors in its reports—which, of course, do occur occasionally (but very rarely)—such complaints typically involve claims, usually by the targeted governments and their partisans, that other countries with equally bad or worse records are not comparably targeted or that the violations identified are somehow justified in the case in question.

During the Cold War, such complaints were the staple of Communist Party state dictatorships and military dictatorships of both the Right and the Left. Today, when a Robert Mugabe in Zimbabwe, an Alexander Lukashenko in Belarus, or a Vladimir Putin in Russia makes such complaints, he is largely ignored. But particularly in the United States, Human Rights Watch has in recent years been a special target of defenders of Israel's antiterrorism policies and its policies in the Occupied Palestinian Territories (see §8.6). The ensuing debates provide a useful lens on the nature of nonpartisan human rights advocacy.

Nonpartisan does not mean nonpolitical. In fact, human rights advocacy is and must be intensely political. It is principally about how a state treats its own nationals and others over whom it exercises legal jurisdiction. Demands to stop human rights violations are demands for changes in legal and political practices. When violations are severe and systematic, human rights advocacy in effect demands that a regime either fundamentally transform its character or put itself out of business.

The vital question, then, is whether (political) advocacy for human rights is carried out in a nonpartisan fashion; that is, in a way that is not based on or intended to promote any particular party, person, or cause (other than human rights itself). Human rights advocates might properly be called partisans for human rights. They claim, though, to pursue their activities in an otherwise nonpartisan fashion. And nonpartisan action is central to the legitimacy and the power of NGO advocates in particular, who have few resources on their side other than their single-minded commitment to human rights.

Let us grant, for the sake of argument, the accuracy of the principal complaints of the "friends of Israel" who condemn Human Rights Watch: that many other regimes with human rights records comparable to and even much worse than Israel's—including most of Israel's enemies—have not been comparably criticized.[3] Let us also acknowledge that the government of Israel claims that many of the practices for which it receives international criticism are undertaken in the name of antiterrorism (which was central to Israeli policy decades before 9/11). But criticisms of inaccuracy are largely unjustified. Although reasonable people may disagree about the reliability of particular sources, virtually every particular claim is sourced, and, despite extensive efforts to debunk HRW's reporting, only rare and isolated errors have ever been identified, most of which have been connected with difficulties imposed by the Israeli government and its military in gathering and verifying information. And nothing in these facts indicates partisanship in HRW's criticism of Israeli human rights practices.

A few governments engage in human rights violations that they do not seek to justify in any serious fashion. Most, though, claim a higher purpose that justifies unfortunate sacrifices being imposed on individuals and groups in their society. Whether such arguments are persuasive is, ironically, a political question—and usually an inescapably partisan one. Most human rights advocates self-consciously refuse to engage such issues of partisan politics. Rather, they decry the violations, independent of any and all alleged justifications.

Human rights advocates do not look at all sides of a partisan political conflict. Such "balanced" or "evenhanded" approaches may be appropriate for others. But the job of human rights NGOs is to focus narrowly (and perhaps single-mindedly) on human rights, period. And that focus is essential to nonpartisan action. If there is a legitimate justification, the government in question can present that to its people, its friends and allies, and the international community.

There is a danger, certainly, of selecting (otherwise legitimate) targets of criticism based on partisan criteria. In the case of Human Rights Watch, however, there is no evidence of such partisanship. Its reach is truly global, as reflected not only in its annual report but also in the list of recent reports above. And its work on Israel falls well within its regional and substantive mandates. Furthermore, its extensive work on human rights in the United States, where it is based, shows an admirable willingness to look at human rights violations at home, not only abroad. (The U.S. section of Amnesty International similarly targets American domestic human rights practices—much to the chagrin of many Americans.)

HRW's work on gay, lesbian, bisexual, and transgender rights actually raises more questions about partisanship. (Compare Problem 3.) Such rights are *not* part of established international human rights law. Therefore, targets may respond, with a certain degree of plausibility, that they are being held to standards that neither they in particular nor the international community in general have endorsed. This, for example, has been the response of Iran (when its president and other officials have not foolishly denied the existence of homosexuals in Iran).

This brings us back to the central contribution of the Universal Declaration to human rights advocates, namely, providing almost universally agreed-upon standards of international human rights. NGOs that stay within the substantive scope of the Universal Declaration are protected against charges of partisanship (on the grounds of the substance of their concerns). Those who go beyond settled international human rights law do risk (not il)legitimate charges of attempting to impose their values on others. Although the charge of imposition is ludicrous, given that the only power being exercised is that of publicity, advocacy on behalf of disputed values is very different from advocacy on behalf of settled principles of international human rights law.

4. Other Advocacy Actions: Celebrity and Consumer Campaigns

As we mentioned in the case of Amnesty International, celebrities have been important actors in raising the visibility of many transnational human rights advocacy efforts. Consider, for example, the powerful symbolism of American First Lady Michelle Obama holding up a sign with the Twitter hashtag #BringBackOurGirls, in response to the 2014 kidnapping of 276 schoolgirls by Boko Haram, an ISIS-affiliated extremist group operating in northern Nigeria, Chad, Niger, and Cameroon in Western Africa. (Unfortunately, most of the girls are still missing.)

Celebrity campaigns such as this help bring wider visibility to human rights problems around the world. In 2002 former U.N. secretary-general Kofi Annan remarked, "Whenever you put your name to a message, you raise awareness far and wide, among policy makers and among millions of people who elect them."[4]

As some observers have noted, however, there is a cynical—and perhaps darker—side to the involvement of celebrity figures in transnational human rights activism. Lilie Chouliaraki argued that the success of celebrity-based humanitarianism depends on spectacle, and that Western audiences in particular must be shocked into pity, as that is the only thing that will elicit an effective response.[5] According to these critics, campaigns such as these are geared toward conveying a manipulated image of suffering that is tailor-made for audiences that cannot possibly understand the real suffering of faraway strangers nor really alleviate their suffering. They instead give the illusion that a small donation or other easy and convenient acts of acknowledgment and financial support to a worthy cause will be enough to solve the problem—a phenomenon we have come to know as "slacktivism." Celebrity soundbites presuppose that a problem has a quick fix. To keep public attention, campaigns have to be simple.

The popularity of these campaigns, however, shows the rise of populist forms of diplomatic activity. And even the deeply state-centric United Nations has endorsed these initiatives, with the establishment in recent years of celebrity goodwill ambassadors, showing that celebrity diplomacy can occupy public space and affect credible diplomatic interventions throughout the international community.

The dangers of misdirected effort and even abuse, however, are starkly illustrated by the Kony 2012 campaign, organized by Invisible Children, Inc. This now-defunct nonprofit was founded in 2004 to raise awareness about the capture and forced induction of child soldiers by the Lord's Resistance Army (LRA), a small (and now mostly nonexistent) rebel group originally operating in Uganda. In March 2012, Invisible Children (IC) launched a thirty-minute "documentary" video entitled *Kony 2012* as the opening salvo in a larger campaign to galvanize public opinion (mostly in the United States) to secure the capture of the LRA's cultish leader, Joseph Kony, who had been indicted in 2005 by the International Criminal Court for war crimes and crimes against humanity.

The video immediately went viral, with more than 100 million views (on YouTube, Vimeo, and the IC website) within six days (the shortest length of time for a video to reach that benchmark). The U.S. Senate was galvanized to adopt a resolution condemning Kony and supporting the Obama administration's prior decision to send military advisors to support those countries actively searching for LRA commanders and those communities that had been affected by the LRA. The video also called for a nationwide Cover the Night action on April 20 (a poor choice of date, considering it was the anniversary of the 1999 Columbine shootings and Adolf Hitler's birthday)—with Invisible Children supplying posters, buttons, T-shirts, bracelets, and stickers to community organizers.

Kony 2012 attracted significant star power. It was immediately endorsed by numerous celebrities, including Taylor Swift, Justin Bieber, George Clooney, Bill Gates, Angelina Jolie, and, most importantly, Oprah Winfrey. The film was generally praised by the White House, researchers and advocates from Human Rights Watch and Amnesty International, and Nicholas Kristoff, the *New York Times* columnist noted for his attention to human rights and humanitarian issues.

These positive assessments, however, were matched and ultimately overwhelmed by a storm of criticism that itself went viral. Critics pointed out that the film's information was out of date (the LRA had long ceased significant operations in Uganda by 2012); that its portrayal of victims was exploitative; and that its message, delivered by white, American-based activists without any significant immersion in the field, failed to address the complex and nuanced circumstances in the areas where the LRA had been active. Furthermore, the consciousness raising did little more than foster "clicktivism" by (especially young, white American female) viewers, which enriched Invisible Children but did nothing to actually solve the problem of child soldiering, assist in the rehabilitation or reintegration of child soldiers, or assist the communities victimized by the LRA.

Alex de Waal, a scholar and development advocate with long experience working in Africa, criticized Invisible Children for providing little more than an "echo chamber" for Kony's own celebrity "as the embodiment of evil." In his view, *Kony 2012* "peddled dangerous and patronizing falsehoods" about the situation of child soldiering in Africa.[6] Mahmood Mamdani of Makerere University in Uganda, who wrote an influential book about the Rwandan genocide, argued that the film's message only promoted militarism in the central African region.

In response, Invisible Children quickly released a follow-up video (in April) entitled *Kony 2012: Part II—Beyond Famous* (even the title sounds like a sequel). By then, though, the furor over the original film had overtaken the cause. The new video received only 1.7 million views in eleven days—less than 2 percent of the views of the original just a month earlier. The Cover the Night action in late April was, by most accounts, a bust: after people got their posters and buttons and bracelets, they failed to show up to events in their hometowns.

After hundreds of millions were briefly captivated and spent millions of dollars in donations and for media kits (Invisible Children reported net revenues of $26.5 million in 2012, up 50 percent from the prior year), nothing happened. Kony remains at large. In 2014, Invisible Children announced it was undergoing a reorganization and essentially went dark.

Although the globalization of economics and communication has enabled consumers to put pressure on transnational businesses, providing "a useful way to carry radical ideas into diverse personal life spaces, as well as across national and cultural borders,"[7] consumer campaigns are not without problems. The influx of new actors trying to help often is not organized effectively, making it difficult for pressure to be asserted strategically—undermining the methods that NGOs have used to make so much headway on human rights issues.

We should ask ourselves whether these examples of twenty-first-century advocacy, in an age of social media and "click-it-and-forget it," are a good thing for human rights. We would argue that the verdict is not yet in. On the one hand, more people are more aware of more human rights violations, abuses, and deficiencies throughout the world. And these organizations and campaigns have made it easier for us to respond with the click of a smartphone. On the other hand, the groups and organizations running these campaigns have created a space for themselves as a kind of middleman: slick and enticing publicity machines, or worse, "merchants of suffering." What kinds of questions should we ask about transnational advocacy efforts emanating from global civil society? The following section will examine some key questions that we should consider when assessing the role and impact of nongovernmental transnational human rights advocates.

5. NGO Legitimacy

This discussion raises the broad issue of the legitimacy of NGOs and their advocacy. To put it bluntly, who authorized NGOs?

The simple answer is, international human rights law. Human rights NGOs, in their typical work of reporting and advocacy, merely draw attention to practices that are, at least on their face, inconsistent with uncontroversial principles of international law. Furthermore, they are simply engaging in the collective exercise of the rights of freedom of expression of their members. Target governments may persecute such organizations and activities in their own territories—they may even criminalize them—but that is simply an expression of the problem to which human rights NGOs are drawing attention.

Yet the picture is not quite that simple. As noted above, human rights advocacy is intensely political. And when external actors criticize governments that have considerable local political legitimacy, the issue of NGO legitimacy may be more than just a smoke screen behind which vicious governments seek to hide.

Here nonpartisanship becomes essential. International human rights law has considerable international, transnational, and national legitimacy in the contemporary world. So long as human rights INGOs operate in a nonpartisan fashion within the confines and on behalf of established international human rights principles, they partake of that legitimacy—particularly when, as is usually the case, their activity is focused on publicizing evidence of violations.

The legitimacy of external actors is further enhanced when their advocacy parallels or supports that of national actors. In democratic and other relatively open regimes, the existence of genuinely nonpartisan local human rights NGOs making parallel arguments enhances the legitimacy of international actors. And where levels of repression do not allow space for local human rights NGOs, indirect evidence that international actors are supporting local advocates serves a similar role.

Human rights INGOs are important and legitimate actors in the global human rights regime. They lack the legal and political authority of states and the international legal authority of multilateral actors. As advocates, however, they have the moral and legal authority of international human rights law behind them. And as long as they engage in truly nonpartisan action within their mandate, they are not merely legitimate but important members of the international community.

Problem 6: Human Rights Obligations of Multinational Corporations

The Problem

Multinational corporations (MNCs) are immensely powerful actors that are becoming increasingly global in character (not simply multi- or international). Doesn't it make sense, then, to impose direct human rights obligations on MNCs? Why should their immense and growing economic power not be matched with direct human rights responsibilities? Isn't this especially the case because their globalization has restricted the ability of welfare states to provide economic and social rights for their citizens?

In 2011, Human Rights Council Resolution 17/4 endorsed a set of guiding principles regarding businesses and human rights. These guiding principles affirm that states are obliged to prevent corporations from committing human rights abuses and that corporations are obliged to refrain from either committing human rights abuses or contributing indirectly to human rights abuses by other countries. Furthermore, the guiding principles establish that states are obliged to provide remedies to individuals who have been harmed as a result of corporate human rights abuses.

These guiding principles were a product of the work of the U.N. special representative on business and human rights. Following the adoption of Resolution 17/4, the special representative's mandate expired and his position was replaced by a U.N. Working Group on business and human rights, which has taken the lead in implementing guiding principles.

The leading source of substantial controversy within the U.N. system regarding multinational corporations and human rights is the question of what obligations a multinational corporation's home country has to prevent that multinational corporation from committing human rights abuses in host countries. Some countries, particularly Ecuador and South Africa, have urged the international community to examine the possibility of creating an international instrument to clarify these obligations, as well as to strengthen the right to remedy.[8]

A Solution

Such a change would involve fundamentally altering the existing system of national implementation of international human rights. Globalization does pose serious problems for this system, as we will discuss in some detail in Chapter 11. Imposing special direct human rights responsibilities for MNCs, however, is the wrong solution.

Recall the distinction drawn in Chapter 2 between duties not to deprive, duties to protect from deprivation, and duties to provide. *All* social actors, including MNCs, have duties not to deprive. But we can see no reason MNCs should have *special* duties.

It might be argued that MNCs are specially situated to deprive and therefore should be specially obliged. But is that true? Is there any evidence, for example, that *multinational* corporations are worse for human rights than are local corporations? Whether we consider wages, working conditions, or environmental practices, local firms can be, and often are, at least as bad as their multinational colleagues. And multinational firms that produce branded goods, because of their relatively high profit margins, often are able to provide better conditions for their workers and neighbors than local commodity producers. (Nike can afford to pay more than manufacturers of house-brand sneakers.) In fact, protecting the value of their brand may demand not merely meeting but exceeding local norms.

This might suggest, though, a special human rights duty not to deprive for *all* firms. But we already enforce such an obligation, in the form of health and safety regulations, minimum-wage legislation, and environmental rules. And there is no special reason to single out commercial firms. Nonprofit organizations, for example, should not be held to lower standards on working conditions or wages. Private individuals have no more of a right to pollute than corporations.

Corporations, both local and foreign, often do use their power in harmful ways, both directly harming their workers and communities and through their influence over local and national governments. The solutions to such problems, however, are standard legal and political solutions, not new human rights duties.

Turning to duties to protect and to provide, direct human rights obligations for corporations, whether national or multinational, are even more problematic. Do we really want corporations protecting our rights? As private, profit-making enterprises, they would seem to be particularly poorly suited to carrying out such duties. Even in their areas of operation, self-regulation is likely to be a recipe for disaster. Some states might be overly exuberant, misguided, or inept in their exercise of their duties to protect. But there is no reason to suspect that firms would systematically do a better job.

As for duties to provide, the best that can be said is that some states may reasonably choose to rely on corporate provision for some economic and social rights. But the reliance of the United States on employer-provided health insurance is hardly a promising model. And the Japanese system of firm-based provision, which worked well in the 1960s, 1970s, and 1980s, has come under considerable strain. Furthermore, even where firms are the first line of provision, states are ultimately responsible.

Nothing we have said is an argument against aggressive efforts to ensure corporate social responsibility. There may even be very good reasons for states to legislate greater corporate social responsibility (for both local and foreign firms). But these are matters of social justice, not human rights duties—which returns us to another central theme from Chapter 2, namely, that not all good things are a matter of human rights.

There may even be good reasons for developing global or regional codes of conduct for MNCs. But it is hardly unproblematic to argue that foreign firms should be held to higher standards than local firms. And although there may be very good reasons for countries to impose certain standards on the international operations of their firms—the United States has long done this through the Foreign Corrupt Practices Act, originally adopted in 1977—this would be a matter of social justice and public policy, not a new system for implementing human rights. And we should not overlook the theoretical problem of extraterritorial jurisdiction (however attractive we may find it in this particular case).

Further Problems

Privatization of government functions has been a major area of discussion—in different ways in different regions—for the past few decades. Is there any reason to believe that profit-making businesses are better able to provide human rights than states? Which kinds of rights? What about nonprofit organizations?

Now ask the same questions about *protecting* human rights.

Is the mix between state and nonstate provision one of those areas where we should not merely expect but positively value international variations based on local culture, history, and politics? What, though, are the limits on designing a system of provision that makes unusually heavy use of private provision by corporations and not-for-profit providers?

Discussion Questions

1. How should we evaluate the impact of traditional human rights advocacy (e.g., what Amnesty International and Human Rights Watch do) versus newer forms of social-media-based advocacy, like consumer campaigns? Is it better that human rights advocacy efforts move from the complex research- and data-driven report to direct actions that are easy to access,

understand, and respond to? Or should effective human rights advocacy require more work?

2. Is there a better way for NGOs to achieve international legitimacy? Is the issue of legitimacy a truly serious one or primarily a diversion raised by the targets of transnational advocacy?

3. Grant that human rights INGOs have a certain kind of legitimacy, as do states. How should we deal with the resulting conflicts? Are there good general rules? Or does it depend on the particular NGO and the particular state?

4. The distinction between *political* and *partisan* that we have drawn may be clear in theory. Is it so clear in practice? How can action addressed against a government really be nonpartisan? Are there multiple senses of *nonpartisan* operating in such discussions?

5. Consider the Kony 2012 case mentioned in the chapter. What should be the role of a campaign such as this one (that uses a documentary style to raise awareness about a human rights problem)? Is this legitimate advocacy, or does it manipulate people to engage in clicktivism? Is that worse than doing nothing or not knowing about human rights problems in other parts of the world?

Suggested Readings

Chapter 7 of David P. Forsythe, *Human Rights in International Relations,* 3rd ed. (Cambridge: Cambridge University Press, 2012), addresses human rights NGOs. It is a natural place to go first after this chapter. Peter R. Baehr, *Non-governmental Human Rights Organizations in International Relations* (New York: Palgrave Macmillan, 2009), provides a comprehensive analytical survey.

Stephen Hopgood, *Keepers of the Flame: Understanding Amnesty International* (Ithaca, NY: Cornell University Press, 2006), offers an excellent analysis of AI that, although deeply sympathetic to the work of the organization, is often critical of its practice. Ann Marie Clark, *Diplomacy of Conscience: Amnesty International and Changing Human Rights Norms* (Princeton, NJ: Princeton University Press, 2001), is also a valuable study of this iconic organization. William F. Schulz, *In Our Own Best Interest: How Defending Human Rights Benefits Us All* (Boston: Beacon Press, 2001), is an impassioned argument by a longtime advocate.

Philip Alston, ed., *Non-state Actors and Human Rights* (Oxford: Oxford University Press, 2005); and George Andreopoulos, Zehra F. Kabasakal Arat, and Peter Juviler, eds., *Non-state Actors in the Human Rights Universe* (Bloomfield, CT: Kumarian Press, 2006), are the best broad scholarly studies. Although somewhat dated, Claude E. Welch Jr., ed., *NGOs and Human Rights: Promise and Performance* (Philadelphia: University of Pennsylvania Press, 2001), is still worth consulting. The *Journal of Human Rights Practice,* published by Oxford University Press, in an excellent resource for current research in the field of human rights advocacy.

NGO activism, however, is not without its problems. David Kennedy, *The Dark Sides of Virtue: Reassessing International Humanitarianism* (Princeton, NJ: Princeton

University Press, 2004), is a brilliant analysis of the pitfalls of advocacy that matches its potent criticisms with a genuine sympathy and commitment to a more just and humane world. Michael Ignatieff's *Human Rights as Politics and Idolatry* (Princeton, NJ: Princeton University Press, 2001) offers a powerful warning about the dangers of excessive self-righteousness and rigidity, again from the perspective of a sympathetic scholar-activist. Mahmood Monshipouri, ed., *Information Politics, Protests, and Human Rights in the the Digital Age* (Cambridge: Cambridge University Press, 2016) and Tristan Anne Borer, ed., *Media, Mobilization, and Human Rights: Mediating Suffering* (London: Zed Books, 2012) canvass the promises and pitfalls of media-based advocacy.

PART THREE

Contemporary Issues

10

Humanitarian Intervention

A primary organizing principle of a system of sovereign states is the norm of nonintervention (see §2.8). International human rights law and its corresponding obligations conform with that principle. Participating in human rights regimes does not entail a loss of sovereignty. Quite the contrary, states exercise their sovereignty when they choose to be bound by international human rights obligations and agree to be scrutinized by international human rights institutions (see Chapter 5). But, as we have seen, this is a system of mild monitoring that only the overly sensitive (or guilty) would call "interference." Nothing in the array of human rights law and institutions authorizes intervention, let alone coercive punishment, for noncompliance with human rights norms.

The principal exceptions are systematic, massive, and flagrant violations of certain key rights that lead to significant loss of life and destruction of livelihoods. Such violations may rise to the level of international crimes. And under certain circumstances the international community may be empowered to intervene coercively. This chapter looks at the issue of humanitarian interventions against genocide and other humanitarian crimes.

This chapter is a long one. It is written, though, so that it can be read in parts. Sections 2, 3, and 4, dealing with Bosnia, Rwanda, and Kosovo, can be read separately (or skipped as time or interest dictates). The same is true of the case studies in Sections 6 (East Timor), 8 (Libya), and 9 (Sudan). Similarly, Sections 5, 7, and 10, which address the authority to intervene, the dimensions of the right to humanitarian intervention, and issues of justifiability can also be read a la carte. Our advice, if you are not planning to read the whole chapter, is, after reading the next section, which defines genocide and humanitarian crimes, to look first at a couple of the case studies, as your interests dictate, and then pay careful attention to Section 7, which sketches the meaning and the parameters of the right to humanitarian intervention (and the responsibility to protect) in contemporary international law and politics. We also think that most readers will find the general assessment in Section 10 of interest.

1. Genocide and Crimes Against Humanity

The Convention on the Prevention and Punishment of the Crime of Genocide was adopted by the U.N. General Assembly on December 9, 1948, the day before the Universal Declaration. This reflected the central role of the Holocaust in crystallizing international concern with human rights. The Genocide Convention defines genocide as a crime and creates a separate set of obligations for addressing it. (Genocide is not mentioned in either the Universal Declaration of Human Rights or the International Human Rights Covenants.)

The Convention defines genocide, whether committed in time of peace or of war, as a crime under international law: "the intent to destroy, in whole or in part, a national, ethnical, racial, or religious group." This includes killing members of the group; causing serious mental or physical harm to members of the group; deliberately inflicting conditions on the group "calculated to bring about its destruction"; imposing measures intended to prevent births within the group; forcibly transferring children of the group to another group; and conspiracy to commit genocide, direct and public incitement to commit genocide, and complicity in genocide.

The Convention establishes several obligations of states with respect to *preventing* genocide and *punishing the perpetrators*. Article VIII of the Convention also allows signatories to call upon competent organs of the United Nations to prevent or suppress acts of genocide. It does not, however, establish any specific parameters for doing so. And by implication it does not empower states to take action outside the framework of the U.N. Charter to intervene.

By the 1990s, however, genocide and other humanitarian atrocities in Europe, Africa, and Asia led to the development of a *practice* of armed **humanitarian intervention,** arising from a combination of a new geopolitical environment, in which rivalry between the superpowers no longer prevented humanitarian action, and the unusually brutal character of the conflicts. These atrocities resulted from wars within, rather than between, states. They also largely ignored the traditional distinction between civilians and soldiers, often intentionally targeting the civilian population of the other side—even defining those civilians as "the enemy."

Unlike genocide, which is a crime whose characteristics are clearly defined by a legal convention to which states have agreed, there is no similar convention on crimes against humanity. Rather, these crimes are defined in a variety of international legal instruments that make up the corpus of **international humanitarian law** or the law of armed conflict. Emerging out of customary international law, the humanitarian strand of the laws of war has been codified in the Hague Laws and Geneva Conventions, the practice of the post–World War II Nuremburg and Tokyo war crimes tribunals, and the ad hoc tribunals for the former Yugoslavia and Rwanda, the Statute and practice of the International Criminal Court, and the actions of various other bodies (e.g., U.N. Security Council Resolution 1820 of 2008, which established that rape could be a war crime and a crime against humanity).

All of these mechanisms, however, at best punish individual perpetrators. They have no legal power or authority to prevent or suppress violations of human rights or humanitarian law. As we move forward though the chapter, this is an important point to keep in mind.

We begin by looking at cases from the 1990s that led to the emergence of a new set of norms on humanitarian intervention. In addition to the former Yugoslavia, particularly Bosnia-Herzegovina and Kosovo (which introduced **ethnic cleansing** to the world's vocabulary), we also discuss the dramatically contrasting examples of Rwanda and East Timor. Together, they document the acceptance, in barely a decade, of a right to armed humanitarian intervention. After examining the codification of these changes in the language of the responsibility to protect (§7), we turn to a discussion of the complexities of these emerging norms and practices in two more recent cases, Sudan and Libya. Then, after addressing the surprisingly problematic notion of justifying humanitarian intervention, the chapter concludes with a discussion of the ongoing war in Syria (Problem 7).

2. Case Study: Bosnia

Yugoslavia was created at the end of World War I, an assemblage of the previously independent states of Serbia and Montenegro; the former Austro-Hungarian territories of Slovenia, Istria, Dalmatia, Croatia-Slavonia, Vojvodina, and Bosnia-Herzegovina; and Macedonia, taken from the Ottoman Empire's last European holdings. Although the dominant Serbs actively discriminated against other ethnic groups, different groups lived together more or less harmoniously (except under Nazi occupation during World War II, when Serbs were targets of genocide by the Ustasha, a local fascist group operating a puppet regime in Croatia).

After World War II, the communists, the strongest force in the resistance to Nazi rule, reorganized Yugoslavia under the leadership of Josip Broz Tito. In a country in which every ethnic group was a minority (roughly two-fifths were Serbs and a fifth Croats), a federal political system granted substantial power to six republics (Serbia, Croatia, Slovenia, Bosnia-Herzegovina, Macedonia, and Montenegro) and two autonomous regions within Serbia (Kosovo and Vojvodina).

For three decades, the system worked tolerably well. (The principal exception was the treatment of ethnic Albanians in the Kosovo region of Serbia.) Tito's death in 1980, however, removed the final arbiter from a system with immense potential for squabbling and deadlock. The accumulated inefficiencies of decades of control by nine separate communist bureaucracies (six republics, two autonomous regions, and the federal government) ended the economic growth that had greased the system. By the mid-1980s, Yugoslavia faced a political and economic crisis well beyond the capabilities of its ruling communist functionaries.

A. The Breakup of Yugoslavia

In 1987, Slobodan Milošević seized on Serbian nationalism to consolidate his rapid rise to power in the Serbian republic. Milošević skillfully manipulated memories of Ustasha brutality, fostering hatred of Croats. He also invoked the quasi-mythic grandeur of Serbia's fourteenth-century Nemanjid dynasty. He aimed to paint Muslims, who made up about one-sixth of the country's population, as enemies, successors of the Turks who had defeated medieval Serbia.

Using tactics made famous by Hitler, Milošević and his front group, the Committee for the Protection of Kosovo Serbs and Montenegrins, organized more than one hundred mass protest demonstrations with average turnouts of more than 50,000 people. By February 1989, the last vestiges of regional autonomy in Vojvodina and Kosovo were eliminated. In addition, Milošević allies had been installed in Montenegro, leaving him in firm control of half the country. Kosovo, whose population was 90 percent ethnic Albanian, was particularly severely repressed.

The other republics, especially Slovenia and Croatia, had the legal and political power to block this protofascist Serbian imperialism. But this only led Milošević to rely increasingly on extralegal means. For example, arms shipments for the Yugoslav National Army (JNA) "inexplicably" began appearing in Knin, Croatia's principal Serbian city, in the fall of 1990. After negotiations to maintain a loose federal system failed, Slovenia and Croatia, fearing the worst, declared independence on June 25, 1991.

Slovenia was ethnically homogeneous and prosperous and did not share a border with Serbia. Within weeks, it had established its effective independence with the support of the European Community (the predecessor to the current European Union). In the last four months of 1991, however, Serbs and Croats fought a brutal war that targeted opposition civilians no less than opposing armies. And when the fifteenth cease-fire—reached on January 2, 1992, and supported by 14,000 peacekeepers of the United Nations Protection Force in the former Yugoslavia (UNPROFOR)—held, international attention shifted to the even more brutal conflict in Bosnia-Herzegovina (hereafter referred to as simply Bosnia).

Bosnia was in many ways a microcosm of Yugoslavia, itself a republic of minorities. In the 1991 census, 44 percent of the population identified themselves as ethnic Muslims, 32 percent as Serbs, 17 percent as Croats, and 7 percent as Yugoslavs or other. In fact, Bosnia was the only Yugoslav republic without an ethnic majority.

Although Bosnia had been a place of considerable ethnic tolerance, especially in the capital of Sarajevo, when war did come it hit with unprecedented ferocity. And Bosnia's Muslims were particularly vulnerable because they lacked the support of neighboring conationals.

Separatist Serbs gained control of two-thirds of the territory of Bosnia. They perfected and popularized the strategy of ethnic cleansing, introduced by Croatian Serbs the preceding year, which aimed to rid "Serbian" territory of Muslim (and Croat) residents through systematic terror and sporadic murder. Relief supplies were blocked. Villages and cities were shelled from a distance when they could not be shot up and burned at close range. Captured men were routinely tortured or murdered, often en masse. Women, children, and the elderly were sometimes shot, often physically abused, but more typically "merely" forced to flee. And Serbian soldiers systematically, on orders from superiors, raped young Muslim women, to degrade them and shame their families.

B. Responding to the Bosnian Genocide

The international community was often, and in many ways justly, criticized for doing too little, too late. However, it did not sit by and idly watch the genocide, as it had during the Cold War in places like Uganda and Cambodia.

The U.N. Security Council imposed an arms embargo on all parties and placed Serbia under a comprehensive economic embargo. A special war crimes tribunal was created. Peacekeepers were sent to protect civilians and facilitate the delivery of humanitarian assistance. And much of the international community exerted considerable diplomatic and political pressure on Serbia and its Bosnian allies. When a peace agreement was finally signed at Dayton in December 1995, there were 50,000 U.N. peacekeepers in the former Yugoslavia, at an annual cost of about $2 billion; 3,000 humanitarian workers were in the field; and the Office of the United Nations High Commissioner for Refugees alone was spending $500 million a year on humanitarian assistance.

Initial responses, however, were timid and largely reflected geopolitical concerns, especially keeping Yugoslavia intact. The international community was willing to allow immense suffering to prevent Yugoslavia from becoming a precedent for an even more catastrophic breakup of the Soviet Union—which, it must be remembered, had not yet dissolved. (There was no way of knowing then that its breakup would be anywhere near as peaceful as it ultimately proved to be.) By the time the war entered its Bosnian phase, however, the Soviet Union had already broken up, and the European Community had recognized the independence of Croatia and Slovenia. Although geopolitical concerns continued to intrude, for the remainder of the conflict the United States, Europe, the United Nations, and even Russia maintained sustained efforts in human rights, humanitarian assistance, peacekeeping, and diplomacy that were without parallel during the Cold War.

i. Multilateral Human Rights Agencies

In August 1992, at the first special session in its history, the U.N. Commission on Human Rights appointed Tadeusz Mazowiecki, former prime minister of Poland, as special rapporteur. Never before had the Commission responded with anything even close to such speed. And the vigor of its response was equally striking. The Security Council also acted (relatively) rapidly and with resolve. An arms embargo and trade sanctions were followed by the creation, in February 1993, of the International Criminal Tribunal for the former Yugoslavia, which by 1996 was actively prosecuting war criminals.

These initiatives, however, responded to, rather than stopped, the genocide—because there was no appetite among any of the great powers to use force to stop the conflict. And, barring armed intervention, there was no way to stop Croatia, Serbia, or Bosnia's Serbs from seeking to realize their objectives by force.

ii. Humanitarian Assistance

Humanitarian assistance aims to cope with some of the most pressing human consequences of war (and other political and natural disasters). Humanitarian workers seek not to prevent violence but to ease the burden on civilian victims. Even these limited tasks, though, undercut the Serbian strategies of pursuing ethnic cleansing in the countryside and strangling Sarajevo. The Bosnian Serbs therefore saw humanitarian assistance as intensely political—which it was, given their strategy—and consistently used all means in their power, including force, to stop international relief from reaching its targets. (Muslim and Croat forces much more irregularly prevented aid deliveries.)

The international humanitarian response in Bosnia was swift, sustained, and relatively effective. The United Nations used strong diplomatic pressure and (limited) force to deliver aid to more than 2 million people. Nonetheless, the suffering in Bosnia was horrible. More than one-third of Bosnia's people were forced to flee their homes. Most of the Bosnian Muslims who did not flee were forced to endure extended Serbian sieges. The more than 200,000 deaths in Croatia and Bosnia were proportionally equivalent to the deaths of about 5 million Americans.

But to have dramatically reduced this suffering, those providing assistance would have had to issue a credible military threat to enter the conflict on the side of Bosnia's Muslims. Leading states simply were not willing to endorse such an option, preferring instead to rely on diplomacy, humanitarian assistance, and sanctions short of the punitive use of force.

iii. Peacekeeping

The soldiers that the United Nations sent in under the banner of UNPROFOR were peacekeepers. **Peacekeeping** involves interposing neutral forces *with the permission of the belligerents* in order to monitor or maintain a truce or settlement. Peacekeepers are lightly armed and are authorized to use force only for self-defense. The aim of peacekeeping is not to repulse or punish an aggressor. That is a job for collective security enforcement, as in the Gulf War of 1991.

UNPROFOR's mandate was restricted to limiting the extent and severity of the fighting. The international community condemned ethnic cleansing. It was willing to prosecute those responsible once the fighting ended. But it would not take the military steps necessary to end the conflict.

The task of UNPROFOR was less to prevent war (soldiers shooting soldiers) than to prevent war crimes (soldiers massacring civilians). To the Serbs, however, UNPROFOR represented a hostile external world frustrating their objectives, which they were well on their way to achieving when the United Nations intervened. They thus focused their efforts on subverting UNPROFOR and completing the ethnic cleansing of "their" country. This was a near-certain recipe for disaster.

The compromised mission of UNPROFOR came to be embodied in the institution of United Nations Protected Areas (UNPAs), or "safe areas." First established in 1992 in Croatia, they were extended to Bosnia in 1993. In July 1995, however, the "protected area" of Srebrenica was overrun, as an appalled and ashamed U.N. contingent found itself able only to stand by and watch. Adult men were separated from the rest of the refugees, who were sent fleeing. Of the total "protected" population of about 40,000, more than 7,000 were slaughtered and buried in mass graves.

With people now dying as an unintended but very real consequence of the "best efforts" of the international community, the West, and particularly the United States, finally intervened. NATO's intensified air strikes, coupled with the Croatian victories in Krajina and renewed pressure applied to Milošević, forced the Bosnian Serbs to the negotiating table. A marathon three-week session at Wright-Patterson Air Force Base in Dayton, Ohio, backed by immense U.S. pressure, produced a peace agreement on December 14, 1995.

iv. Assessing the Bosnian Intervention

Viewed in isolation, Bosnia appears as largely a failure of international action. Nonetheless, Bosnia and its people were, quite literally, kept alive. More than 2 million people received humanitarian assistance. International action helped to keep Sarajevo from falling, thus averting an even greater disaster. The arms embargo prevented an even larger bloodbath (especially if one attributes part of the relatively good record of the Bosnian Muslims to their lack of opportunities to exact revenge). And U.N. peacekeepers sent to the border of Macedonia in December 1992 stopped the fighting from moving east and south.

Taking a comparative perspective, this suggests that Bosnia was not merely a success but a major breakthrough. *Relatively* strong international action came *relatively* rapidly. In the end, armed force was brought to bear. And international action was decisive in ending the conflict. Bosnia marked a crucial step in transforming international responses to genocide.

Precedents, however, are made by later actions that treat them as constraining. They do not automatically cause comparable action in the future. Furthermore, their meaning changes as they become embedded in streams of action. The meaning of Bosnia emerged only as the international community confronted new genocides in Rwanda, Kosovo, and East Timor.

3. Case Study: Rwanda

If Bosnia is the success story of the early 1990s, Rwanda was the great, and horribly tragic, failure.

Ethnic conflict in Rwanda was in large measure the creation of Belgian colonial rule. After receiving control over Rwanda from Germany after World War I, the Belgians exacerbated the tensions between the two main groups in the territory, the majority Hutu and the minority Tutsi. After having purged Hutus from the largely Tutsi elite, the Belgians used the Tutsi as an instrument of colonial domination, provoking understandable resentment from the Hutu majority.

In 1959, as independence was approaching, the Belgians decided to switch their support from the Tutsi to the Hutu, whose resentment turned into the violent assertion of political dominance once they took over the colonial state. Some 20,000 Tutsis were massacred, and another 200,000 were forced to flee. In the ensuing years, sporadic ethnic violence, with short bursts of genocidal killing (particularly in 1964 and 1974), marked politics in Rwanda, as well as in neighboring Burundi. The staggering scope of the violence that occurred in 1994, however, was unprecedented.

The prelude to genocide began in October 1990 when the Rwandan Patriotic Front (RPF), made up primarily of Tutsis living in refugee camps in Uganda, invaded

Rwanda. The Hutu-dominated military government of Juvénal Habyarimana portrayed this as an attempt to (re)impose Tutsi domination and responded with increased repression. A cease-fire to this inconclusive conflict was finally negotiated in the summer of 1992. In August 1993, a fragile peace agreement was signed in Arusha, Tanzania (the Arusha Accords).

Meanwhile, the Habyarimana government and its radical Hutu supporters established a network of Hutu militias (interahamwe), which by the spring of 1994 numbered about 30,000. Radio stations, especially the government-controlled Radio Mille Collines, spread increasingly virulent anti-Tutsi propaganda. From the national cabinet down to local mayors, preparations were laid for a massive, organized campaign of violence against Tutsis and political opponents of the regime. The killings began on the night of April 6, 1994, after the plane carrying the presidents of both Rwanda and Burundi was shot down. (Responsibility remains a matter of considerable controversy, but forensic evidence points to radical elements within the Rwandan Armed Forces.)

Individual contingents of the United Nations Assistance Mission in Rwanda (UNAMIR), a peacekeeping force observing implementation of the Arusha Accords, tried to shelter some civilians. The formal mandate of UNAMIR, however, restricted the troops to monitoring. In any case, U.N. peacekeepers themselves quickly became targets. Ten Belgian soldiers were captured on April 7, tortured, and murdered.

Two weeks later, the Security Council unanimously agreed to cut the UNAMIR force from 2,500 to 270, despite estimates that more than 100,000 civilians had already been massacred. Not until April 30, when hundreds of thousands had been killed, did the Security Council even condemn the violence. Even then it pointedly refused to call it a genocide, admitting only that "acts of genocide" had been committed. The United States, as late as June, also continued to refer only to "acts of genocide," wary of the international legal obligation under the Genocide Convention to respond.

The world stood by and watched while more than 750,000 Rwandans out of a prewar population of about 6,750,000 (proportionally the equivalent of roughly 30 million deaths in the United States) were butchered in a little more than three months. And butchered is a brutally accurate term: the machete was the weapon of choice of many of the génocidaires. Another 2 million Rwandans fled to Zaire (now the Democratic Republic of the Congo).

All of this was particularly troubling because information was available—in the media, at the United Nations, and in the major governments involved (France, the United States, and Belgium)—that genocide was imminent. In January 1994, the commander of the U.N. force, General Roméo Dallaire, asked for, but was denied, permission to confiscate the weapons of the interahamwe. Throughout February and March, General Dallaire pleaded, with increasing desperation, for reinforcements and a more robust mandate, but the Security Council refused.

As we have noted, the United Nations is an intergovernmental organization, made up of and controlled by its member states. The Security Council is dominated by its five permanent members (China, France, Russia, the United States, and the United Kingdom), each of whom can veto Security Council action. In the case of

Rwanda, four of the permanent powers actively opposed U.N. action—especially France. The United States had recently been forced to make a humiliating withdrawal from Somalia and was unwilling to consider involvement in another small, fractious African country. France, which considered itself to have special geopolitical interests in central Africa, had particularly strong relations with the Habyarimana government and had substantially increased its military support to the Rwandan government in response to the RPF invasion in 1990. Britain appeared willing to consider stronger action but had no desire to lead on the issue of Rwanda. Russia and China had "principled" objections, insisting that the conflict was an internal Rwandan matter (and China was the primary source of the machetes that were the principal weapon of choice in the genocide). All these political forces conspired against U.N. intervention. And in a cruel irony, Rwanda happened to occupy one of the ten rotating seats on the Security Council and used this position to try to minimize the scope and severity of the problem.

During the hundred-day genocide, most of the killing occurred in the first six weeks. By the time the Security Council did finally act, in late June 1994, most of the killing had ended, and the RPF had secured most of the country. The Security Council authorized a French-led intervention—Operation Turquoise—ostensibly to protect civilians from further genocidal acts and from RPF countermeasures. France established a "safe zone" in the southwest of the country to quell the growing tide of Hutu who were beginning to flee the advance of the RPF. The result, however, was that this operation allowed tens of thousands of perpetrators to escape into neighboring Zaire, under the protection of French military forces.

Because of the low-tech nature of the genocide, even as few as several thousand troops could have stopped much, probably even most, of the killing. However, those states with the knowledge and power to do something chose inaction. In their defense, few expected anything like the scope of violence that occurred—although a willingness to tolerate tens of thousands of deaths is still shameful. As the tragedy unfolded, though, and appreciation grew of the opportunity for humanitarian action that had been forfeited, a deep sense of shame spread through the international community.

4. Case Study: Kosovo

When the next major humanitarian crisis arose, in Kosovo in 1998 and 1999, the contrasting lessons of Bosnia and Rwanda weighed heavily on the minds of decision makers and public opinion. Key international actors, led by the administration of President Bill Clinton in the United States and the government of Prime Minister Tony Blair in Britain, seem to have learned from Bosnia and Rwanda that successful humanitarian intervention was both (politically and logistically) possible and (morally, perhaps even politically) necessary.

Kosovo, as noted above, had been an autonomous region of Serbia, not a republic of Yugoslavia. This was crucial, because when Yugoslavia (and then the Soviet Union) broke up, it did so according to the old internal boundaries. Thus, federal republics (such as Serbia, Bosnia, and Slovenia and, in the USSR, Russia, Kazakhstan, and Georgia) easily received local and international recognition of their independence. Other internal units, such as Kosovo in Serbia (Yugoslavia) and Chechnya in Russia (USSR), did not.

As discussed above, this left Kosovo's ethnically Albanian population under the increasingly brutal domination of Serbia. Throughout the mid-1990s, the Kosovo Liberation Army carried out sporadic, quite ineffective guerrilla operations that had little popular support. The Serbian government, however, responded with increasingly brutal repression, including attacks on civilians. The Serb massacre of fifty-eight people in Perkazi in February 1998 initiated a spiral of escalation. In the following twelve months, about a thousand people, mostly ethnically Albanian Kosovar civilians, were killed. Perhaps even more ominously, more than 400,000 were forced to flee their homes.

Some debate remains about the intent of the Milošević government. The prevailing opinion in much of the West by early 1999 was that ethnic cleansing had begun in earnest. Efforts to get the Security Council to act were nonetheless blocked, primarily by Russia.

The Clinton administration, however, continued to argue, forcefully, that the lessons of Bosnia and Rwanda proved that early action was necessary. Britain and some other European states agreed. The problem was determining who would act, on what rationale, in the absence of Security Council authorization. Rather than act unilaterally or create an ad hoc coalition, they decided to use NATO, the old Cold War alliance against the Soviet Union that had been trying to reinvent itself as a new kind of regional security organization.

A land invasion was ruled out, as the costs, in terms of troops mobilized and lives lost, were anticipated to be more than Western publics would accept. This left only airpower. From March 24 to June 19, 1999, NATO forces carried out an increasingly punishing campaign of aerial bombardments, including repeated attacks on the Serbian capital of Belgrade.

The Serbian authorities took advantage of the attacks to put into action a well-coordinated campaign of ethnic cleansing. About 10,000 people were killed, and nearly 1.5 million people were forced to flee their homes. The speed and efficiency of the Serbian actions clearly indicated Milošević's rather elaborate plan, which he had been waiting for the right moment to implement.

Three features of the Kosovo intervention deserve special mention. First, it was undertaken as genocide began, or perhaps even before. In Bosnia, intervention occurred when genocide was well under way. Second, the intervention was undertaken despite the fact that the number of deaths was *relatively* low. (The Serbian strategy of ethnic cleansing, which used exemplary violence to coerce people into fleeing the territory to be cleansed, seems to have been, in part, a calculated attempt to stay under a perceived killing threshold for an international response.) Third, regional powers acted on humanitarian grounds, in the absence of Security Council authorization or any other particularly powerful legal justification. In effect, the negative precedent of Rwanda—something had to be done—took priority over the usual requirements of authorization and legality.

5. The Authority to Intervene

Who is entitled to intervene on behalf of (potential) victims of genocide? We can distinguish interveners by their mode of action (unilateral or multilateral) and the scope of the community within or for which they act (global or regional).

The authority of multilateral interveners arises from legal, political, or moral recognition by the political communities that the organization or its members represent. Multilateral intervention necessitates the building of political coalitions across states, which, even if it does not entirely eliminate the influence of national selfishness, substantially increases the likelihood of genuinely humanitarian motivation. At the very least, it makes the political self-interests involved somewhat less narrow. When the multilateral forum is the Security Council—which can act only with both a majority of its membership and the consent of the five permanent members—any use of force that is authorized is likely to have a very central humanitarian dimension to it.

Unilateral actors—which include ad hoc coalitions—may or may not have comparable recognition by broader political communities. It is an empirical question whether a great power acting unilaterally intervenes with authority or merely as a result of its superior power. Great powers have engaged in far more *anti*humanitarian than humanitarian interventions. Multilateral intervention thus is the preferred alternative, for practical as well as theoretical reasons.

Unilateral action by a great power with highly mixed motives nonetheless may save lives that would be lost while waiting for a more pure multilateral intervention that never comes. (Classic Cold War examples include the conflict between India and East Pakistan [Bangladesh] and that of Vietnam in Cambodia.) Furthermore, unilateral actors, being politically autonomous, may be able to intervene when multilateral action is blocked. And when unilateral actors intervene as de facto representatives of both victims and broader regional or international political communities, their actions may acquire considerable informal legitimacy.

The second dimension of this typology, the distinction between regional and global interveners, concerns the appropriate level for action within the international system. Regional and global actors may have different capacities and authorities. For example, regional multilateral action may be easier because of greater common interests within the region. Regional actors may also have the advantage of superior knowledge or authority because they are closer to the problem. But if a regional organization is dominated by a regional hegemon (for example, Nigeria in the Economic Community of West African States), it may be (perceived as) a captive of that state, undermining its legitimacy.

Let us apply this typology to Kosovo. Global multilateral action was effectively blocked. China and Russia had a deep and relatively principled opposition to multilateral intervention. In addition, Russia had much more selfish political interests in its long-term historical relationship with Serbia.

The Organization for Security and Co-operation in Europe, the most obvious regional actor, lacked the unified political will needed to act in this particular case—let alone the legal authority to use force. A similar political situation also precluded action through either the European Union or the Council of Europe. Furthermore, unilateral action by the United States was definitely unacceptable to most, if not all, of the states of the European Union, as well as most states outside of Europe.

Nonetheless, the states of the European Union were unwilling—at least after a lot of political lobbying—to stand by and allow genocide to occur in Kosovo. NATO provided a convenient organizational forum for needed action that could not be authorized elsewhere. Faced with a genuine dilemma, the members of NATO decided that intervention was the lesser of two evils.

Assuming that preemptive humanitarian intervention will generally be blocked at the global level, concerned states seem to be left with the uncomfortable alternatives of inaction, unilateral action, or regional multilateral action. This is a recipe for uneven and selective responses to humanitarian crises. There are large parts of the world where there is neither a viable regional actor nor a unilateral actor that has the necessary power, legitimacy, and commitment. Selectivity is further increased by the effective exemption of the permanent members of the Security Council from U.N. action and a comparable regional exemption of leading local powers such as Nigeria and India (and their allies). Kosovo also raises the specter of what might be called coercive regionalism, in which the target of action is not a member of the intervening regional community. Furthermore, the 2005 intervention of the African Union in Sudan—to which we will return—suggests that relying on (ineffective) regional intervention may be a way for global actors to avoid taking difficult or costly action.

But as long as we retain an international system structured around sovereign states—that is, for the foreseeable future—we are not likely to be able to evade these problems of authority and inequality. We are beginning to grapple with them, though, with a certain degree of success. And the U.N.-authorized intervention in East Timor later in 1999 largely removed doubts that a right to humanitarian intervention was being established as a matter of positive international law.

6. Case Study: East Timor

The island of Timor was divided during the colonial era into East Timor and West Timor, held respectively by Portugal and the Netherlands. When Indonesia achieved independence, it received (only) the Dutch holdings in the East Indies (including West Timor, but not East Timor). Neither then nor in 1960, when the United Nations reorganized its decolonization machinery and classified East Timor as a Portuguese colony, did Indonesia claim East Timor.

In 1974, a coup removed the military government in Portugal, the only Western state still holding a substantial colonial empire (most notably Angola and Mozambique). Taking advantage of the situation, East Timor declared independence.

Indonesia, however, had other ideas. It invaded East Timor on October 16, 1975. Indonesian rule was viewed as illegal by most countries. It was rejected by most of the local population. Nonetheless, the government in Jakarta attempted to consolidate its rule through often brutal repression, punctuated by special regional development assistance that suggested material benefits would follow from compliance.

Particularly striking was the Dili Massacre of November 12, 1991. Indonesian troops opened fire on peaceful proindependence demonstrators, killing at least 271 and wounding at least another 275. In addition, more than 250 people disappeared. Besides being unusually brutal, the Dili Massacre was widely publicized, galvanizing international attention in many countries previously uninterested in East Timor's plight (analogous to the impact of the Sharpeville Massacre on international responses to South Africa).

Eventually, international pressure induced Indonesia to permit a U.N.-sponsored referendum on independence. In the election, held on August 30, 1999, more than three-quarters of the votes favored independence. Indonesia, however, balked. Local militias, which were already operating with the acquiescence, and often the active assistance, of Indonesian military authorities, went on a sustained rampage that increasingly appeared to have genocidal aspirations. A fifth to a quarter of the population were forced to flee their homes, with thousands tracked down and killed in churches, schools, and public buildings where they sought refuge.

On September 15, 1999, the Security Council unanimously created the International Force for East Timor, an Australian-led force that, in combination with intensive international political pressure and diplomatic activity, restored order and produced Indonesian acquiescence to Timorese independence. On October 25, 1999, the Security Council established the United Nations Transitional Administration in East Timor. A week later, the last Indonesian troops left East Timor. On May 20, 2002, East Timor achieved full independence.

The technical illegality of Indonesia's occupation of East Timor facilitated such a strong response. Many countries that would have otherwise been reluctant to accept a U.N. military operation were able to view this as a decolonization issue more than a humanitarian intervention. Leading international actors, however, had Kosovo (and Rwanda) very much in mind. East Timor was widely understood as a turning point, completing the transformation of Bosnia from an isolated exception to a precedent in a continuing stream of customary law formation that in some complex way also included Kosovo.

The power of the emerging norm of humanitarian intervention against genocide is illustrated by the fact that almost all the conventional political and material considerations counseled inaction. Indonesia is a large, strategically located country (the world's largest majority-Muslim country) with considerable oil resources and a strong record of support for, and by, the West. In addition, there were well-founded fears, both within and outside Indonesia, about the susceptibility of the country to secessionist movements, some of which had been carrying on armed struggles for decades. East Timor, by contrast, is small, poor—whatever its oil resources, they are dwarfed by those of Indonesia—and of little material interest to anyone except its own people. Nonetheless, in the end, and with surprisingly little controversy, the major Western powers and the rest of the Security Council agreed to send soldiers to protect the Timorese people and enforce their decision to attain independence— in part because they had an international legal right to independence, but in large measure because the international community was unwilling to allow their forced incorporation to be maintained through genocide.

7. The Right to Humanitarian Intervention and the Responsibility to Protect

At the beginning of the 1990s, positive international law clearly did not authorize armed humanitarian intervention, even in response to massive genocide. Not a single intervention against genocide had been widely endorsed as legal. The Security Council had the authority to determine that genocide represented a threat to international peace and security. In practice, though, it never exercised that authority. The standard pattern, right through the end of the Cold War, was for the international community to wring its hands in anguish as genocide played itself out in places like East Pakistan (where in 1971 several hundred thousand were killed and some 10 million people put to flight in calculated ethnic violence), Cambodia (where more than 1.5 million people—about one-fifth of the total population of the country—died at the hands of the Khmer Rouge between 1975 and 1979), and Uganda (where more than a quarter-million people died during the rule of Idi Amin in the 1970s). Neighboring states, usually with powerful geopolitical interests, sometimes intervened. None of these interventions, however, was accepted as legal. And most were not even presented as primarily humanitarian by the interveners.

By the end of the millennium, however, the Security Council had authorized not only humanitarian interventions in Bosnia and East Timor but also peacekeeping operations in Sierra Leone, Liberia, the Central African Republic, and the Democratic Republic of the Congo that had a central humanitarian component. And, in the first decade of the twenty-first century, additional operations were conducted in Liberia, Côte d'Ivoire, Sudan, Burundi, Afghanistan, and Haiti. Today we have both a well-established norm and a surprisingly clear pattern of practice of Security Council–authorized humanitarian intervention against genocide. And the example of Kosovo suggests considerable international toleration for genuinely humanitarian interventions taken in response to Security Council inaction.

NATO's Kosovo intervention provoked the Canadian government to convene an independent commission to explore the changing nature of humanitarian law and humanitarian intervention in light of state sovereignty. The International Commission on Intervention and State Sovereignty (ICISS) was cochaired by Gareth Evans (an Australian lawyer and politician) and Mohamed Sahnoun (an Algerian diplomat) and included independent diplomats and lawyers from several countries, including Russia, Germany, the Philippines, Guatemala, India, and the United States. The ICISS completed its landmark report, *The Responsibility to Protect,* in December 2001.

The ICISS posed a central question: If state sovereignty is a shield that protects states from intervention, as a matter of law, what are the limits (if any) of the duty of nonintervention? Does international law protect states that are very clearly engaged in massive and flagrant violations of human rights, especially including genocide and crimes against humanity?

The Commission began by noting changes since World War II in the makeup of the international system, especially the proliferation of sovereign yet weak states that are vulnerable to internal strife and violence. It also noted that the normative environment of international relations had changed in recent decades. In particular, the concept of state security had been supplemented by human security, and the ambit of human rights and humanitarian law had grown dramatically in extent and importance. These changes, the Commission argued, demanded a reconceptualization of sovereignty, especially in relation to human security.

The main conceptual problem, the Commission wrote, was one of framing the question, which begins with nonintervention as the default condition. The norm of nonintervention is enshrined in Article 2.7 of the U.N. Charter, which essentially prohibits any interference by the United Nations (or other states) in matters "essentially within the domestic jurisdiction" of member-states. However, that prohibition does not apply to actions taken by the Security Council, under its Chapter VII powers to authorize both nonmilitary and military action against states found to be a threat to international or regional peace and security.

The ICISS thus suggested that the right of noninterference was conditional, rather than absolute—that the first responsibility of all states is to protect their populations from grave harm. If states are unwilling or unable to undertake that responsibility, the duty to do so shifts from the state to the international community, which is then empowered to act. The doctrine of "the responsibility to protect" provided not only that there is a *right to intervene* in situations of grave breaches of human rights and humanitarian law but rather that intervention under such circumstances constituted *a duty (responsibility)* of the international community.

The ICISS outlined several criteria, rooted in traditional "just war" theory, that would trigger the responsibility to protect (R2P).

1. The intervention had to be primarily for a *just cause*: to halt, avert, or prevent large-scale loss of life from, for example, ethnic cleansing, genocide, or other crimes against humanity. The violations must be gross and systematic, and documented by clear evidence from credible sources.

2. States or other actors that intervene must do so with *right intention*; that is, the just cause must be the principal motive to action. This does not mean that the interveners need to have purely humanitarian motives. Any *other* motives, however, must be clearly secondary to the humanitarian motive (and are inherently suspect).

3. The intervention must be a *last resort*. Other actions must have already been tried and have failed.

4. Under R2P, any armed intervention must be *proportionate,* and have *reasonable prospects for success.* This is one of the biggest hurdles that any state or group of states that is considering an armed humanitarian intervention must take into account. Discussions about duties versus consequences often get hung up on this point, as there is always a danger that an intervention in a complex humanitarian emergency or crisis, if not done right, could easily spin out of control and lead to even worse humanitarian outcomes than would have been the case with not intervening.

5. Finally, the interveners must have *legitimate authority* to act. Authorization by the U.N. Security Council unquestionably provides such

authority. The Commission, however, saw the NATO intervention in Kosovo as "illegal yet legitimate," a very interesting gray area.

In the case of Kosovo, there was widespread agreement in the Security Council that the threshold criteria for action were in evidence. Four Security Council resolutions had been adopted, demanding an end to the violence by the Serbian regime (a legal requirement, not a recommendation), and Serbia had been shown to be a consistent violator not only of human rights and humanitarian law but of the demands of Security Council resolutions. In the eyes of NATO, the action was genuinely a last resort, because it was clear that Russia and China were not willing to move to a military action under Chapter VII. Furthermore, the vote taken by NATO to intervene was unanimous, among eighteen member-states that were widely considered to be good citizens of the United Nations. Finally, after the intervention achieved its goals, NATO returned as quickly as possible to working within the U.N. Charter frame to establish a cease-fire and begin the difficult work of postconflict rebuilding (in U.N. Security Council Resolution 1244).

The R2P doctrine—with caveats—was accepted unanimously by the international community at the 2005 World Summit, a major policy summit coinciding with the sixtieth anniversary of the adoption of the U.N. Charter. The 2005 summit endorsed the basic principle that sovereignty cannot act as a shield to protect states from scrutiny with respect to the gravest of human rights and humanitarian crimes, but it did not endorse the notion that the international community had a specific and unquestioned responsibility to intervene.

One legal analysis[1] concluded that, when considered to its fullest extent, the R2P norm is still fairly shallow. At one end of the spectrum, the ideas that (a) the first responsibility of the state is to protect its people and (b) that sovereignty is a weak defense against violating that responsibility are widely held by states. Slightly fewer states agree that outside actors have a right to intervene nonforcibly, and still fewer, that states may use coercive means to uphold the responsibility to protect. *Very few* states accept the notion that outside actors have a positive *duty* to intervene. A *responsibility* to protect, is, at best, an aspiration that few if any states with the capabilities to participate in protective actions are willing to acknowledge.

Furthermore, the existing right to humanitarian intervention applies only to genocide and crimes against humanity. There is no evidence to suggest that it is spilling over into other, more common, human rights violations, even in cases of torture and slavery, where national courts are increasingly applying international human rights norms.

This poses a moral paradox. We seem willing to respond to certain kinds of graphic and concentrated suffering but to tolerate substantially greater suffering so long as it remains more diffuse. This paradox is by no means restricted to genocide. Consider, for example, the contrast between the relatively strong international reaction to the 1989 Tiananmen Square massacre in China, where hundreds of people died in a relatively telegenic way, and the weak reactions to the systematic and severe daily violations of the human rights of hundreds of millions of Chinese citizens. Even more striking is the substantial international willingness to respond to famines but a parallel unwillingness to deal with the far more severe problem of malnutrition.

If we take seriously the unity of all human rights and if we take seriously the idea that human rights are about a life of dignity, not mere life, then the restriction of humanitarian intervention to genocide and other humanitarian crimes is highly problematic. There are, however, powerful practical, and even ethical, reasons to restrict humanitarian intervention to the most severe atrocities.

Psychologically, the restriction acknowledges the realities of mobilizing an international response adequate to bearing the considerable costs associated with military humanitarian intervention, especially if that intervention is not to be restricted to high-altitude bombing. Furthermore, a narrow humanitarian exception reflects the continuing priority of local and national communities. It remains rare—but no longer unheard of—for states and citizens to be willing to bear the costs of rescuing foreigners from the depredations of their own governments. An active sense of cosmopolitan moral community remains very, very thin.

The international community may have a *moral* obligation to prevent and respond to the most serious breaches of humanitarian law. It might even be argued that such a duty is implied by the very structure of the global human rights regime. National implementation of internationally recognized human rights, if it is more than a political compromise with the reality of state power, must assume that states are capable and not unwilling to protect the human rights of their citizens. But this is patently absurd in the case of genocidal regimes. In fact, it appears as a cruel hoax to continue to act on such an assumption. In such cases, as the ICISS suggested, residual responsibility reverts to the international community.

Nonetheless, international law recognizes only a right to humanitarian intervention. As with any right, the Security Council may choose not to exercise it; the Council is free to intervene, or not, as it sees fit. And the grounds for both acting and not acting may legitimately appeal to a variety of nonmoral considerations, to which we will turn at the end of the chapter.

First, though, let us look briefly at two case studies from the 2000s that challenges the relatively optimistic picture derived from these cases in the 1990s.

8. Case Study: Libya

In conjunction with Arab Spring uprisings in Tunisia, Yemen, Egypt, Syria, and Morocco, mass protests broke out in Libya on February 17, 2011, against the government of Mu'ammar Gaddafi. The largest was in the city of Benghazi, in the west of the country. The crackdown by the regime was swift and ruthless. Gaddafi proclaimed that those rebelling against his rule would be "hunted down street by street, house by house, and wardrobe by wardrobe." By February 22, several NGOs were reporting mass atrocities against civilian protesters, including mass killings, and the U.N. Security Council acknowledged that "possible" crimes against humanity were occurring in Libya. That same day, the League of Arab States, which traditionally has been immensely respectful of the sovereignty of systematic human rights violators, voted to suspend Libya's membership.

On February 25, the Human Rights Council adopted a resolution establishing a commission of inquiry to explore whether the actions of the Gaddafi regime constituted crimes against humanity, and it recommended that the U.N. General Assembly consider suspending Libya's seat on the Human Rights Council (to which it had just been elected). The following day, the Security Council unanimously adopted Resolution 1970, which, among other things, imposed an arms embargo on Libya and imposed travel bans and asset freezes on senior officials of the Gaddafi regime. The Security Council also referred the situation in Libya to the prosecutor of the International Criminal Court, an action it very rarely takes.

Such rapid and wide-ranging action was as impressive as it was unusual. Only a minority of voices from the West (mostly the United States, United Kingdom, and France), however, argued for more proactive measures. A majority of the Security Council and other regional actors urged restraint.

The tide toward intervention, however, began to turn on March 12, when the League of Arab States stated that the Gaddafi government had "lost its sovereignty" and urged for the establishment of a no-fly zone as a way to protect civilians while also maintaining the principles of sovereignty and territorial integrity, as such an action would preclude a boots-on-the-ground-style intervention. After deliberations within the Obama White House on March 15, the United States agreed to cosponsor a Security Council resolution (with France, Lebanon, and the United Kingdom) authorizing the protection of civilians using "all necessary measures," including the establishment of a no-fly zone and NATO enforcement of the arms embargo. This new resolution—1973—was adopted on a vote of 10–0, with Brazil, China, Germany, India, and Russia abstaining.

This action was seen to fall within the doctrine of R2P, a language that was used extensively both by those favoring intervention and those who were initially reluctant or opposed. It seemed to be a textbook case of the "responsibility to react" as outlined by the ICISS: there was just cause, a sense of imminent danger, and the intervention seemed to be a last resort. The scope of the intervention seemed to have also met the criteria for proportionality and prospects for success. It was even carried out with the legitimate authority of the U.N. Security Council.

The criterion of right intention, however, was contentious. As the practicalities of enforcing a no-fly zone become clearer—in particular as the diversion of government resources threatened to shift the balance of power—China and Russia began to suspect that the real intention was regime change: removing rather than restraining Gaddafi. And this view today continues to compete with a more benign reading of NATO actions.

The more serious problem, though, has been the ultimate failure to fulfill—some would argue even a lack of effort concerning—the third pillar of R2P, the "responsibility to rebuild." Gaddafi and his family are gone. Libya today is a failed state, fragmented and practically ungovernable. Small-scale conflicts and widespread human rights abuses continue on a daily, if disorganized, basis.

In fact, one might speculate that China and Russia permitted the Libyan intervention (by abstaining rather than vetoing action) in order to expose R2P for what it really is, in their view: a violation of national sovereignty and of international law, under the cloak of humanitarianism. One only needs to look at the situation in Syria to draw this conclusion (see the Problem on page 193).

In any case, Libya has made it clear that protection through armed intervention is far more difficult than Kosovo and East Timor may have initially suggested. And, like Iraq, Libya tragically demonstrates that establishing even basic political order, let alone a rights-protective regime, is extraordinarily difficult in a country that has suffered under a brutal personalist military dictatorship for decades. When politics has been that badly broken, neither national nor international actors are likely to have the knowledge, resources, or commitment to fix much. Although this is not an argument for allowing brutal dictators to continue to abuse their people, it does suggest that sometimes—and probably more often than we would like to admit—the best that can reasonably be hoped for from humanitarian intervention is a moderately civilized form of postconflict politics that limits rather than seeks to remove gross and systematic human rights violations and that leaves space, and perhaps provides some foundations, for future progress. In other words, humanitarian intervention may often be merely the lesser of two evils. And, if it is not done well, it is maybe not even that, especially in the short and medium run.

We thus must give greater attention than has often been the case to the fact that international actors not only have a responsibility to protect but are responsible for the consequences of their protective actions. When a relatively easy quick fix, such as was carried out in East Timor, is not possible, the character of humanitarian intervention changes fundamentally. And when local actors are in no position to rebuild their society for themselves, the vital responsibility is to rebuild—a burden that most foreign peoples and their governments are not willing to undertake with the serious long-term commitment of effort and resources that it requires.

9. Case Study: Sudan

The roots of Sudan's humanitarian crises go back to its colonial creation, which combined a largely Arab and Muslim North with a largely black and Christian and animist South. When the country attained formal independence on January 1, 1956, Sudan was already in the midst of a civil war between North and South that continued until 1972—only to break out again in 1983, continuing, more on than off, until 2005. About half a million people died in the first phase of the civil war (out of a population of about 10 million at independence). Perhaps another 2 million died in the second phase. Although there was considerable brutality on both sides, most of the suffering was caused by military action by the North that targeted civilians and used the denial of food, even in times of famine, as a standard tactic.

This particular humanitarian disaster was finally brought to an end in 2011. In January, the people of southern Sudan overwhelmingly voted for independence. In July 2011, the new country of South Sudan peacefully seceded—although peace between the two Sudans is hardly secure and perhaps not even likely.

Sadly, though, this solution seems to have been facilitated by the emergence of a new humanitarian crisis, beginning in 2003, in Darfur, the western region of Sudan, which like the South is primarily non-Arab and non-Muslim (although with a much more substantial Arabized minority). The Darfur conflict initially went in favor of the rebels, who handily outmaneuvered the government army (which was stretched thin to begin with by the conflict in the South and another conflict in the East). The government, however, quickly switched to a counterinsurgency strategy based on *janjaweed* militias, composed of local mounted herders armed by the government, supported by government helicopters. Many thousands were killed, and more than 100,000 refugees were put to flight by the time the conflict moved to the forefront of international attention in 2004.

The violence directed at the non-Arab population was reminiscent of Serbian ethnic cleansing in Bosnia and Kosovo. A conscious effort seems to have been made both to limit the killing, which was aimed primarily at causing targeted populations to flee, and to engage diplomatically with critics in order to forestall an effective, full-scale multilateral intervention. But even this "restrained" violence forced more than 2.5 million people—40 percent of the prewar population—to flee and killed perhaps a third of a million people (three-quarters of those deaths being from disease among refugees).

The international response was in many ways rapid and robust. In April 2004, Chad brokered a cease-fire. In August 2004, the African Union (AU) sent 150 Rwandan troops to monitor the cease-fire. They were soon joined by 150 Nigerians. The following month, the Security Council condemned the government for its actions in Darfur. In 2005, the AU peacekeeping force was expanded, first to more than 3,000 troops and then to almost 7,000. A peace agreement between the government and some rebels was signed at Abuja, Nigeria, in May 2006. At the end of August 2006, the Security Council authorized a force of more than 17,000 peacekeepers. Numerous efforts at cease-fires and final resolution were undertaken, by both bilateral and multilateral actors, both inside and outside of the region, including prominently the United States. A major NGO response mobilized substantial pressure both on Sudan and especially on Western governments. Charges were even brought in the International Criminal Court against leaders of the violence, including the sitting president of Sudan, Omar al-Bashir. And a new, more promising, peace agreement was signed by all the major parties in Doha, Qatar, in July 2011.

Compared to Kosovo and East Timor, though, these responses were somewhat timid and noticeably unsuccessful. The United States, already bogged down in wars in Afghanistan and Iraq, was unwilling to lead a more robust response. Without a substantial American commitment, a significantly larger force could not be raised. And even if it had been committed, no other power or group of powers had the logistical capabilities to support it in the field.

Darfur is a huge area (more than 190,000 square miles, roughly the size of Spain) with primitive infrastructure. The substantial majority of the population lives in widely scattered villages in a flat, semiarid terrain. A large and difficult ground operation thus would have been required to provide protection. (A small lightly armed force, such as would have made a huge difference in Rwanda, could not provide protection against mobile militias backed by air support.)

The international politics were further complicated by China and Russia being even more reluctant than usual to permit armed intervention. China had major economic interests in the region, especially oil. And Russia was both locked in its own brutal separatist war in Chechnya and happy to take the opportunity to sell arms to Sudan's government, despite the U.N. embargo.

The regional environment also undercut stronger action. The AU was more than willing to intervene. But it lacked any substantial moral authority in Sudan, and it lacked the resources to do an effective job. Furthermore, its efforts were undermined by the indirect support that Sudan received from the Arab League.

The government in Khartoum was an astute and effective opponent. It appears to have carefully studied previous interventions. And it had a clear appreciation of the strengths of its position. Khartoum thus calibrated its actions, both internally and externally, to allow it to continue the ethnic cleansing of Darfur.

All of the above suggests that Kosovo and East Timor may have been *relatively* easy cases that created unrealistic expectations. Being forced out of East Timor was deeply embarrassing for the Indonesian government. But it had little material cost, especially because it has not in fact strengthened secessionist movements elsewhere in the country. Indonesia, in other words, was *relatively* open to international pressure and in the end not willing to fight further to keep a territory to which it had a questionable claim in the first place—especially given the internal political changes that were taking place within Indonesia, leading toward its effective democratization over the following several years. Furthermore, the Australian intervention in East Timor was successful, with a force more than one-third smaller than the clearly inadequate force the Security Council authorized for Darfur.

As for Kosovo, the NATO bombing campaign was not foreordained to succeed. In fact, almost up to the moment that it finally succeeded, it appeared to be failing. The loss of Kosovo, although a much more severe blow to Serbia than the loss of East Timor was to Indonesia, was not decisive, given its broader range of objectives, especially closer integration into Europe and the material (and psychological) benefits that would provide. And there was an internal opposition within Serbia that pressed the government to alter its policy.

The government in Khartoum, by contrast, had demonstrated itself willing to carry out decades-long massacres of people that, although technically fellow citizens, it viewed as culturally, ethnically, and racially inferior. It had the oil resources to support such policies, both internally and externally. It brooked no opposition to its rule, which even in the North of the country was highly repressive (although much less violent). It did not care much what the rest of the world thought of its actions. It needed nothing from outside (other than to sell its oil, which proved no problem). And it pursued its policies with considerable skill.

In other words, Sudan shows that a relatively effective and committed government can largely flout the international community, so long as it is willing to inflict sufficient suffering on its people. North Korea, Burma, and Zimbabwe present different variants of this pattern—which has no connection at all with genocides in "failed" states such as Somalia and Congo. Politically possible actions simply were inadequate to stop the killing.

But, even in Darfur, the international response had a (limited) positive impact. The number of people directly killed numbered "only" several tens of thousands (though there were a couple hundred thousand deaths from war-related disease).

Horrible as that figure is, it almost certainly would have been much higher had the international community not been watching carefully.

New violence, however, erupted in 2014, with many villages destroyed, men arrested, people beaten, and women systematically raped. In the fall of 2016, chemical weapons appear to have been used against civilians. In December 2016, the chair of the South Sudanese Commission on Human Rights, Yasmin Sooka, addressed the twenty-sixth special session of the U.N. Human Rights Council, recounting mass atrocities that are being committed—the early warning signs of an impending genocide. Again the lesson seems to be that international action in Darfur and South Sudan has been able to limit but not eliminate targeted political violence against civilians. And whether this counts as a success or a failure is a question over which reasonable people may reasonably disagree.

10. Justifying Humanitarian Intervention

As the above cases illustrate, justifying humanitarian intervention in contemporary international politics involves a complex interaction of morality, law, and politics. The moral case for humanitarian intervention against genocide is relatively unproblematic. In §3.3, we used John Rawls's notion of overlapping consensus to circumvent disputes over foundational theories of human rights. In much the same way, we can see today an overlapping consensus on the use of armed force against genocide. Whatever their differences, most contemporary moral and religious doctrines agree that genocide is the kind of international crime that in principle justifies armed humanitarian intervention. Across a very wide range of common moral theories and principles, *this* kind of suffering cannot be permitted.

Yet states and international organizations are not unencumbered moral agents. They are also subjects of international law and deeply political actors. And international law and politics impose their own standards of justification. Throughout the Cold War, morality justified humanitarian intervention against genocide, but international law, emphasizing sovereignty and nonintervention, prohibited it. Today, law and morality largely converge. But, as Rwanda and Kosovo illustrate, states still face a problem when the substantive standard of protecting victims of genocidal conflicts with the international legal requirement of U.N. Security Council authorization.

Justification becomes even more complicated when we recognize that states are also political actors. National leaders are *supposed* to take into account the political standard of the national interest. In addition to acting in accordance with the demands of law, morality, and humanity, they should consult the interests of their own state (and perhaps the interests of international society).

Political interests may justify inaction that is morally demanded and legally warranted. In fact, it is essential that potential interveners consider the material and political costs, to themselves and others, of undertaking a morally and legally justifiable intervention. No less important, political interests—or at least the absence of competing political interests—may be a crucial final element in reaching a decision to act on moral and legal justifications.

How we balance these competing standards is, of course, a matter of intense controversy, both in general and in any specific case. But justifying humanitarian intervention requires that we take into account the full range of relevant moral, legal, and political principles—making justification a remarkably complex matter in many cases.

This is particularly true because most interventions arise from mixed motives. Humanitarian interventions typically are costly, both financially and in the risks to which they expose soldiers. States may occasionally accept such risks for purely humanitarian reasons. A number of states are even coming to see preventing or stopping systematic gross human rights violations as part of their national interest. But purely moral motives have been, and are likely to remain, rare.

Nonhumanitarian motives, however, do not necessarily reduce the justifiability of an intervention. Some political motives do not conflict with either humanitarian norms or international law. And, even when they do, we need to *balance* the competing considerations. So long as there are significant humanitarian motivations, interventions undertaken with mixed motives will be either contested or excused by various motivated parties.

Issues of justification are also connected with questions of (in)consistency (see also §7.4.B). Critics often present the impure as trumping the pure: because one did not intervene in A, which is in all essential ways similar to B, intervening in B is somehow unjustified, or at least suspect. Such an argument, however, reflects an absurd perfectionism that would paralyze states not just in cases of humanitarian intervention but in almost all areas of endeavor.

Inconsistency arguments do have real force when they point to blatant partisanship: for example, supporting a practice among friends but intervening when an enemy does the same thing. Consistency per se certainly is desirable, for all kinds of political, psychological, and perhaps even moral reasons. But as Peter Baehr nicely put it, "One act of commission is not invalidated by many acts of omission."[2] Inconsistent need not mean unjustified.

Problem 7: The War in Syria

The Problem

Since 2011, the war in Syria has devolved into the most protracted and grave humanitarian crisis since the Second Congo War (1998–2003). The United Nations estimates that around 400,000 have been killed since the outbreak of the conflict in 2011; around 88,000 of those were civilians. It appears that 2014 was the worst year of the war in terms of deaths and casualties—around 70,000. The Syrian Observatory for Human Rights estimated the 2016 death toll was nearly 50,000, including 13,617 civilians. As a result of the conflict, nearly 5 million refugees (nearly half Syria's population) have fled to camps in Turkey, Lebanon, and Jordan. About 1 million have sought asylum in Europe.

The war in Syria has not elicited any credible claims of genocide. The United Nations, however, reports that the war has been "characterized by a complete lack of adherence to the norms of international law." The United Nations and numerous human rights NGOs alike have found that human rights violations, war crimes, and crimes against humanity have been committed by both the regime of Bashar al-Assad and by rebel groups trying to remove him from power, although the vast majority of violations have been perpetrated by government forces. The human rights violations, war crimes, and crimes against humanity are numerous, among them torture and extrajudicial killing; mass arbitrary arrests; use of chemical weapons and poison gas; the targeting of civilian sites, including schools and hospitals; the systematic denial in some areas of access to food and water; recruitment of child soldiers; and murder of religious minorities.

In November 2016, the United Nations estimated that nearly 1 million Syrian civilians were living under siege. The most tragic case of these has been the siege of eastern Aleppo, which began in July 2016, trapping more than 275,000 civilians. In late December 2016, the al-Assad government had reclaimed the last rebel-held areas of the city.

So far, the international community has been paralyzed—except for Russian military intervention in support of al-Assad. The responsibility to protect is often invoked. But neither the Security Council nor any ad hoc coalition of powers has been willing to authorize or provide the kind of massive armed intervention that would be necessary to stop these atrocities.

Why not? What would have to change in order to bring these atrocities to an end?

The war in Syria is really four different conflicts occurring in the same place. The core conflict is between the al-Assad regime and Syrian rebels trying to oust him. A second conflict is between al-Assad and Syria's ethnic Kurdish minority, whose goal it is to declare an independent Kurdish state in Northern and Eastern Syria, a long-standing goal of the Kurds in Turkey as well.

A third conflict involves the Islamic State (ISIS, or ISIL, or Daesh), which in 2014 captured significant territory in Syria and Iraq. ISIS has no allies and is essentially at war with all other factions involved in the conflict.

Finally, the entire situation in Syria (which, because of ISIS, crosses over into Iraq) is complicated by numerous outside actors, all of which are supporting one or another of the various local actors engaged in the conflict. Al-Assad's government is supported by Iran, Russia, and the Lebanese militant group Hezbollah. Various rebel groups (and there are dozens of them, some working together, others opposed to each other) are being supported by the United States (working with what it calls "the moderate opposition") and Saudi Arabia (the Saudis are intensely concerned about Iran's influence in Syria). Other Arab states—Jordan, Qatar, and the United Arab Emirates—are also supporting the rebels.

Security Council (in)action is rooted in the involvement of Russia and the United States in the conflict. The Council was able to unanimously adopt resolutions in 2013 and 2014 calling for the removal of chemical weapons from Syria (Resolution 2118). A second unanimous resolution (2139) demanded access for the delivery of humanitarian aid. All mention of sanctions, however, was stripped from the resolution to secure Russia's vote. Since then, the Russian military has significantly stepped up its support of the Assad regime in the form of direct military engagement (mostly by its air forces), under the guise of combatting ISIS and terrorism.

In October 2016, both U.N. secretary-general Ban Ki-moon and U.S. secretary of state John Kerry alleged Russian complicity in war crimes, insofar as its air campaign has deliberately targeted schools, hospitals, and other civilian targets. The Russians vetoed a 2014 draft resolution that would have referred the situation in Syria to the ICC prosecutor, based on a call by the Human Rights Council's Independent International Commission of Inquiry that all alleged violations of international human rights law be investigated. Russia (often with the support of China) has vetoed a number of other Security Council resolutions that would have demanded a halt to Syrian troop movements, the use of heavy weaponry in heavily populated areas, and overflights of cities such as eastern Aleppo and that would have levied sanctions on the al-Assad government for noncompliance. In each case, the Russians have called these resolutions "one sided" and blatant attempts to predetermine a political outcome—namely, the removal of the al-Assad regime from power. After the October 2016 veto, the U.N. emergency relief coordinator, Stephen O'Brien, told the Security Council, "I am more or less at my wits end as a human being. . . . [S]hame on all of us for not acting to stop the annihilation of Eastern Aleppo and its people and much of the rest of Syria." And there is no reason to expect 2017 to be any better as the government's use of chemical weapons in April in Khan Shaykun indicates.

Possible Solutions?

The case of Syria confronts us with a very harsh reality: without political will, of the international community cannot respond effectively to even the worst of human tragedies. The Syrian conflict is a perfect storm in many respects: it is in a highly unstable region, it involves many regional actors that are using the conflict to exert influence over the outcome (especially Turkey, Iran, and Saudi Arabia), and the conflict involves two of the most powerful states in the world—the United States and Russia—both of which will avoid finding themselves face to face on the ground or in the skies over Syria. The ghosts of Cold War–era politics walk in Syria.

The problem in Syria is not legal; it is political. The United States acted timidly throughout the early years of the crisis, only threatening to intervene as a coercive measure to compel the al-Assad regime to dismantle its chemical weapons stockpiles. This so-called "red line" response, however, received lukewarm domestic support in the United States and (perhaps thankfully) was taken off the table when Russia intervened diplomatically and convinced al-Assad to agree to join the Chemical Weapons Convention and allow Syria's stockpiles to be removed from the country. And Russia appears quite satisfied with how the situation is developing.

This example thus reminds us not to confuse international action with action by international organizations. Those organizations, which indeed usually are the most effective mechanisms for carrying out humanitarian interventions, can act only when the leading powers allow them to. And when it comes to the use of military force, great power backing—or at least the willingness of great powers not to veto acting—is essential. The problem of humanitarian inaction is essentially a problem of states not being willing to accept the costs necessary to solve the problem—or, as in the case of Russia in Syria, preferring to intervene in a conflict for geopolitical rather than humanitarian reasons.

Finally, it is worth taking seriously the possibility that Syria represents a process of successful learning from the debacles of intervention in Iraq and Libya. Debate will continue to rage over whether more aggressive action early in the civil war could have produced, if not a desirable outcome, a result far better than what actually occurred. There was no evidence of American or other Western willingness to shoulder a large and long-term burden of rebuilding a Syria that quite likely would have been wrecked by regime change. Quite the contrary, there was considerable evidence of unwillingness. Therefore, it is not clear that the very limited action Western states have been willing to undertake should be considered unjustified. If international actors are probably unable or unwilling to fix a problem, is nonintervention the better course of action?

Syria thus may be a reminder that sometimes *all* the politically viable options are unacceptable. This appears to be the justification of the Obama administration for its policies. And although it is by no means clear that such a justification should be accepted, it is no clearer that it should be rejected. Politics, both national and international, is, at best, the art of the possible. When the desirable is not realistically possible, the only question may be which tragedy will we participate in, through what particular combination of (ultimately unjustifiable) action and inaction.

Discussion Questions

1. How do you interpret the rapid switch from ethnic tolerance to violent ethnic mobilization in the former Yugoslavia? Clearly, we are not dealing with primordial animosities, especially in the case of Serbs and Croats, who had no significant political contact with one another until the twentieth century. But what do you imagine the relative mix was between deep but repressed animosities and the opportunistic manipulation of differences that led to social and political discrimination? Which explanation is more frightening?

2. Is there any moral or theoretical significance in the sharp discrepancy in responses to genocide and responses to other kinds of human rights violations? What *dangers* are posed to international human rights policies when we respond forcefully only to unusually photogenic suffering? In thinking about this issue, consider the analogy of relatively strong international responses to famine but much more modest responses to the more serious problem of malnutrition.

3. In recent years, there has been much talk of a clash of civilizations and the development of anti-Islamic attitudes in the West, especially in the United States. How does Bosnia fit into such arguments? Some have charged that the West did not do more because the Bosnians were Muslims. Others have pointed to the responses in Bosnia and in Kosovo to

show how the West was able to distinguish between politicized Islamists and ordinary adherents of one of the world's great religions. Which reading seems more correct?

4. The former Yugoslavia has been used in arguments about the place of race in contemporary Western foreign policies. Here the comparison is with Rwanda. Did the West do more to stop genocide in Croatia and Bosnia, because the victims were white, than in Rwanda, where the victims were black? What other explanations might there be? Is it as simple as the fact that the killing in Rwanda was over quickly? Remember the length of time it took to get the West seriously involved in Bosnia.

5. Bosnia and Rwanda illustrate a willingness to respond to genocide *after* it has occurred. Why is there no comparable international willingness to respond to *prevent* genocide? Is Kosovo the exception that proves the rule?

6. The war crimes tribunal for the former Yugoslavia, the parallel process for war crimes in Rwanda, and the creation of the International Criminal Court have finally introduced an element of personal international legal responsibility to human rights violations, at least in the case of genocidal warfare. This is obviously of great symbolic significance. But what is its practical value? In the particular cases? In the future? In answering these questions, try to recall the earlier discussions of the role of normative transformation and the relative strengths and weaknesses of individual petition procedures.

7. What *are* the lessons of Sudan and Syria? To what extent do these cases undercut the progress of the 1990s? Is this a question that can be answered confidently before we know what comes next?

8. Would the world be a better place if there were a responsibility to protect victims of genocide? What would the *costs* be? What about protection for victims of other human rights violations? Again, consider both benefits and costs.

9. Is justification for humanitarian intervention really as complex as suggested in this chapter? Or is it more a simple case of choosing between the obvious moral obligation to act against genocide and crimes against humanity and the unwillingness to pay the costs of discharging that obligation?

Suggested Readings

Readers looking for introductory book-length discussions have a number of choices. Two of the best are Thomas G. Weiss, *Humanitarian Intervention: Ideas in Action*, 3rd ed. (Cambridge: Polity Press, 2016); and Aidan Hehir, *Humanitarian Intervention: An Introduction*, 2nd ed. (Houndmills, UK: Palgrave Macmillan, 2013).

Although this chapter focuses its attention narrowly on international responses to genocide, readers are likely to be interested in further sources on the broader issue.

Adam Jones, *Genocide: A Comprehensive Introduction*, 2nd ed. (New York: Routledge, 2011), is a good starting point. Dinah L. Shelton, ed., *Encyclopedia of Genocide and Crimes Against Humanity* (Detroit: Macmillan Reference, 2005), is an authoritative three-volume reference work. Dale C. Tatum, *Genocide at the Dawn of the Twenty-First Century: Rwanda, Bosnia, Kosovo, and Darfur* (New York: Palgrave Macmillan, 2010), covers most of the cases considered in this chapter in more detail. Cathie Carmichael, *Genocide Before the Holocaust* (New Haven, CT: Yale University Press, 2009), provides historical background.

William A. Schabas, *Genocide in International Law: The Crime of Crimes*, 2nd ed. (Cambridge: Cambridge University Press, 2009), is authoritative. Ronald C. Slye and Beth Van Schaack, *International Criminal Law: Essentials* (New York: Aspen, 2009); and David Luban, Julie R. O'Sullivan, and David P. Stewart, *International and Transnational Criminal Law* (New York: Aspen, 2010), tackle the issue from the perspective of international criminal law more broadly.

Those with an interest in moral and political theory should profit from consulting Terry Nardin and Melissa S. Williams, eds., *Humanitarian Intervention* (New York: New York University Press, 2006); John K. Roth, ed., *Genocide and Human Rights: A Philosophical Guide* (Houndmills, UK: Palgrave Macmillan, 2005); and Larry May, *Genocide: A Normative Account* (Cambridge: Cambridge University Press, 2010).

Two brief readings stand out for thinking ethically about the broad issue of humanitarian intervention. The essential starting point is Michael Walzer, *Just and Unjust Wars* (New York: Basic Books, 1977), 53–63, 101–108. This classic book lays out a strong ethical-legal defense of sovereignty (as a reflection of the rights of individual and communal self-determination) and then argues no less powerfully for a limited right to humanitarian intervention in cases of enslavement or massacre that shock the moral conscience of mankind. Terry Nardin, "The Moral Basis of Humanitarian Intervention," *Ethics and International Affairs* 16 (2002): 57–70, is also essential reading, contrasting more statist defenses such as Walzer's with an alternative tradition that makes direct appeals to substantive principles of natural law and justice.

Much recent debate has been structured around *The Responsibility to Protect,* the report of the International Commission on Intervention and State Sovereignty (available online at http://responsibilitytoprotect.org/ICISS%20Report.pdf), which can be read as an effort both to codify the normative progress of the 1990s and to begin a conversation over a more robust doctrine of armed humanitarian intervention. For recent discussions of the responsibility to protect (R2P), see Cristina G. Badescu, *Humanitarian Intervention and the Responsibility to Protect: Security and Human Rights* (New York: Routledge, 2011); Philip Cunliffe, ed., *Critical Perspectives on the Responsibility to Protect: Interrogating Theory and Practice* (London: Routledge, 2011); Ramesh Thakur, *The Responsibility to Protect: Norms, Laws, and the Use of Force in International Politics* (London: Routledge, 2011); James Pattison, *Humanitarian Intervention and the Responsibility to Protect: Who Should Intervene?* (Oxford: Oxford University Press, 2010); and Alex J. Bellamy, *Responsibility to Protect: The Global Effort to End Mass Atrocities* (Cambridge: Polity Press, 2009).

There is now an immense international legal and political literature on humanitarian intervention. J. L. Holzgref and Robert O. Keohane, eds., *Humanitarian*

Intervention: Ethical, Legal, and Political Dilemmas (Cambridge: Cambridge University Press, 2003); and Jennifer M. Welsh, ed., *Humanitarian Intervention and International Relations* (Oxford: Oxford University Press, 2004), provide excellent statements of most leading mainstream perspectives. Nick Wheeler's *Saving Strangers: Humanitarian Intervention in International Society* (Oxford: Oxford University Press, 2000) is perhaps the best single book on the topic considered as an issue in international relations. It is particularly strong on Cold War–era practice and its transformation in the 1990s. Brendan Simms and D. J. B. Trim, eds., *Humanitarian Intervention: A History* (Cambridge: Cambridge University Press, 2011), provides historical context for contemporary practice.

On the broader U.N. role in armed humanitarianism, see Edward Newman, Roland Paris, and Oliver P. Richmond, eds., *New Perspectives on Liberal Peacebuilding* (Tokyo: United Nations University Press, 2009); William J. Durch, ed., *Twenty-First-Century Peace Operations* (Washington, DC: U.S. Institute of Peace and the Henry L. Stimson Center, 2006); and Mats Berdal and Spyros Economides, eds., *United Nations Interventionism, 1991–2004* (Cambridge: Cambridge University Press, 2007).

Among more critical perspectives, David Chandler's *From Kosovo to Kabul: Human Rights and International Intervention* (London: Pluto Press, 2002) is notable. He offers a spirited reading of the rise of so-called humanitarian interventions as an expression of American hegemony. David Rieff is a prolific journalist who has long been an insightful critic of armed humanitarianism. Two good examples of his work are *At the Point of a Gun: Democratic Dreams and Armed Intervention* (New York: Simon & Schuster, 2005); and *A Bed for the Night: Humanitarianism in Crisis* (New York: Simon & Schuster, 2002). Aidan Hehir, *Humanitarian Intervention After Kosovo: Iraq, Darfur, and the Record of Global Civil Society* (Houndmills, UK: Palgrave Macmillan, 2008), challenges the idea that a fundamental transformation took place in the 1990s.

Samantha Power, *"A Problem from Hell": America and the Age of Genocide* (New York: Basic Books, 2002), is a well-written, thoughtful, and engaging, even gripping, account that includes extended case studies of Bosnia, Rwanda, and Kosovo. Norrie MacQueen, *Humanitarian Intervention and the United Nations* (Edinburgh: Edinburgh University Press, 2011), focuses on Africa, the Balkans, and East Timor.

On the Kosovo intervention, Albrecht Schnabel and Ramesh Thakur, eds., *Kosovo and the Challenge of Humanitarian Intervention: Selective Indignation, Collective Action, and International Citizenship* (Tokyo: United Nations University Press, 2000), is the essential starting point. This remarkable volume not only covers broad issues such as sovereignty, citizenship, and responsibility but also includes a dozen excellent brief chapters on the foreign policies of the great powers as well as those of many smaller powers. The other essential source is the report of the Independent International Commission on Kosovo, available online at http://reliefweb .int/sites/reliefweb.int/files/resources/6D26FF88119644CFC1256989005CD392 -thekosovoreport.pdf.

The literature on Bosnia is extensive, but there is no obvious place to start, as with the volume on Kosovo by Schnabel and Thakur. Among the more useful books are Sabrina P. Ramet, *Balkan Babel: The Disintegration of Yugoslavia from the Death of Tito to the Fall of Milosevic,* 4th ed. (Boulder, CO: Westview, 2002); Tom Gallagher, *The Balkans After the Cold War: From Tyranny to Tragedy* (London: Routledge, 2003); Paul Mojzes, *Balkan Genocides: Holocaust and Ethnic Cleansing in the Twentieth Century* (Lanham, MD: Rowman & Littlefield, 2011); and Gerard Toal and Carl Dahlman, *Bosnia Remade: Ethnic Cleansing and Its Reversal* (New York: Oxford University Press, 2011). Misha Glenny, *The Balkans: Nationalism, War, and the Great Powers, 1804–1999* (New York: Viking, 2000), is a very readable volume that places the conflict in a broad historical setting. Jon Western, "Bosnia," in *Implementing U.S. Human Rights Policy,* edited by Debra Liang-Fenton (Washington, DC: U.S. Institute of Peace Press, 2004), is a good brief account of the American response.

On Rwanda, Michael Barnett, *Eyewitness to a Genocide: The United Nations and Rwanda* (Ithaca, NY: Cornell University Press, 2002), is excellent on the role of the United Nations. Christian P. Scherrer, *Genocide and Crisis in Central Africa* (Westport, CT: Praeger, 2002), places the genocide in a broader regional context. Mahmood Mamdani, *When Victims Become Killers: Colonialism, Nativism, and the Genocide in Rwanda* (Princeton, NJ: Princeton University Press, 2001), provides an excellent account of the development of ethnic conflict, showing very clearly that there was nothing "primordial" about it. See also Lee Ann Fujii, *Killing Neighbors: Webs of Violence in Rwanda* (Ithaca, NY: Cornell University Press, 2009).

For a good brief account of American (in)action, see Alison Desforges, "Learning from Disaster: U.S. Human Rights Policy in Rwanda," in Liang-Fenton, *Implementing U.S. Human Rights Policy,* 29–50. More broadly, see Linda Melvern, *A People Betrayed: The Role of the West in Rwanda's Genocide* (London: Zed Books, 2009); Andrew Wallis, *Silent Accomplice: The Untold Story of France's Role in the Rwandan Genocide* (London: I. B. Tauris, 2006); and Roméo Dallaire, with Brent Beardsley, *Shake Hands with the Devil: The Failure of Humanity in Rwanda* (New York: Carroll & Graf, 2005), by the U.N. commander in the field who saw the genocide coming, pleaded for additional forces, and was ignored.

On East Timor, the *Final Report of the Commission for Reception, Truth, and Reconciliation in East Timor* (available online at https://www.etan.org/news/2006 /cavr.htm) is a good place to start for further reading. See also Geoffrey Robinson, *"If You Leave Us Here, We Will Die": How Genocide Was Stopped in East Timor* (Princeton, NJ: Princeton University Press, 2010); Joseph Nevins, *A Not-So-Distant Horror: Mass Violence in East Timor* (Ithaca, NY: Cornell University Press, 2005); and Michael G. Smith and Moreen Dee, *Peacekeeping in East Timor: The Path to Independence* (Boulder, CO: Lynne Rienner, 2003).

Finally, the more recent cases (especially Sudan and Libya, but others as well) have generated considerable debate about the promises and pitfalls of the responsibility to protect doctrine. A full issue of the journal *Global Society* (Taylor & Francis), published in January 2016, was devoted to the topic of contesting and shaping the norms of protection with an emphasis on some of these recent cases. Another recent volume, Kurt Mills and David Karp, eds., *Human Rights Protection in Global Politics: Responsibilities of States and Non-State Actors* (Houndmills, UK: Palgrave Macmillan, 2015), devotes considerable attention to R2P and includes a full chapter on the Libyan case.

11

Globalization, the State, and Human Rights

It is difficult to talk about international relations today for more than a few minutes without at least raising the issue of globalization. (The other unavoidable issue, terrorism, is the subject of the next chapter.) What are the implications of globalization for human rights? We will focus on the web of interconnected processes that challenge the political, economic, and cultural primacy of the state, which, as we have seen, has principal responsibility for implementing human rights. Is globalization undermining the enforcement of human rights?

1. Globalization

Globalization is generally understood literally to mean the creation of structures and processes that span the entire globe. People, goods, and ideas increasingly move and interact across—even irrespective of—national territorial boundaries. Markets, politics, and culture become transnational, even global, rather than national.

Globalization, understood as the spread of capitalist markets and the growing transnational integration of systems of production and distribution, goes back at least to the maritime expansion of the West that began in the late fifteenth century. Similarly, today's telecommunications revolution, involving high-speed digital networks with ever-growing bandwidth, has a lineage that stretches back not just through television, radio, telephone, and telegraph but to steamships, railroads, and clipper ships. The globalizing spread of ideas and practices of electoral democracy and individual human rights builds on the centuries-old spread of sovereign territorial states and the incorporation of the entire globe into what was originally the European-states system.

Nonetheless, not only is it plausible to suggest that the pace of change has accelerated dramatically, but, moreover, important qualitative differences became evident in the decades on either side of the year 2000. Social, political, economic, and cultural action above, below, outside, around, and even without much concern for the state is much more of a practical reality for a much greater number of individuals and groups, in a much greater number of arenas and areas of concern, than it was for the preceding few centuries—which in many ways looks like the era of the nation-state.

Particularly striking is the interaction of material, institutional, and ideational change. For example, the growing transnational consolidation of capitalist markets has been accompanied by the spread of market ideologies and their enforcement by multilateral agencies (such as the World Bank, International Monetary Fund, and the World Trade Organization) and multinational banks and corporations. The spread of American or Western economic and political power has been matched by the spread of initially Western economic and political ideas and models—including human rights. Revolutions in telecommunication and transportation have even begun to alter how we conceive of ourselves and the communities in which our lives are embedded and how we relate to governmental power.

Sovereign states may have been the optimal size for economic, political, and social organization in the nineteenth and twentieth centuries. That is changing.

On the one hand, today they increasingly seem too small. Ever larger and stronger business enterprises are adopting a truly global form and outlook, causing even powerful states to lose control over aspects of their economies and polities, which they have been accustomed to dominating. Regional and international organizations increasingly influence, and sometimes even make, decisions that once were unquestionably the province of states. Transnational nongovernmental organizations now exert powerful and sophisticated pressures on states (and businesses) on issues such as human rights and the environment.

On the other hand, globalization often makes the state too large. Local and regional autonomy has become a common theme, especially (but not only) in Europe. Spain has perhaps gone the furthest among nonfederal states in devolving spending and decision-making powers to regional authorities, not just in the Basque and Catalan regions but throughout the country. Consider also the creation of the Scottish and Welsh Parliaments in the United Kingdom (and the nearly successful independence referendum in Scotland in 2014), the emergence of the Northern League as a powerful political force in Italy, and the revival of regional languages such as Breton in France and Frisian in the Netherlands. In many countries of the global South as well, demands for greater autonomy are often focused on an intrastate region rather than on creating a separate state. "Localization" has become another dimension of globalization.

In fact, the local and the global are increasingly linked without the intermediation of the state. Multinational business provides the most obvious example. But new information and transportation technologies also allow the disenfranchised to leap over their own (often hostile or indifferent) states. For example, Alison Brysk has shown how indigenous peoples in the Americas are able to interact with their colleagues and allies across the globe, dramatically improving their bargaining position vis-à-vis their own state.[1] This is a striking example of what Margaret Keck and Kathryn Sikkink call the "boomerang" model of transnational advocacy: local actors direct information and appeals to transnational colleagues, foreign states, and regional and international organizations, who respond by mobilizing external pressure on resistant states.[2]

Some of these new flows of structures, processes, and opportunities are empowering. The spread of human rights ideas, and their rise to global preeminence in the post–Cold War era, can be seen as an element of globalization. More prosaically, individuals and groups with shared interests increasingly are able to interact, in real time, over immense distances, without regard to the boundaries between (or the interests of) states. The Internet and modern transportation networks have allowed a growing number of communities in the global South to exploit the benefits of agricultural and craft cooperatives, fair-trade products, and alternative crops such as miniature vegetables for high-profit markets in developed countries. Mobile phones allow even small entrepreneurs in poor countries to make connections with customers and suppliers that open up previously unimagined possibilities for business and a better life for themselves and their families. Even antiglobalization protests have been significantly facilitated by global communications and transportation technologies.

However, other global flows that circumvent the state have a much darker side. Consider, for example, burgeoning transnational criminal enterprises, transnational human trafficking, sex tourism in Southeast Asia and the Caribbean, the use of social media to radicalize and recruit people to join terrorist groups, and the growing market in private security services. There is also an ominous side to the ability of large global firms to accumulate wealth and power that escapes national or international regulation.

No single chapter can even begin to approach the full range of human rights issues posed by globalization. Here we focus on one, namely, the challenge that economic globalization poses to the liberal democratic welfare state and to economic and social human rights.

2. States and Human Rights

States have done and will continue to do many nasty, even horrible, things to their citizens. In the 1970s and 1980s, such abuses were the focus of most human rights advocates. That made considerable sense then. Globalization, however, suggests that we might do well to focus more on the essential role that states play in implementing and protecting human rights.

As we have seen, most people enjoy their internationally recognized human rights, particularly when they require coercive enforcement, as a result of action taken by their own state. Even Europe's strong and effective regional human rights regime, as we saw in §6.1, is largely a supplement and spur to national action. In fact, the struggle of dispossessed groups has typically been a struggle for full legal and political recognition by the state, and thus inclusion among those whose rights are protected by the state. Human rights advocacy is in many ways aimed at transforming the state from predator to protector of rights.

This is no less true of economic and social rights than it is of civil and political rights. Classical political economists across the political spectrum, from Adam Smith to Karl Marx, stressed that market systems of production and distribution, by freeing productive forces from political constraints, have immensely liberating potential. But Smith no less than Marx also recognized that these same productive forces (and those who control them) are typically indifferent to the fates of individuals unable to compete successfully in the predatory world of capitalist competition. Historically, the only mechanism that has been able to protect individual rights in market systems has been the state.

Thus, a human rights perspective on the state is neither statist nor antistatist. Rather, human rights advocates seek to promote a specific type of state. The struggle for human rights has in many ways been a struggle to transform the state from the protector of a dominant economic and political elite into a guarantor of basic rights and equal concern and respect for all.

Globalization threatens "good" states as well as "bad" states. If liberal democratic welfare states are undermined by globalization—and if we fail to create alternative mechanisms for implementing and enforcing human rights—then the substantial achievements of the human rights movement since the end of World War II will be at risk.

3. Markets and Liberal Democratic Welfare States

The state envisioned by contemporary international human rights norms is liberal; that is, its legitimacy rests on protecting the human rights of its citizens. It is democratic, in the sense that it is committed to universal political participation and, within the limits of the human rights of all, vests political power in the people. It is also a welfare state, with extensive economic and social obligations to protect and promote the well-being of all citizens. As we saw in Chapter 4, the state has a wide variety and range of obligations and duties with respect to economic and social rights, from creating and maintaining economic conditions that are conducive to sustained economic activity, to regulating markets, to serving as "provider of last resort" for those in absolute dire need.

In practice, though, the experience of the Cold War and decolonization eras showed that economic and social rights can be widely and sustainably provided only to the extent that markets are central to the national economy (which today is increasingly integrated into a global market-based economy). The inefficiencies of centrally planned or command economies almost always swamp any equity benefits, at least in the medium and long runs. Countries such as Cuba and Sri Lanka did achieve notable short- and medium-run success in the 1960s and 1970s. In the long run, though, neither growth nor equity has proved to be possible within a command economy. A considerable degree of economic efficiency, and thus reliance on markets, is necessary for *sustainable* progress in implementing economic and social rights.

States, however, have at least two vital economic roles. They must facilitate the operation of markets, in order to foster growth. And they must redistribute resources and opportunities, to ensure that growth contributes to the enjoyment of economic and social rights by all.

Markets, by design, distribute the benefits of growth without regard for individual needs and rights (other than property rights). Markets seek economic efficiency—that is, maximizing the total quantity of goods and services produced with a given quantity of resources. Markets promise to produce more overall, not more for all.

Market distributions take into account only economic value added, which varies sharply across individuals and social groups. Free markets thus *necessarily* produce gross economic inequalities. The poor tend to be "less efficient": as a class, they have fewer of the skills valued highly by markets. Their plight is then exacerbated when political disadvantage contributes to a vicious rights-abusive cycle. Efficient markets improve the lot of some—ideally even many—at the cost of (relative and perhaps even absolute) deprivation of others. And that suffering is concentrated among society's most vulnerable elements.

Advocates of markets readily admit that some are harmed, especially in the short run. Everyone, though, is supposed to benefit in the long run from the greater supply of goods and services. "Everyone," however, does not mean each and every individual. Rather, economists refer to the *average* individual, an entirely abstract per capita entity. And even the average person is assured of significant gain only at some point in the future. Here, now, and in the near future, many real flesh-and-blood individual human beings and families suffer. Even worse, because markets distribute the benefits of growth without regard to short-term deprivations, those who suffer adjustment costs—lost jobs, higher food prices, inferior health care—acquire no special claim to a future share of the collective benefits of efficient markets.

Although markets rely on individual initiative, they ground a collectivist, utilitarian political theory. Markets are justified by arguments of collective good and aggregate benefit, not individual rights (other than, perhaps, the right to economic accumulation). Free markets are an economic analogue to a political system of majority rule without minority rights. The welfare state, from this perspective, is a device to ensure that a minority that is disadvantaged in or deprived by markets is still treated with minimum economic concern and respect. Only when the pursuit of prosperity is tamed by economic and social rights—when markets are embedded in a welfare state—does a market-based economy merit our respect.

Without welfare states (or other comparable redistributive mechanisms), there is no necessary connection between market-led growth and development and the enjoyment of economic and social rights or *human* development and welfare. This is the basis of the welfare states that Westerners take for granted. All existing liberal democracies use the welfare state to compensate (some of) those who fare less well in the market.

Individuals who are harmed by the operation of social institutions (markets and private property rights) that benefit the whole are entitled to a fair share of the social product their participation has helped to produce. The collectivity that benefits in the aggregate has an obligation to look after individual members who are disadvantaged in or harmed by markets. The welfare state guarantees *all* individuals certain economic and social goods, services, and opportunities, irrespective of the market value of their labor.

In fact, one of the great human rights achievements of the past century has been the humanization of capitalist markets by welfare states. State regulation of hours, wages, and working conditions is widely accepted (in theory at least) in most countries throughout the world. Furthermore, the citizens of most states—not simply those with developed market economies—consider their governments to be obliged to provide minimum levels of subsistence, housing, health care, and social services to those unable to acquire them through family or market mechanisms.

The welfare state today, however, is under assault from economic globalization. As an international division of labor continues to develop, leading to a growing separation between locales of production and consumption, firms are increasingly free to move offshore, in whole or in part, to escape the higher costs imposed by welfare state guarantees of economic and social rights. States, by contrast, for all their power, remain largely tied to and limited by a particular territory. The resulting threats to economic and social rights are equally evident in the developed market economies of the global North, where benefits have already begun to erode, and in much of the developing world, where market-based reforms targeting waste and inefficiency also typically reduce social welfare expenditures. And in both North and South, growing numbers of voters are increasingly unwilling to support the state budgets necessary to assure all economic and social rights for all. (Health care in the United States is a particularly striking example.)

4. Market Democracy and American Foreign Policy

One result of these changes has been a very particular convergence of markets, human rights, and political power in the idea of "market democracy," a vision of national and international political legitimacy that is arguably a central part of the process of globalization in the early twenty-first century. Although markets and democracy certainly are good things, especially when contrasted to the alternatives of command economies and authoritarian or totalitarian rule, we will emphasize that they are not the same good things as human rights.

A. Democracy, Democratization, and Human Rights

Democracy answers the question of *who* should rule. Democracy empowers the people and seeks to realize their collective good. Human rights, by contrast, address *how* governments should rule. Human rights empower autonomous individuals. They seek to ensure that personal and societal goals, including democratically defined goals, are pursued within the confines of guaranteeing every individual certain minimum goods, services, opportunities, and protections.

Human rights define the range within which democratic decision making is allowed to operate. They are concerned with each rather than all, aiming to protect every person, against majorities no less than against minorities. Human rights ordinarily take precedence over the wishes of the people, no matter how intensely even the vast majority of society desires to abuse some individual or group. In fact, in procedurally democratic states, where the majority is relatively well positioned to care for its own rights and interests, the *principal* function of human rights is to limit democratic decision making.

The post–Cold War world has seen the continued spread and deepening of electoral democracy. For the first time in history, the majority of people on this planet live under democratically elected governments. This momentous achievement is a source of legitimate satisfaction. We must not, however, overestimate its human rights significance. In particular, we must not confuse decreased tolerance for old forms of repressive rule with support for, let alone institutionalization of, rights-protective regimes. We can distinguish three levels of political progress toward respect for internationally recognized human rights.

Liberalization involves a decrease in human rights violations and an opening of political space for at least some previously excluded groups—roughly, progress in civil and political rights short of democratization. China has undergone periodic limited liberalizations. Poland liberalized in the 1980s, initially under the pressure of the Solidarity movement, before it democratized in 1990. South Korea liberalized in the 1980s before establishing electoral democracy in the 1990s.

By *democratization,* we mean the process of establishing electoral democracy, which involves a qualitative leap beyond liberalization. When "soft" authoritarian regimes allow truly fair and open elections (not just once or if they win), the political system is fundamentally transformed.

A *rights-protective regime* both makes the protection of internationally recognized human rights a central element of its mission and, through extensive, intense, and sustained effort, has achieved considerable success in realizing this aspiration. This is *liberal* democracy. If one insists on using the language of democratization to describe transitions from electoral to liberal democracy, one might talk about the "deepening" of democratization—although it is respect for human rights, rather than for the will of the people, that deepens.

Although only the second of these three processes is centrally connected with democracy understood in the core sense of rule of the people—the distinction between electoral and liberal democracy concerns not who rules but how (within what limits), and liberalization too is concerned with the limits on government rather than who rules—the term *democratization* is often used to cover all three kinds of change, on the assumption that they are phases of a single, largely linear process of development. Political development, however, is not naturally driven toward a single end. Resistance to authoritarian rule is often not a transition to democracy, or anything else, but a reaction against injustice—Egypt in the wake of the 2011 Arab Spring provides a perfect example. Regimes that have liberalized often resist democratization. Even fair and moderately open elections may produce governments that violate human rights.

One of the most disturbing lessons of democratization in Eastern Europe and Central Asia since the end of the Cold War is that many people see voting as a device for acquiring prosperity and a sense of control rather than a way to ensure widespread protection of human rights. Even more disturbing are the cases where the majority seeks electoral power to oppress a minority—or a minority hijacks the electoral process to oppress the majority.

Electoral democracy may be a necessary condition for liberal democracy. Liberalization and electoral democracy may even foster liberal democracy by allowing human rights advocates political space and opportunities. But there is no natural, inescapable evolution. Electorally democratic governments may use their power in ways that violate, threaten, or fail to defend internationally recognized human rights. (Consider the reductions in access to health care promised by Republicans in the wake of the 2016 national elections in the United States.) Especially in times of crisis or disillusionment, electoral democracy may even be prone to populist, protofascist demagoguery. (This sentence, we want to note, remains unchanged from the fourth edition of 2013.)

Elections are only a device. They have very different meanings in different political contexts. All other things being equal, it is a good thing if leaders are freely chosen and speak for the people. What is most important, though, is whether human rights are secure. Only when supported by rights-protective political attitudes and institutions will elections lead toward deeply liberal democratic regimes.

The danger, especially in U.S. foreign policy, is that we will forget that democratization is, at best, a good start on realizing human rights. Americans seem inclined to the convenient but dangerous illusion that, once elections have been held, the struggle for human rights—or at least America's part in the struggle—is largely over. Often, in fact, that is when the real struggle begins.

B. Market Democracy and Economic Rights

Americans also too often forget how heavily the U.S. government is involved in regulating markets and attempting to counteract the social inequities they produce. Not even Ronald Reagan proposed returning to anything even approximating a true free-market economy. Twentieth-century liberal democracies were distinguished from free-market capitalism by redistributive policies that protect individual rights and seek social justice. And although in this postfact era we sometimes hear free-market pundits and politicians call for crippling or even dismantling government regulatory agencies, most really seek only to reduce state intervention and regulation. (For example, Senator Rand Paul speaks for almost no one other than mine owners—and perhaps not even a majority of them—when he calls for abolishing federal mine safety regulations and regulators.) Furthermore, most such pleas (suspiciously) affect the enjoyment of the rights of others, not the rights of the advocates of such measures.

Despite all the gaps in its coverage, the United States is a huge welfare state. For example, workers and employers together are taxed one-seventh of an employee's income just to fund a single social welfare program: state-supported old-age pensions (Social Security). The protection of robust benefits through Medicare (health insurance for the elderly) is even more sacred. Even Americans, who are more individualistic and antistatist than most Europeans, see their welfare state as an essential part of the American political ideal.

In American foreign policy, however, sometimes it seems as if all one hears about is markets. When dealing with countries still shaped by the legacy of command economies, the allure of the market is perhaps understandable. However, American advocacy of markets in the former Soviet bloc and the Third World ignores their significant human costs. There is a disturbing parallel with Cold War anticommunism: excessive focus on the problem (communism, command economies) yields inattention to the unintended consequences of the solution (dictators, markets).

This was particularly true for American support of IMF-imposed structural adjustment programs in the 1980s and 1990s. Structural adjustment almost always had immediate and detrimental short-term effects on the enjoyment of economic rights by large segments of the population. Reductions in state spending on education and health, retrenchments in public-sector employment, declining real wages, and programs to privatize land leave the poor even more vulnerable than they were before. In addition, the political unpopularity of often-punitive cuts in social services may disrupt the pace and process of political liberalization and democratization.

We do not mean to suggest that even punishing structural adjustment, or today's penchant for austerity, is always the wrong course of action, all things considered. Each country is unique. There are difficult trade-offs that need to be made between competing goals and time frames. Furthermore, practice shows that program implementation is at least as important as program design in determining human rights consequences. But such problems need to be confronted, seriously and directly, rather than brushed aside with appeals to the general virtues of markets.

Neither do we mean to belittle the problems faced in implementing economic and social rights or the contribution of properly regulated markets. Markets, to repeat, are necessary. It is essential, though, to give equal emphasis to the fact that they are not sufficient.

We do not even want to deny that some countries may face a tragic choice between growth and equity. But where victims of market-driven growth truly cannot be prevented (at a reasonable cost), they must be acknowledged and mourned. Instead, in their enthusiasm for sweeping away the old, Americans too often seem not to see, let alone be troubled by, the problems in the new.

5. An Alliance of States and Human Rights Advocates?

If the welfare state is increasingly unable to ensure economic and social rights for all, regional or global institutions might seem to present an obvious solution. The problem, of course, is that there is little evidence of the imminent emergence of global (or, outside of Europe, even regional) redistributive institutions. Virtually all states, including even well-to-do and committed liberal democratic welfare states, remain extremely reluctant to transfer substantial authority or resources to supranational political institutions.

Nonetheless, interstate mechanisms are not necessarily doomed to failure. For example, the harmonization of social policies in the European Union can be viewed as a collective regional effort to reduce the incentives of individual states to compete for jobs by dismantling the welfare state. Europe, however, looks very much like the exception that proves the rule. And even the Europeans seem uninterested in using the Organisation for Economic Co-operation and Development, or some new institution, to spread cooperation on social policy across a wider range of developed market economies. The Eurozone crisis of 2011–2013 suggests a deep reluctance to bear substantial costs even on behalf of other EU members. And the 2016 decision by voters in the United Kingdom to leave the European Union (Brexit) demonstrates that economic globalization can provoke a democratic nationalist backlash—in this case, seeing workers from the rest of the Union as a threat to the economic security of Britain (and especially England outside of relatively cosmopolitan London).

Transnational actors offer another potential mechanism for revitalizing economic and social rights. Human rights NGOs, trade unions, women's groups, environmentalists, indigenous peoples, and a host of other groups in civil society share a common interest in (re)asserting welfare state control over global markets and multinational business. Civil society actors, however, are at an extreme disadvantage, both because of their relative lack of economic and political resources and because they face far greater problems in forming national and transnational alliances. In addition, although not as territorially bound as states, they are usually less mobile than the businesses against whom they are pitted.

The current international situation with respect to economic and social rights has parallels to conditions in Western Europe in the mid-nineteenth century, where business had the upper hand and skillfully used its resources to protect its interests. Contemporary multinational businesses also have the advantage of being able to play country against country—and in the United States, because of its federal system, state against state. Those seeking to strengthen the welfare state, by contrast, face the daunting task of (re)establishing control. Multinational businesses need only evade regulation.

Advocates of economic and social rights, however, have resources of their own, including national electoral power and advanced communications technologies that increase their capabilities for national and transnational organization. Efforts such as these were particularly effective—to an extent—at raising awareness at home about growing income inequality in the United States in the aftermath of the 2008–2009 financial meltdown. Furthermore, unlike in the nineteenth century, they can draw on the moral force of authoritative international human rights norms and the accumulated experience of many decades of welfare state policies.

In addition, advocates of internationally recognized economic and social rights share a common interest with at least some government elites in controlling transnational business. Especially in highly institutionalized liberal democratic welfare states, human rights advocates and states share a deeply rooted desire to temper the efficiency of markets with rights-based concerns for at least minimally equitable distributions of social goods, services, and opportunities. Of course, state elites often seek control over business for their own selfish, even predatory, purposes. But even then their shared desire to gain greater control over corporate practices and profits provides the basis for at least tactical political alliances with human rights advocates.

Once again, the issue is not the state per se but the *type* of state. Transnational businesses are using economic globalization to press for a state that gives greater emphasis to markets, the domain of social action where their power and skills are greatest. On the other side, human rights advocates and allied elements of civil society are seeking to use their electoral, organizational, and moral power on behalf of welfare states. Thus, the fate of human rights is likely to depend, in the early twenty-first century, as in the late nineteenth and early twentieth centuries, on who controls the state and how they use that control. In those countries where human rights advocates are maintaining or strengthening their position, an alliance with the state may prove the best way to reestablish the social control over markets necessary to ensure economic and social rights for all—although the rise of populist nationalism in Europe and the United States in 2015 and 2016 has weakened the position of national as well as transnational human rights advocates.

The fundamental fact of globalization, however, is that, like it or not, no individual state acting alone is able to impose new regulations or even hold onto its former ability to control its own firms, let alone its own economy. States and other international actors must cooperate, regionally and internationally, if they are to have a chance of humanizing global markets. And they must forge new alliances with national and transnational civil society actors. Whether this is practically possible, however, is by no means clear.

My enemy's enemy is my friend, the old rule of realist international politics, applies today to states and human rights advocates. Whatever their past animosities, today they face a new common enemy. The future of human rights just might be determined by their ability to develop new forms of cooperation that protect the state as an essential mechanism for realizing human rights—at least until new mechanisms are created, which still seems, at best, very far off in a speculative future.

A central purpose of human rights advocacy has always been to empower people to force their state to treat them as they deserve to be treated—shaping states into instruments to protect, rather than ignore or even trample on, the human rights of their citizens. This has always required states and citizens to stand up to, and attempt to exert control over, transnational and global, not merely national, forces. That struggle continues. Human rights demand that it must continue. At the beginning of 2017, though, we worry that some of the hard-won human rights progress of the twentieth century may be at significant risk and that, in the near future at least, more of the work of human rights advocacy will be about holding the line rather than about raising the bar.

Problem 8: The Global North and South and Market Redistributions

The Problem

Globalization has eroded the capacity of welfare states in the global North to provide economic and social rights at the levels to which their populations had become accustomed. Other factors, including demographic changes and politically motivated overcommitments to beneficiaries, are also part of the explanation. But the new global division of labor has undoubtedly reduced the number of well-paid, low- and moderately skilled jobs available in developed market economies. This simultaneously creates new demands for benefits and restricts the ability of states to fund those benefits by taxing increasingly peripatetic firms.

But is this really a global human rights problem, all things considered? Aren't the same global market forces dramatically raising incomes in numerous countries in the global South? In fact, given the much greater marginal utility of improvements for poor people in the global South compared to the losses likely to be suffered by middle-class beneficiaries in the global North, is not the net human rights impact of economic globalization positive?

A Solution

The extension of market efficiencies to regions previously suffering under closed or command economies certainly is a good thing for economic and social rights. It creates new goods, services, and opportunities that can be mobilized to better provide economic and social rights for a much greater segment of the population (and perhaps also improve their capacities to demand and enjoy civil and political rights as well). But there is no *automatic* mechanism that ensures that the losses of relatively privileged workers in the global North will be transformed into improved economic and social rights for large numbers of people in the global South.

We must not confuse a transfer of resources from North to South with improvements in the enjoyment of economic and social rights in the South. The crucial question is how those transferred resources are distributed in particular southern countries. Were most of the benefits to go to a small elite—which is a particularly plausible possibility in the case of mineral and timber resources—the net effect might even be negative.

In addition, some portion of the resources lost by workers in the global North is going into the pockets of northern capitalists, rather than workers in the global South. Much depends on questions such as wage rates and working conditions in the new countries of production and the tax and spending policies of their governments. And those are a function of both local conditions and the possibility of firms moving their production to more "business-friendly" environments.

On balance the living conditions of workers in many countries in the global South have improved dramatically as a result of the new global division of labor. This has been most striking in several rapidly growing Asian countries, especially China, where between 1981 and 2010 *nearly 700 million people(!)* escaped extreme poverty, largely due to economic globalization, reducing the percentage of the Chinese population forced to endure a life of extreme poverty from more than 80 percent to barely 10 percent. But it is increasingly true in other regions as well. For example, over eight of the past ten years, Africa grew more rapidly than did Asia (including Japan). And even when governments have not been particularly concerned with redistribution or directly providing economic and social rights, in numerous countries their people are enjoying better food, better housing, better health care, and better protection against economic fluctuations. (Remember that private provision is central, even the norm, for many economic and social rights, even in the global North.)

This has been dependent on the fact that, so far at least, globalization has been a highly positive sum game; that is, it has increased the total pie, not just redistributed it. For example, real global gross domestic product (GDP), measured in 2005 dollars, increased from about $29 trillion in 1990 to almost $78 trillion in 2014. Some significant part of this growth can be attributed to the increasing globalization of production. And that has made available the aggregate resources necessary to support widespread improvements in the enjoyment of economic and social rights.

Any deterioration in the enjoyment of any human rights by anyone anywhere is a legitimate matter of concern for human rights advocates, not to mention the people whose rights are at issue. Nonetheless, these particular losses of northern workers—which, especially in Europe, have so far been extremely modest—would seem, on balance, to be a matter of relatively low concern in a broad, global human rights assessment. Nevertheless, populist rhetoric concerning the effects of globalization on domestic labor markets has led to victories at the ballot box for more inward-focused, nationalistic, and xenophobic candidates who promise to challenge these trends—as in the United States with President Donald J. Trump's assertion that he will "make America great again."

Further Problems

We should not, however, confuse averages, or even the norm, with every case. Consider, for example, Nigeria, which has largely squandered its immense oil wealth in a kleptocratic orgy by a tiny elite. Teodoro Obiang Nguema Mbasogo, who has held power in Equatorial Guinea since 1979, is another egregious example—one of the most impoverished countries of the world led by a brutal dictator with a net worth of more than $600 million.

Economic globalization can be, but need not be, a boon to human rights. This is another way of saying that markets are a necessary but not sufficient condition for sustained improvements in economic and social rights.

Furthermore, it is not obvious that sacrifices by northern workers, either to date or in the future, are *necessary* for the improvement of economic and social rights in the global South. Fair trade rather than free trade *might* be a better formula for improving human rights for all.

Finally, the prospect of global firms being able to redirect a growing percentage of the benefits of national and international markets to themselves needs to remain a major concern of human rights advocates. In the long run, mechanisms comparable to national welfare states will be necessary to ensure that capitalism does not revert to the gross inequalities and inequities that led *all* developed market economies to establish highly redistributive welfare states. As the world begins to work itself out from the global recession of the late 2000s, this may prove to be the most important issue it faces for the future of economic and social rights.

Discussion Questions

1. When you use the term *globalization,* what exactly do you mean? Is it a recent phenomenon or a long-term process? What are its dimensions? Is the global spread of human rights itself a phenomenon of globalization?
2. Human rights advocates typically focus on states as a threat to human rights. This chapter suggests that globalization is forcing human rights

advocates to emphasize the role of the state as protector. Has there really been a change? Has not the role of the state as protector always been central?

3. Is the welfare state really such a wonderful achievement? Is globalization making a positive contribution by freeing economic initiative from the shackles of excessive welfare state regulation? Can we not see the shift produced by globalization in the balance of power away from states as basically a positive trend? Why do advocates of liberal democratic welfare states want the state in our lives economically but out of our lives in other domains?

4. How would you evaluate the distinction drawn among liberalization, democratization, and creating a rights-protective regime? Applying this distinction and the post–Cold War history of the former Soviet bloc, what does it say about other countries in the global South that regularly hold elections? Are we correct that this distinction is especially (or only?) important for Americans, who tend to focus on the formalities of democratization, often to the exclusion of the real substance of protecting human rights?

5. Why are Americans, who claim to be so individualistic, so attracted to democracy and markets, which are fundamentally collective systems of political justification? What kind of individualism is it that Americans really value?

6. The United States and several countries in (Western) Europe have recently turned toward more conservative or right-wing politicians, largely because of slow recoveries and job losses associated with the recent financial crisis, austerity measures, and globalization in general. In their own way, these political actors promise economic rights in terms of new jobs garnered by closing the tap on globalization pressures. Is this the right way forward, for economic recovery/growth *and* for human rights?

Suggested Readings

Perhaps the best discussion of human rights and globalization available is Rhoda E. Howard-Hassmann, *Can Globalization Promote Human Rights?* (University Park: Pennsylvania State University Press, 2010). Her answer to the title question is a strong but qualified yes—if the efficiencies of global markets can be harnessed to human development in ways comparable to those used by liberal and social democratic welfare states in the twentieth century. An article-length version of Howard-Hassmann's argument is also available: "The Second Great Transformation: Human Rights Leap-frogging in the Era of Globalization," *Human Rights Quarterly* 27 (February 2005): 1–40. A similar and in many ways complementary argument is developed in David Kinley, *Civilising Globalisation: Human Rights and the Global Economy* (Cambridge: Cambridge University Press, 2009). For a much more negative assessment, see Neve Gordon, ed., *From the Margins of Globalization: Critical Perspectives on Human Rights* (Lanham, MD: Lexington Books, 2004). For a balanced assessment of structural adjustment, see M. Rodwan Abouharb and David Cingranelli, *Human Rights and Structural Adjustment* (Cambridge: Cambridge University Press, 2007).

Good and generally wide-ranging discussions can be found in the following books: Wolfgang Benedek, Koen De Feyter, and Fabrizio Marrella, eds., *Economic Globalisation and Human Rights* (Cambridge: Cambridge University Press, 2007); Janet Dine and Andrew Fagan, eds., *Human Rights and Capitalism: A Multidisciplinary Perspective on Globalisation* (Cheltenham: Edward Elgar, 2006); Jean-Marc Coicaud, Michael W. Doyle, and Anne-Marie Gardner, eds., *The Globalization of Human Rights* (Tokyo: United Nations University Press, 2003); and Alison Brysk, ed., *Globalization and Human Rights* (Berkeley: University of California Press, 2002).

On the huge topic of the movement to establish human rights obligations for corporations, good introductions are available in Chapter 3 of Allison Brysk, *Human Rights, Private Wrongs* (New York: Routledge, 2005); and Chapter 8 of David P. Forsythe, *Human Rights and International Relations*, 3rd ed. (Cambridge: Cambridge University Press, 2012).

On the ethical dimensions of the topic, good places to start are Thomas Pogge, ed., *Freedom from Poverty as a Human Right: Who Owes What to the Very Poor?* (Oxford: Oxford University Press, 2007); and Daniel E. Lee and Elizabeth J. Lee, *Human Rights and the Ethics of Globalization* (New York: Cambridge University Press, 2010). Among the more interesting sustained explorations we would single out David Miller, *National Responsibility and Global Justice* (Oxford: Oxford University Press, 2007) and Thomas Pogge, *World Poverty and Human Rights: Cosmopolitan Responsibilities and Reforms* (Cambridge: Polity Press, 2008).

For interesting discussions that link democracy, globalization, and human rights, see Deen K. Chatterjee, ed., *Democracy in a Global World: Human Rights and Political Participation in the 21st Century* (Lanham, MD: Rowman & Littlefield, 2008); and Nicolas Guilhot, *The Democracy Makers: Human Rights and International Order* (New York: Columbia University Press, 2005).

12

(Anti)Terrorism and Human Rights

Since September 11, 2001, the rise of terrorism as a threat to states and international order has raised significant challenges for human rights. We have experienced an ongoing and somewhat coordinated global response to terrorism, especially by the United States and Europe, that has included armed military interventions to "disrupt and destroy" terrorist groups and activities in many parts of the world. The targets of these efforts have been both states (e.g., Afghanistan in 2001–2002) and (usually Islamist) terrorist organizations or groups based in a variety of weak or recalcitrant states, including Boko Haram in Nigeria, AQIM (Al-Qaeda in the Islamic Maghreb) in Algeria and Mali, al-Shabaab in Somalia, AQAP (Al-Qaeda in the Arabian Peninsula) in Yemen, Jabhat Fateh al-Sham (formerly al-Nusra) in Syria, and ISIL/ISIS in Iraq and Syria.

The *Oxford English Dictionary* notes that originally "terrorist" practices were used by governments or ruling groups, usually through paramilitaries, to maintain control over their population. It defines *terrorism,* though, as "the unofficial or unauthorized use of violence and intimidation in support of political aims." We adopt this definition here—not because state terrorism is not an important problem but because it is both a different problem and a problem that can best be seen as basically an extreme form of ordinary human rights violations.

This chapter explores the special challenges for human rights in our era of the "war on terror." In many countries, the threat of terrorism has provided a convenient excuse to thwart efforts to improve the enjoyment of human rights. Even in well-established liberal democracies, the ways in which terrorism is framed as a threat (e.g., use of the term *radical* Islamic *terrorism*) has created an atmosphere of fear, prompting government policies that violate internationally recognized human rights.

After a brief overview of terrorism and human rights law, we will closely examine the post-9/11 environment, focusing on American policy. The war on terror initiated by the Bush administration after 9/11 brought down two governments (in

Afghanistan and Iraq) and, in its unilateral exuberance, threatened others as well. The early Obama years saw a somewhat more nuanced approach to antiterrorism. Since 2012, however, new challenges have arisen, which we discuss at the end of the chapter.

1. International Human Rights Law and the Dilemmas of Counterterrorism

Terrorism poses a threat to internal order and security. As this strikes at the heart of the primary purpose of the state, an aggressive response by states is not only understandable but demanded. Even well-meaning responses, however, often sit uncomfortably with respecting and protecting human rights.

International human rights law recognizes that human rights are not absolute. Most notably, Article 4 of the International Covenant on Civil and Political Rights allows a state to suspend or curtail *some* human rights to respond to situations that "threaten the life of the nation."

In such circumstances, however, there must be a public declaration (e.g., of a state of emergency) and the measures must be of limited duration. In addition, infringements of human rights may not be arbitrary and must respect the rule of law (for example, by allowing judicial oversight or review of actions undertaken by governmental authorities). And Article 4 absolutely prohibits derogations (legally justifiable infringements or denials) of many of the rights enumerated in the Covenant, including rights to life; recognition as a person before the law; freedom of thought, conscience, and religion; and protections against torture, slavery, and ex post facto laws (which criminalize behavior that was not a crime at the time the act was committed).

The U.N. Security Council, Human Rights Council, and General Assembly have adopted numerous resolutions in an attempt to balance the real security needs of states with their human rights obligations. For example, the General Assembly noted[1] the following counterterrorism actions that states have undertaken that are highly problematic in terms of human rights:

- The detention of persons suspected of acts of terrorism in the absence of a legal basis for detention and due process guarantees
- The deprivation of liberty that amounts to placing a detained person outside the protection of the law
- The trial of suspects without fundamental judicial guarantees
- The illegal deprivation of liberty and transfer of individuals suspected of terrorist activities
- The return of suspects to countries without individual assessment of substantial grounds for believing that they would be in danger of subjection to torture
- Limitations to effective scrutiny of counterterrorism measures

And, of course, measures such as torture and arbitrary execution, which international human rights law holds can never be legally permissible, have been undertaken in the name of combatting terrorism, as well as less extreme but equally impermissible measures that discriminate on the basis of religion (especially the Muslim faith), ethnicity, or national origin.

Nonetheless, in thinking about terrorism and human rights, the starting point must be the fact that even the most genuine desire to respond to unquestionable threats posed by self-identified terrorists can *at most* justify only modest and short-lived restrictions on some (but not all) internationally recognized human rights—and then only to the extent that such restrictions are both necessary and proportional. In many countries, most antiterrorism efforts have indeed fully respected international human rights obligations, especially when it is the rights of citizens that are at stake. Even there, though, most governments and their citizens have struggled with their natural inclination to sacrifice human rights to the imperatives of combatting terrorism. In other countries, antiterrorism has become just one more excuse to expand a regime's repertoire of rights-abusive practices. And we are aware of no country with an extensive antiterrorism program that has not seen some of its practices subjected to legitimate questions about an unjustifiably negative impact on the equal enjoyment of all human rights by all citizens and others under its jurisdiction.

In other words, antiterrorism poses real challenges to respecting human rights even when a government has the best of intentions. And when it does not, antiterrorism has become a new twenty-first-century language that states use to claim that *they* really are not bound to respect internationally recognized human rights.

2. The War on Terror and the Retreat of Human Rights

Although terrorism is hardly new, the spectacular nature of the attacks on New York and Washington, DC, on September 11, 2001, where al-Qaeda operatives slammed two hijacked planes into the World Trade Center and a third into the Pentagon, shocked the world. Within a week, in unscripted remarks, President George W. Bush called for a "crusade, [a] war on terrorism." On September 20, in a speech to a joint session of Congress, Bush remarked that "our 'war on terror' begins with al-Qaeda, but it does not end there. It will not end until every terrorist group of global reach has been found, stopped, and defeated."

Three days after the attacks, the U.S. Congress passed a sweepingly broad authorization for the president to use "all necessary and appropriate force against those nations, organizations, or persons he determines planned, authorized, committed, or aided the terrorist attacks that occurred on 11 September 2001, or harbored such organizations or persons, in order to prevent any future acts of international terrorism against the United States by such nations, organizations or persons." This authorization of both punitive/retributive and preventative action, which remains in force to this day, initiated a dramatic shift in American foreign policy priorities.

Since the first few years of the war on terror, we have witnessed significant changes in orientation on terrorism, from the initial crusade toward more nuanced policies late in the Bush administration and early in the Obama administration and, more ominously, a shift to more hard-line policies with the rise of ISIS/ISIL in Iraq and Syria. In sharp contrast to the golden age of the first decade of the post–Cold War era, which saw a clear and even dramatic increase in the attention paid to international human rights and democracy, international human rights policies often have not fared well when they ran up against the war on terror.

Initially, as during the Cold War, countries formerly considered to be inimical or hostile to American interests were suddenly transformed into allies. Consider Pakistan, which in the official American representation went from a retrograde military dictatorship—and one that, in addition, was a major supporter of international terrorism, the preceding decade's most flagrant violator of the nuclear nonproliferation regime, and a bellicose threat to regional security in South Asia—to a leading American ally. And, despite the lack of any substantial human rights improvements or any progress toward real democracy in Pakistan, the American embrace continued, far beyond what the war in Afghanistan demanded.

Much more generally, governments, especially in the first few years following 9/11, took advantage of the rhetoric of antiterrorism to intensify their attacks on domestic and international enemies. In 2012, Human Rights Watch reported that more than fifty governments had revised existing antiterrorism laws, and another eighty had adopted new policies, many of which represented a "broad and dangerous expansion of government powers to investigate, arrest, detain, and prosecute individuals at the expense of due process, judicial oversight, and public transparency."[2] These policies have included limitations on free expression and peaceful assembly; the expansion of police powers (warrantless searches and seizures and random searches in "designated areas"); extending precharge police custody to periods up to a month or longer, or without judicial authorization; incommunicado detention (including restrictions on access to legal counsel and delayed notification of family members); restricting the rights of detainees to legally challenge their detention; reducing police accountability (including specific immunity provisions for terrorism suspects); preventative detention and "control orders"; the use of military or special courts; and the application of the death penalty or other forms of capital punishment for nonlethal crimes.

Like anticommunism during the Cold War, antiterrorism became less a material interest of foreign policy than a crusade against evil to be pursued without too much concern for the ordinary restraints of law and conventional limits on the use of force. Where the conflict has been militarized, classic just-war restrictions have eroded or been ignored: noncombatants are directly targeted, proportionality is ignored, and the very idea of innocent civilians is undermined by direct and indirect attributions of collective responsibility and guilt. Where the struggle is carried out through the institutions of law and order and the internal security forces, human rights are the price exacted not just from terrorists but from peaceful political opponents, members of groups that are feared or despised, and ordinary individuals accidentally or arbitrarily caught up in the security apparatus.

These relatively dramatic examples, which involve the positive enabling of rights-abusive policies, were matched by a modest and uneven but real decline in American attention to human rights and democracy promotion during the Bush years. Although the United States remains committed to human rights and democracy, these objectives have moved toward the background in a number of particular cases. The decline was substantially less dramatic than during the Cold War. (An analogy with the impact of the war on drugs on U.S. policy in the Andean region is closer to the mark.) Nonetheless, the decline was real and important. And in some ways it has persisted until today.

Support for these changes was by no means restricted to the nationalist political Right. Many supporters of American international human rights policies, from both major parties, did not object to the Bush administration's antiterrorism policies. Although some domestic measures, such as the restrictions on civil liberties in the USA PATRIOT Act, were criticized by prominent figures in both parties, criticism of their international dimensions was largely restricted to human rights NGOs and figures on the fringes of the political mainstream.

Nevertheless, even the Bush administration did not mount a general attack on human rights and democracy objectives, which have remained goals of American foreign policy. One need not be overly charitable to suggest that this reflects genuine commitment to these values. At the very least, it indicates that important domestic and international constituencies continue to take them seriously. (Hypocrisy is effective only to the extent that it taps into widely and genuinely held values.)

In an important sense, then, the relative decline of human rights in American foreign policy has been largely unintended. The explicit aim has been not to harm or even slight human rights but rather to pursue security objectives that are deemed to be more important. This does not, however, in any way lessen American responsibility. The negative human rights consequences have been very real, were easily anticipated, and are now well known. The lack of intent, though, is important for thinking about the prospects for reversing these trends.

In particular, we should expect a resurgence of American international human rights policies as space is opened by the retreat of competing security objectives—just as happened after the end of the Cold War. And in fact during the early years of the Obama administration, we witnessed glimpses of such a reopening.

That opening, however, was very short lived. The rapid deterioration of stability in the Middle East and North Africa, fueled in part by the rise in the number of terrorist organizations linked to ISIS, has resulted in a dramatic increase in the frequency and severity of terrorist activity, especially in Europe. The war in Syria has resulted in a massive refugee crisis that looms over European policies. And the increasingly barbaric actions of the Russian-backed Syrian regime, culminating in the collapse of Aleppo in December 2016, have given the cause of antiterrorism brutal new life fifteen years after 9/11.

3. Human Rights, Security, and Foreign Policy

A defender of the war on terror might argue that the story we have told so far is a simple one of competing foreign policy objectives: major security interests have appropriately pushed human rights and democracy promotion to the sidelines. We suggest, however, that the actual dynamic has been rather different. In this section, we focus on qualitative substantive changes in the understanding of security—that is, the American tendency to conceive new threats in moralized terms and to respond with an irrational exuberance for a militarized crusade.

Up to this point we have talked of *security* as if its meaning was obvious and constant. Protecting the national territory from invasion may fit this description. However, most other security interests are more thoroughly constructed and variable. What is to be secured—the state (national security) or citizens (personal security)? Where does the threat lie—externally or internally? And what is the nature of the threat—material or moral/ideological?

The relatively constant and uncontroversial dimensions of security address external material threats to the state. Security thus understood is indeed plausibly seen as an appropriately overriding concern of foreign policy. Without national security from external material threats, all other interests and values are at risk. As we move away from this relatively simple case, however, security becomes more obscure and its priority more contentious. In addition, its conceptual and normative relationships to human rights vary considerably.

Although the security of individual citizens has strong connections with human rights, state security is not necessarily connected to individual human rights; it depends on the character of the state being protected and the means used to secure it. To oversimplify, human rights are about protecting citizens from the state. National security is about protecting the state from its (perceived) enemies. Those enemies may themselves be citizens. And even when the enemies are primarily external, the rights of citizens may need to be sacrificed to carry out defensive measures.

An antagonistic relationship between (national) security and human rights is especially likely when security is seen in moral rather than material terms and to the extent that threats are perceived to lie in internal subversion. This was a common perception during the Cold War. With security understood almost exclusively as a matter of *national* security (which was understood to have a significant ideological dimension), U.S. foreign policy was extremely tolerant of regimes that systematically sacrificed the human rights of their citizens to the (alleged) imperatives of protecting the nation from communist attack and subversion.

The post–Cold War redefinition of American security interests in less ideological terms has eliminated the American incentive to court repressive regimes in order to keep them out of the communist camp. At the same time, it undermined the principal rationale for repression by rightist dictatorships. Taken together, these changes greatly reduced the antagonism between human rights and security in American foreign policy.

In other words, not only were security concerns reduced in number, but the concept of security changed. Russia still posed most of the same material threats in 1995 that it did in 1985; the end of the Cold War, and the dramatic *perceived* decline in the Russian threat, did not coincide with a substantial reduction in Russian military power. Rather, the ideological threat posed by communism disappeared with glasnost and new thinking, the collapse of the Soviet bloc, and the dissolution of the Soviet Union.

In addition, there was a partial move toward a conception of security with more of a personal dimension—or, in the language that became popular in the 1990s, *human security* (compare §10.7). Human security never displaced national security on the American foreign policy agenda. It did, however, acquire a significant place. This is perhaps most evident in the rise of armed humanitarian operations that received strong American support, from Somalia and Bosnia through Kosovo and East Timor (see Chapter 10). More broadly, the concept of peace building (not just peacekeeping) was added to the international security lexicon, and a human rights dimension was incorporated into a number of postconflict peacekeeping operations.

Terrorism has modestly increased the material threat to the United States. The biggest change, however, has been in the other dimensions of security. The war on terrorism has led to a significantly more ideological vision of security—a theme pursued in greater detail in the next section. The focus on personal security has receded in favor of a renewed emphasis on national security. And the internal dimensions of security have moved to the forefront, as expressed in the language of *homeland security*. As during the Cold War, security and human rights have again increasingly come to be seen as competing rather than reinforcing concerns.

4. The Axis of Evil

The implication of the preceding section is that human rights and democracy promotion have lost out less as a result of carefully considered trade-offs of competing interests and more because of a decision to reorient American policy around an ideological crusade. In this section we suggest, by examining the case of the "axis of evil," that this introduced a substantially irrational element into American policy.

In his 2002 State of the Union address, President Bush announced a refocusing of American foreign policy on an "axis of evil" composed of Iraq, Iran, and North Korea. In fact, though, not only were there no significant connections among these three countries, but Iran and Iraq were bitter enemies and North Korea was not closely linked to either of the other two regimes (or any other country in the world, for that matter, with the possible exception of China). This new enemy was constructed out of a hodgepodge of very different (and largely unrelated) concerns—most notably terrorism, proliferation, regional security, and general anti-Americanism—held together largely by antiterrorist hysteria.

Nationals of these countries—in sharp contrast to those of Saudi Arabia, for example—were not involved in terrorist attacks on Americans. In fact, only Iran actively supported international terrorists. And their contribution to global terrorism paled in contrast to that of America's ally Pakistan, which supported the Taliban in Afghanistan (prior to its post-9/11 about-face) and continued to support particularly violent terrorism in Kashmir.

Much the same is true of the other "crimes" of these regimes. Consider proliferation. North Korea has indeed been guilty of breaching international nonproliferation norms, as well as particular agreements with the United States. But, again, our ally Pakistan was the most flagrant proliferator of the 1990s, both domestically and by supporting North Korea's nuclear program. Iraq's nuclear ambitions had been effectively thwarted by international sanctions and monitoring. And Iran, although a legitimate proliferation concern, was not an imminent threat to the United States and had been much less than clear in its expression of its intentions.

From a human rights perspective, these problems might be forgivable if these "evil" states were the world's leading human rights violators. A strong case can be made that North Korea and Saddam Hussein's Iraq belonged on any top ten list. But the inclusion of Iran in such company was absurd. Iran was in many regards an extremely unappealing regime. The human rights situation, however, was and remains far worse in America's leading ally in the region, Saudi Arabia.

Iran at the time was one of the few countries in the region with a vibrant opposition and real hope for reform. (Although those hopes were violently crushed in 2009, Iran remains today somewhere in the middle of the pack in North Africa and the Middle East with respect to both democracy and human rights.) And women's rights were further advanced in Iran than they were in most Arab countries. Compared to Saudi Arabia, Iran (especially Tehran) was (and remains) a paradise for women's rights.

Particularly tragic is the fact that U.S. policy sacrificed the chance to facilitate the process of reform in Iran, which was especially vibrant during the first Bush administration. Quite the contrary, the bellicose words and actions of the United States made life more difficult for reformers. Rather than recognize the positive (if limited) changes in Iran, the United States chose to single out Iran for special attack. It even sacrificed opportunities to pursue convergent interests cooperatively, most notably in Afghanistan and Iraq, preferring to keep Iran as a demonized enemy.

5. The War Against Iraq

In hindsight, the idea of an axis of evil seems silly. Certainly, the idea that these three second- or third-rate powers were the appropriate focal point of the foreign policy of "the world's only superpower" was patently ludicrous. This silliness, however, had serious negative consequences—not just for reformers and human rights in Iran and the general turn of American attention away from human rights, but in the human rights disaster and regional insecurity arising from the American war on Iraq.

Like the axis of evil, the justification for the invasion of Iraq in 2003 was cobbled together out of a variety of disparate concerns, including weapons of mass destruction, regime change, a history of animosity, and concern over influence and security in the region, held together with a lot of post-9/11 hysteria. The threat of weapons of mass destruction was largely imaginary. Iraq's contribution to international terrorism (before the U.S. invasion and occupation) was minimal, extending not much beyond a totally unsubstantiated (and patently implausible) claim that Saddam Hussein's government had conspired with al-Qaeda cells in Europe. Elsewhere in American foreign policy one can find no hint that even the most vicious behavior of a government is legitimate grounds for a military invasion. And Iraq was no serious threat to its neighbors, having been effectively hobbled by the First Gulf War and a decade of international sanctions.

In addition to the disorder, death, and destruction that have characterized "liberated" Iraq—something in the neighborhood of half a million Iraqi civilians have died from war and the lingering factional violence—the United States has embarked on a series of direct violations of human rights and humanitarian law. Abu Ghraib entered the popular lexicon as a symbol of sadistic political brutality. Clearly, such excesses were not part of official American policy. But many have argued that they have been facilitated, even encouraged, by American policies and practices that suggest that human rights and the rule of law often must be sacrificed to the fight against terror.

The American naval base at Guantanamo Bay, Cuba, has been carved out as a netherworld where neither American nor international (nor Cuban) law applies and where issues of innocence, proof, responsibility, and proportionality are deemed irrelevant. Extraordinary renditions—kidnapping suspected terrorists, transporting them across international boundaries, and delivering them into the hands of "friendly" security services that regularly practice torture—reflected a cynical evasion of even the most rudimentary principles of the rule of law. Although President Bush insisted, with apparent sincerity, that the United States neither practiced nor tolerated torture, Vice President Dick Cheney and his staff campaigned for months against legislation that codified this claim (and existing American legal obligations under the Torture Convention and the Third Geneva Convention). And the list goes on, with the consequence that even America's closest Western allies strongly condemned American lawlessness and violations of human rights.

The invasion of Iraq was in no simple way caused by the war on terror. It did, however, enable a shift in policy, most notably toward unilateralism and the demonization of enemies. And antiterrorism helped to hold together the various justifications that were used to build the political coalitions that backed the war. Without the paranoia over terrorism, it is hard to imagine the Bush administration marshaling the national and international support needed to launch the war against Iraq.

6. Recent Developments: Progress or Retreat?

The Obama administration (2009–2017) was largely a disappointment to civil libertarians and human rights advocates—although whether for lack of effort or due to resistance by Congress and American society is a matter of considerable debate. In its early years, however, the atmosphere was beginning to change. There was a growing lack of enthusiasm for the extreme measures of the Bush administration, even among its continuing supporters. After nearly a decade, it was hard to sustain the sense of crisis that was essential to early American excesses.

In an act of considerable symbolic importance, almost immediately upon assuming office, Obama signed an executive order that officially outlawed the "enhanced interrogation techniques" that had been used during the Bush years. And, also of considerable symbolic importance, he cited international human rights law in support of this new policy. In addition, the Obama administration attempted to close the prisoner camps at Guantanamo Bay but was prevented from doing so by Congress.

Obama also made it a signature priority of his administration to end the U.S. formal combat presence in Iraq, to draw down and end the deployment of the "surge" in U.S. forces that were supporting the new Iraqi government's efforts to quell a counterinsurgency that began in the mid-2000s. This drawdown was completed early in Obama's second term. By the summer of 2014, however, a new insurgency led by ISIS resulted in a near total collapse of the Iraqi army and the loss of key cities, including Mosul. Those events, coupled with the civil war that was raging in Syria (which began, of course, as a series of protests that were part of the Arab Spring of 2011) led to a new terrorism-related crisis that has spawned new human rights challenges.

Since 2012, there has been a significant increase in ISIS-related terrorist activity, especially in Europe. In 2015 in France, there were the Île-de-France attacks (including the *Charlie Hebdo* shootings) and the November 13 attacks in Paris, which killed 130 people, including 89 at the Bataclan theater. In March 2016, in Brussels, suicide bombers struck the airport and a metro station, killing 32 people. And in October 2015, a Russian Metrojet passenger plane was destroyed in midair over the Sinai Peninsula, killing all 217 on board. All these attacks (and dozens of others) were perpetrated by groups claiming allegiance to the Islamic State.

Different governments and societies have responded differently to this uptick in terrorist violence. On the one hand, French and Belgian authorities exercised considerable, and in many ways remarkable, restraint in carrying out their investigations and limiting their infringements of human rights. On the other, the Metrojet incident helped to spur Russia's intervention in the Syrian civil war—although regional influence was a more important motive and Russian involvement was warmly embraced by the al-Assad regime.

But, even in countries that have shown restraint, there has been a substantial resurgence of fear and discrimination against Muslims, especially those from the Middle East. The European migration/refugee crises that have resulted from conflicts in the Middle East and North Africa have been met in some cases with specious claims that these refugees are harboring ISIS cells among them. This has been accompanied by calls for closed borders and the rise of right-wing political parties that promise greater security from the threat of "Islamic extremism" throughout Europe (but especially in Eastern and Southern Europe). In the United States, while on the campaign trail, candidate Donald J. Trump even called for an outright ban on immigration by all Muslims, which was later replaced by an only slightly less chilling call for "extreme vetting," which the administration has attempted to enact, by executive orders, in February and March 2017—despite the fact that no one from the six or seven targeted countries has committed a single terrorist act that has killed a single person in the United States.

It is unclear where all of this is heading. But wars—especially moralized wars—discourage rational calculation. There seems to be something unseemly about inquiring into the costs or consequences of combating evil, resolutely, whatever the consequences. When we stop weighing costs and benefits, though, we leave behind rational calculation. We did that during the Cold War. We did it again in the early years of the war on terror. And in the wake of Trump's attempted travel ban, many people fear that we are moving in that direction again.

None of this is to deny the real dilemmas that terrorism has created for states committed to protecting human rights. Nor does it mean always choosing human rights over antiterrorism. As we noted at the outset, modest restrictions of limited duration on a small range of rights *may* be justifiable. Nonetheless, the international human rights obligations of states remain exactly what they were before 9/11. Therefore, we need to continue to take seriously the demands of human rights in the context of a calmly conceived, efficient, and effective antiterrorism policy based on a sober assessment of real costs and benefits—for the sake of both American foreign policy and international human rights.

Problem 9: The Absolute Prohibition of Torture

The Problem

International human rights law bans torture absolutely. As Article 2(2) of the Convention Against Torture puts it, "No exceptional circumstances whatsoever . . . may be invoked as a justification of torture." In other words, whatever the cost, torture should not be employed. Our experience suggests, though, that few people really believe this—really believe, for example, that if torturing one person could unquestionably save the lives of thousands, tens of thousands, or millions of people (from, say, a chemical or nuclear weapon in the middle of a large city) that the right thing to do, all things considered, would be to let a large number of innocent people die needlessly. Such intuitions suggest that the absolute prohibition on torture ought to be replaced by a more nuanced policy.

A Solution

An absolute prohibition, we will argue, is less problematic than its alternatives. To paraphrase Churchill on democracy, it is the worst policy except for all the others that have been tried. And there are other ways to accommodate legitimate concerns about the perverse unintended consequences of an absolute ban.

Essential to such an argument is the empirical fact that it is extremely rare that torturing a single individual can, with a high probability, save the lives of very large numbers of innocent people. (There may be actual cases where this has been true, but we know of none. And it is telling that, despite the intense debate over this issue during the past decade, there is no widely known historical case where these conditions have been met.) The force of the argument for permitting torture, however, is undercut by decreases in the number of people saved, decreases in the likelihood of success, and increases in the amount of torture required.

A familiar legal maxim states that hard cases make bad law. This is particularly true when the cases are extremely rare. Philosophers may value such cases because they sharply pose a dilemma arising from conflicting principles. Law, however, is at its best when it provides general regulations of broad applicability.

This is especially true because the social utility of torture in all but the "perfect" case is likely to be, at best, both modest and highly speculative. Certainly, this is true of all the cases we know about over the past decade. (And we at least doubt that the cases we have not heard about are any different. Were there really a big and dramatic success for torture, especially by the United States, is it really plausible that it has been kept secret?) And the strong temptations to abuse any explicit exceptions make the case for an absolute prohibition powerful, *even on grounds of social utility*.

But what about that "perfect" case? If you really "know" (have a very well-founded belief) that a single individual has information necessary to save the lives of a great number of people, have a reasonable belief that she can be forcibly compelled to reveal that information in time, and there really is no other plausible option, what do you do? We suggest that the proper course of action is to torture her—and then face the consequences, pleading extenuating circumstances as an excuse.

Recall the discussion in §10.10 of different types of justification. With an absolute prohibition, torture will never be authorized in the strong sense that all relevant norms provide justification. The justifiability of torture will always be, at best, contested. But it may be excusable, in the sense that a prima facie unjustifiable act is, all things considered, defensible, perhaps even the best possible choice given the circumstances.

Treating torture as, at best, excusable ensures that each instance will be examined in a context in which the burden of proof has been placed on the torturer. Legislating exceptions will not provide the same kind of scrutiny and leaves the burden of proof more obscure, perhaps even on the side of the victim. And a justification as "excusable" properly presents every instance of torture as, at best, a tragic infringement of basic values and human rights. It may be the right thing to do, all things considered. But it is only the lesser of evils.

This is another way of saying that rights are trumps—but only prima facie trumps. There is always a possibility of exceptions, all things considered. But law and policy should not be based on rare and dangerous cases. Such cases are better dealt with individually, on an ad hoc basis, should they actually arise.

Further Problems

Grant that there ought to be an absolute prohibition on torture. What *other* internationally recognized human rights merit such an absolute prohibition? Is torture unique or close to unique? If so, why? If not, what are we to do when multiple absolute prohibitions conflict?

Now grant that there ought *not* to be an absolute prohibition on torture. What other internationally recognized human rights should have legislated exceptions? Of what sort? On what grounds?

Consider now the possibility that this whole discussion is misformulated in the sense that every right has within it a set of implicit limitations and exceptions. The problem then becomes specifying what those limitations and exceptions are. Suppose that this analysis is theoretically correct. Is it practically viable in the absence of any authoritative statement of those limits and exceptions? If there were a more robust international human rights jurisprudence, would this be a potentially practical way to deal with these issues?

The argument for excusing violations of an absolute prohibition is that it is less dangerous than legislating exceptions. But is excusing torture in rare, truly "necessary" cases going too far? Does it lead us down a slippery slope?

Problem 10: (Anti)Terrorism and Civil Liberties

The Problem

The war on terror has had domestic as well as international consequences for human rights. Most of the more serious abuses at the hands of American officials have taken place overseas. Nonetheless, personal liberties—especially privacy and due process rights but also the free exercise of religion, freedom of association, and even freedom of speech—have been curtailed. The dramatic expansion of surveillance and the removal of some standard legal safeguards in terrorism cases have come at a cost to human rights that even defenders of those tactics usually acknowledge. Has it been worth it? Is it still worth that cost today?

A Solution

Once more we face an issue of trade-offs, that is, a question of relative weights. And the issue is empirical, not theoretical. How much additional security has been purchased? What is the real cost of the (modest but real) domestic limitations on personal liberties? We want to suggest that American policy has overrated the benefits, undervalued the costs, and acted out of convenience rather than necessity.

As we saw in Chapter 2, rights are trumps. And one of their principal functions is to remove issues from the domain in which simple calculations of social utility rightly determine public policy. If privacy and due process were not basic rights, one might plausibly argue that even minor improvements in homeland security would justify their limitation. But they *are* basic rights. Therefore, those who would claim justifiable infringement must show both a very large benefit and a pressing necessity.

About 3,000 Americans have died from terrorism since 9/11, roughly 200 people a year. This total of 3,000 is approximately the same number of people who die *annually* from drowning in a bathtub. Twice as many people die annually from *accidental* gunshot wounds. Thirty times as many are killed by drunk drivers. Two hundred times as many people die each year from air pollution. Yet we have no war on guns or air pollution—and certainly would not accept restrictions on basic human rights to prevent some portion of these deaths from occurring.

Furthermore, the connection between restricting civil liberties and protecting people against terrorism is unclear at best. And arguments that such restrictions are *necessary* to produce the positive results attributed to them are rarely even made. Instead, it is argued that enhanced surveillance techniques have foiled, and will continue to foil, some not negligible number of significant terrorist plots and that new legal rules have produced, and will produce, more successful prosecutions of terror suspects. But this just is nowhere near enough to justify infringing basic human rights.

Certain limited sacrifices of civil liberties might be justified in some circumstances. The United States over the past several years, however, does not seem to be such a case.

Further Problems

If we grant an antiterrorism exception, why should similar arguments not apply to other types of security? For example, from gun violence? Or from felons that we know have a high probability to reoffend? And why not apply the same arguments to certain nonsecurity goals?

Is there not, though, a qualitative difference between terrorism and other kinds of threats? Suppose that there is. Just what is it? And how much of a sacrifice of human rights does it justify? On what grounds?

Even if antiterrorism policies are justifiable in themselves, do they lead us down a slippery slope? If not, what prevents it?

Discussion Questions

1. How much has the world changed since 9/11? For Americans? Europeans? Muslims? Arabs? Israelis? Palestinians? Iraqis? Syrians? Libyans? Pakistanis? Afghanis? Africans? Latin Americans? East Asians?
2. Is it true that human rights became permanently entrenched in American and broader Western foreign policies in the 1990s? If the war on terrorism drags on, is it not likely to undercut further the progress of the 1980s and 1990s? What if dramatic acts of terrorism become an annual event in the United States? A monthly event? Just how deep does the commitment to international human rights really go?
3. Is there any evidence that human rights may be vulnerable to reactions to the new rise in terrorism and violent extremism?
4. Should we really care all that much about the treatment of terror suspects? Or those who are reliably known to be terrorists? Why should terrorists be entitled to the protections of the rules they seek to overthrow?
5. Are terrorists really forcing us to conceptualize human rights and security as competing concerns? Can a war on terror be effective while respecting the full range of internationally recognized human rights for all? If not, what is the problem with limited, targeted infringements of internationally recognized human rights? Is this not precisely the sort of emergency that justifies overriding the prima facie priority of human rights?
6. What about the *domestic* human rights impact of the war on terror? How significant are the restrictions on human rights that have been imposed since 9/11 in places like the United States and Britain? Are they not actually very modest and probably justifiable (even if controversial)?
7. Grant that the world has become a worse place for human rights since 9/11. Is blaming the United States (or other countries that have borne the brunt of terrorism) tantamount to blaming the victim?
8. Is the decision of this chapter to focus on the war on terrorism rather than on terrorism, and its unquestioned evils, the right one *from a human rights perspective*? Even accepting that it is, is there some broader

moral or political perspective in which combatting terrorism ought to take priority? And even if not, are there *other* ethical, moral, or political concerns that *would* appropriately trump human rights?

Suggested Readings

On the general issue of terrorism and human rights, there are a number of good wide-ranging books, including Andrea Bianchi and Alexis Keller, eds., *Counterterrorism: Democracy's Challenge* (Oxford: Hart, 2008); Richard Ashby Wilson, ed., *Human Rights in the "War on Terror"* (Cambridge: Cambridge University Press, 2005); and Thomas G. Weiss, Margaret E. Crahan, and John Goering, eds., *Wars on Terrorism and Iraq: Human Rights, Unilateralism, and U.S. Foreign Policy* (New York: Routledge, 2004). On the question of how much things have changed for human rights since 9/11, see Michael Goodhart and Anja Mihr, eds., *Human Rights in the 21st Century: Continuity and Change Since 9/11* (Houndmills, UK: Palgrave Macmillan, 2011).

For comparative studies of national antiterrorism policies, see Mary L. Volcansek and John F. Stack Jr., eds., *Courts and Terrorism: Nine Nations Balance Rights and Security* (Cambridge: Cambridge University Press, 2011); Kent Roach, *The 9/11 Effect: Comparative Counter-terrorism* (New York: Cambridge University Press, 2011); and Alison Brysk and Gershon Shafir, eds., *National Insecurity and Human Rights: Democracies Debate Counterterrorism* (Berkeley: University of California Press, 2007).

On the broad issue of trade-offs between human rights and security in the context of combating terrorism, see Christian Walter, ed., *Terrorism as a Challenge for National and International Law: Security Versus Liberty?* (Berlin: Springer, 2004); M. Katherine B. Darmer, Robert M. Baird, and Stuart E. Rosenbaum, eds., *Civil Liberties vs. National Security in a Post-9/11 World* (Amherst, MA: Prometheus Books, 2004); Wolfgang Benedek and Alice Yotopoulos-Marangopoulos, eds., *Anti-terrorist Measures and Human Rights* (Leiden, Netherlands: Martinus Nijhoff, 2004); and Michael Freeman, *Freedom or Security: The Consequences for Democracies Using Emergency Powers to Fight Terror* (Westport, CT: Praeger, 2003).

On American abuses of prisoners, good starting points are David P. Forsythe, *The Politics of Prisoner Abuse: The United States and Enemy Prisoners After 9/11* (Cambridge: Cambridge University Press, 2011); and Laurel E. Fletcher, Eric Stover, Stephen Paul Smith, et al., *The Guantánamo Effect: Exposing the Consequences of U.S. Detention and Interrogation Practices* (Berkeley: University of California Press, 2009). On torture in the United States and U.S. foreign policy, see Karen J. Greenberg, ed., *The Torture Debate in America* (Cambridge: Cambridge University Press, 2006); and Karen J. Greenberg and Joshua L. Dratel, eds., *The Torture Papers: The Road to Abu Ghraib* (Cambridge: Cambridge University Press, 2005).

Notes

Chapter One

1. The U.N. Office of the High Commissioner for Human Rights also considers the treaties on migrant workers and enforced disappearances to be core treaties. We leave them off our list because of their relatively narrow scope and low ratification rate (barely 30 percent of the average of the other seven treaties).

2. The least ratified of the core treaties is the Torture Convention, with 158. The most ratified, the children's rights treaty, has 196 of a possible 197 parties (excluding only the United States).

3. Note that the 1948 Convention on the Prevention and Punishment of the Crime of Genocide is not included in this list. International law has technically defined genocide as a *sui generis* crime outside of the body of human rights law, narrowly and technically defined. For most purposes, though, the reader can adopt the wider ordinary-language sense of human rights that includes not only genocide but also what international law calls crimes against humanity.

Chapter Two

1. This is not exactly correct. Although children are human beings, they usually are not thought to have, for example, a right to vote, on the grounds that they are not fully developed. Once they reach a certain age, however, they must be recognized as holding all human rights equally. Similarly, those who suffer from severe mental illness are often denied the exercise of many rights—but only until they regain full use and control of their faculties. Furthermore, both children and those with severe mental disabilities are denied the protection or exercise of only those rights for which they are held to lack the necessary requisites. They still have, and must be allowed to enjoy equally, all other human rights. And, in the case of children, the 1989 Convention on the Rights of the Child seeks to clarify this special status, including rights to special protections.

2. We can also note that other standard arguments for recognizing only this one economic right fail to stand up to scrutiny. For example, there are many ways other than a right to property to guarantee economic security and economic participation

in society (e.g., rights to work, social insurance, and old-age pensions). In fact, those other mechanisms are vastly more important for most people in modern societies.

3. Henry Shue, *Basic Rights: Subsistence and Affluence in U.S. Foreign Policy* (Princeton, NJ: Princeton University Press, 1996; originally published 1980), 51–64.

4. It did this in a couple of ways. First, the ACA made it illegal for insurance providers to lock out those with preexisting health conditions. It also fostered the creation of marketplaces of insurance providers through state-run exchanges and a national exchange coordinated by the federal government, the point of which was to spur competition to keep premiums as low as possible. Among the biggest sources of controversy with the ACA is the mandate for employers (to provide insurance) and individuals (who must be insured or pay a fine).

5. In what follows, we focus on the "external" dimensions of sovereignty, that is, sovereignty as it appears in the relations of states. Here the emphasis is on the absence of any superior (sovereign) above the state and thus on the sovereign equality of states. The "internal" dimensions of sovereignty concern the supreme authority of the state within its territory. Here the focus is on the legal and political superiority of the state over other actors. In the contemporary world, internal sovereignty is usually seen as resting on the state acting in the name and interests of the people: "popular sovereignty."

6. For an extended discussion of this idea, see Hedley Bull, *The Anarchical Society* (New York: Columbia University Press, 1977).

7. Robert Gilpin, "The Richness of the Tradition of Political Realism," in *Neorealism and Its Critics,* edited by Robert O. Keohane (New York: Columbia University Press, 1986), 305; Hans Morgenthau, *Politics Among Nations,* 2nd ed. (New York: Alfred A. Knopf, 1954), 9.

8. George F. Kennan, "Morality and Foreign Policy," *Foreign Affairs* 64 (Winter 1985–1986): 206; George F. Kennan, *Realities of American Foreign Policy* (Princeton, NJ: Princeton University Press, 1954), 48; George F. Kennan, *The Cloud of Danger: Current Realities of American Foreign Policy* (Boston: Little, Brown, 1977), 45.

9. Herbert Butterfield, *Christianity, Diplomacy, and War* (London: Epworth Press, 1953), 11.

10. Robert J. Art and Kenneth N. Waltz, "Technology, Strategy, and the Uses of Force," in *The Use of Force,* edited by Robert J. Art and Kenneth N. Waltz (Lanham, MD: University Press of America, 1983), 6.

Chapter Three

1. Henry Shue, *Basic Rights: Subsistence, Affluence, and U.S. Foreign Policy* (Princeton, NJ: Princeton University Press, 1996; originally published 1980), 29–34.

2. Dunstan M. Wai, "Human Rights in Sub-Saharan Africa," in *Human Rights: Cultural and Ideological Perspectives,* edited by Adamantia Pollis and Peter Schwab (New York: Praeger, 1979), 116.

3. Hung-Chao Tai, "Human Rights in Taiwan: Convergence of Two Political Cultures?," in *Human Rights in East Asia: A Cultural Perspective,* edited by James C. Hsiung (New York: Paragon House, 1985), 77, 79.

4. Fouad Zakaria, "Human Rights in the Arab World: The Islamic Context," in *Philosophical Foundations of Human Rights,* edited by UNESCO (Paris: UNESCO,

1986), 228. Cf. Abul A'la Mawdudi, *Human Rights in Islam* (Leicester, UK: Islamic Foundation, 1976), 10.

5. Khalid M. Ishaque, "Human Rights in Islamic Law," *Review of the International Commission of Jurists* 12 (1974): 32–38.

6. Manwoo Lee, "North Korea and the Western Notion of Human Rights," in Hsiung, *Human Rights in East Asia,* 129, 131.

7. This scheme is developed in greater detail in Jack Donnelly, *Universal Human Rights in Theory and Practice,* 3nd ed. (Ithaca, NY: Cornell University Press, 2013), §6.3.

8. Robert E. Goodin et al., *The Real Worlds of Welfare Capitalism* (Cambridge: Cambridge University Press, 1999).

9. Other examples, such as pornography and homosexuality, miss the mark. Tolerance of neither is required by international human rights norms (although the Human Rights Council has begun to make some headway on the issue of sexual orientation and gender identity; however, see below in the chapter and n11). Where they are allowed, they involve particular conceptions of the rights to free speech and nondiscrimination that are permitted but not mandated by international human rights norms.

10. The resolution adopted was A/HRC/32/2, 15 July 2016.

11. Incidentally, when the report of the Human Rights Council came up for a vote in the U.N. General Assembly's Third Committee in November 2016, a block of states led by the African group attempted to "defer consideration" of the appointment of the independent expert "in order to allow time for further consultations to determine the legal basis" of the mandate (U.N. Doc A/C.3/71/L.46). That provision was stripped out by an amendment to the draft resolution (A/C.3/71/L.52), but the vote on the amendment was exceedingly narrow: 84–77–17. The attempt to thwart a decision of the Human Rights Council was itself unusual. That the vote was so close reinforces our main argument.

Chapter Four

1. James Nickel, "Rethinking Indivisibility: Towards a Theory of Supporting Relations Between Rights," *Human Rights Quarterly* 30, no. 4 (2008): 986.

2. Craig Scott, "The Interdependence of Permeability of Human Rights Norms: Towards a Partial Fusion of the International Covenants on Human Rights," *Osgoode Hall Law Journal* 27 (1989): 769–875.

3. Emphasis ours. Proclamation of Teheran, Final Act of the International Conference on Human Rights, Teheran, April 22–May 13, 1968, U.N. Doc A/CONF/32/41 (1968).

4. U.N. Doc A/CONF.157/23 (July 12, 1993).

5. Karel Vašák, "A 30-Year Struggle: The Sustained Efforts to Give Force of Law to the Universal Declaration of Human Rights," *UNESCO Courier* (November 1977), 28–29, 32.

Chapter Five

1. Comprehensive information on activities of the council is available at http://www.ohchr.org/en/hrbodies/hrc/pages/hrcindex.aspx.

2. The main UPR gateway page is at http://www.ohchr.org/EN/HRBodies/UPR /Pages/UPRMain.aspx.

3. For more information, see http://www.ohchr.org/EN/HRBodies/UPR/Pages /BasicFacts.aspx.

4. Subhas Gujadhur and Marc Limon, *Towards the Third Cycle of the UPR: Stick or Twist (Lessons Learned from the First Ten Years of the Universal Periodic Review)* (Geneva: Universal Rights Group, July 2016).

5. Ibid., 4.

6. http://www.ohchr.org/EN/Pages/Home.aspx.

7. Located in Bangladesh, Chad, Dominican Republic, Ecuador, Honduras, Jamaica, Kenya, FYR Macedonia, Madagascar, Malawi, Maldives, Moldova, Nigeria, Panama (UNDG-LAC), Papua New Guinea, Paraguay, Philippines, Russia, Rwanda, Sierra Leone, Southern Caucasus (Tbilisi), Serbia, Sri Lanka, Tajikistan, Tanzania, Timor Leste, Thailand (UNDG Asia-Pacific, Bangkok), Ukraine, and Zambia.

8. The United States made the largest single contribution—$16 million, followed by Norway and Sweden, which each contributed about $14 million (which is significantly higher in per capita terms than the U.S. contribution). The European Commission was fourth, at about $13 million.

9. See http://documents.worldbank.org/curated/en/525671468188047741 /World-Bank-budget-FY16.

10. The name of this committee is a historical artifact from the early draft of the then-single "International Covenant on Human Rights," before it was split into the ICCPR and ICESCR. The U.N. never bothered to change the name to Committee on Civil and Political Rights, which would put it in line with the other TMBs.

11. See http://www.ilo.org/global/lang—en/index.htm.

12. See http://en.unesco.org/.

13. See https://www.icc-cpi.int/Pages/Home.aspx.

14. Jean-Philippe Thérien and Philippe Joly, "'All Human Rights for All': The United Nations and Human Rights in the Post–Cold War Era," *Human Rights Quarterly* 36, no. 2 (2014): 378.

15. For more information, see https://undg.org/home/undg-mechanisms/undg -hrm/.

16. For more information, see https://undg.org/home/guidance-policies/country -programming-principles/human-rights/rights-up-front-initiative/.

17. The full text of the Common Understanding is at http://hrbaportal.org/the -human-rights-based-approach-to-development-cooperation-towards-a-common -understanding-among-un-agencies.

18. Thérien and Joly, "All Human Rights for All," 387.

19. Ibid., 388.

20. See http://www.ohchr.org/EN/HRBodies/SP/Pages/Welcomepage.aspx.

21. Much of this section is derived from Marc Limon and Hilary Power, *History of the United Nations Special Procedures Mechanism: Origins, Evolution and Reform* (Geneva: Universal Rights Group, 2014).

22. See http://www.ohchr.org/EN/HRBodies/SP/Pages/Introduction.aspx.

23. Surya Subedi, "Protection of Human Rights Through the Mechanism of UN Special Rapporteurs," *Human Rights Quarterly* 33, no. 1 (February 2011): 212.

24. Ibid., 218.

25. Rosa Freedman and Jacob Mchangama, "Expanding or Diluting Rights? The Proliferation of United Nations Special Procedure Mandates," *Human Rights Quarterly* 38, no. 1 (February 2016): 164–193.

Chapter Six

1. For more information about the Council of Europe, see http://www.coe.int/.

2. The European Court website is at http://www.echr.coe.int.

3. Through 2015. The case law and jurisprudence of the European system can be searched through the powerful Human Rights Documentation (HUDOC) database at http://www.echr.coe.int/ECHR/EN/Header/Case-Law/HUDOC/HUDOC +database/.

4. For more information, see ECHR, *Analysis of Statistics 2015,* http://www.echr .coe.int/Documents/Stats_analysis_2015_ENG.pdf, 4.

5. See Robin R. Churchill and Urfan Khaliq, "The Collective Complaints System of the European Social Charter: An Effective Mechanism for Ensuring Compliance with Economic and Social Rights?," *European Journal of International Law* 15, no. 3 (2004): 417–456.

6. See http://www.osce.org/.

7. See http://www.oas.org/en/iachr/.

8. See http://www.corteidh.or.cr/index.cfm?&CFID=666614&CFTOKEN=6952 0161.

9. See http://interamericanhumanrights.org/background/challenges-and-critici sms/.

10. See http://www.corteidh.or.cr/casos.cfm?&CFID=829208&CFTOKEN=26 959705.

11. Obviously there is a distinction here: Europe is "organization-rich" compared to nearly every other region of the world, as we see in the preceding section of the chapter. Not every country in Europe is a member of the EU, and members of the Council of Europe (whose membership is also not universal) are not required to adhere to the European Social Charter.

12. Paul D. Williams, "From Non-Intervention to Non-Indifference: The Origins and Development of the African Union's Security Culture," *African Affairs* 106, no. 423 (2007): 253–79, http://www.jstor.org/stable/4496441.

13. For more information, see http://www.achpr.org/.

14. Nsongurua J. Udombana, "Toward the African Court on Human and Peoples' Rights: Better Late Than Never," *Yale Human Rights and Development Journal* 3, no. 1 (2000): Article 2.

15. See Amnesty International, "Africa: Malabo Protocol: Legal and Institutional Implications of the Merged and Expanded African Court," January 22, 2016, https:// www.amnesty.org/en/documents/afr01/3063/2016/en/.

16. For the U.S. State Department view, see https://2009–2017.state.gov/r/pa /prs/ps/2012/11/200915.htm. For the views of civil society organizations, see Human Rights Watch, "Civil Society Denounces Adoption of Flawed ASEAN Human Rights Declaration," November 19, 2012, https://www.hrw.org/news/2012/11/19 /civil-society-denounces-adoption-flawed-asean-human-rights-declaration. For the U.N. high commissioner's views, see U.N. News Centre, "UN Official Welcomes

ASEAN Commitment to Human Rights, but Concerned over Declaration Wording," November 19, 2012, http://www.un.org/apps/news/story.asp?NewsID=43536#.VlcfLZMrIdW.

17. League of Arab States, "Memorandum on the Development of Joint Arab Action presented by 37 Human Rights Organizations," March 20, 2012, http://www.cihrs.org/?p=1889&lang=en#; http://carnegieendowment.org/sada/?fa=23951.

18. http://www.icnl.org/research/monitor/las.html.

19. Cecilia Medina Quiroga, *The Battle of Human Rights: Gross, Systematic Violations and the Inter-American System* (Dordrecht: Martinus Nijhoff, 1988), 312.

20. For a detailed—and fascinating, even gripping—account of Argentina's efforts in the United Nations, see Ian Guest, *Behind the Disappearances: Argentina's Dirty War Against Human Rights and the United Nations* (Philadelphia: University of Pennsylvania Press, 1990), Part 2.

Chapter Seven

1. See http://www.state.gov/j/drl/rls/hrrpt/.

2. Henry Kissinger, *Diplomacy* (New York: Simon & Schuster, 1994), 759–761.

Chapter Eight

1. Cynthia Brown, ed., *With Friends like These: The Americas Watch Report on Human Rights and U.S. Policy in Latin America* (New York: Pantheon Books, 1985), 20. Compare with the Watch Committees and Lawyers' Committee for Human Rights, *The Reagan Administration's Record on Human Rights in 1986* (New York: Watch Committees and Lawyers' Committee for Human Rights, 1987), 49, 92–99; and *The Reagan Administration's Record on Human Rights in 1987* (New York: Watch Committees and Lawyers' Committee for Human Rights, 1988), 106. On the Reagan administration's systematic misrepresentation of the facts, see Americas Watch, *Managing the Facts: How the Administration Deals with Reports of Human Rights Abuses in El Salvador* (New York: Americas Watch, 1985).

2. See https://www.hrw.org/asia/burma; and David Scott Mathieson, "A Bridge Too Far for Obama, Crossed Too Early, in Myanmar," Human Rights Watch, November 18, 2012, https://www.hrw.org/news/2012/11/18/bridge-too-far-obama-crossed-too-early-myanmar.

3. See "Obama Orders US Economic Sanctions on Myanmar Lifted," *Al Jazeera,* October 7, 2016, http://www.aljazeera.com/news/2016/10/obama-economic-sanctions-myanmar-161007215716882.html.

4. Such practices are well documented by B'Tselem, the Israeli Information Center for Human Rights in the Occupied Territories. See http://www.btselem.org/.

5. Jim Zanotti, *Israel: Background and U.S. Relations* (Washington, DC: Congressional Research Service, 2016), https://fas.org/sgp/crs/mideast/RL33476.pdf.

6. Ibid.

7. The classic discussion of the Israel lobby is John J. Mearsheimer and Stephen M. Walt, *The Israel Lobby and U. S. Foreign Policy* (New York: Farrar, Straus and Giroux, 2007).

8. Quoted in Charles Cooper and Joan Verloren van Themaat, "Dutch Aid Determinants, 1973–85: Continuity and Change," in *Western Middle Powers and Global Poverty: The Determinants of the Aid Policies of Canada, Denmark, the Netherlands, Norway, and Sweden,* edited by Olav Stokke (Uppsala, Sweden: Almquist and Wiksell International, 1989), 119.

9. Jan Egeland, *Impotent Superpower—Potent Small State: Potentialities and Limitations of Human Rights Objectives in the Foreign Policies of the United States and Norway* (Oslo: Norwegian University Press, 1988), 3, 5.

10. Ibid., 15.

11. *Statements and Speeches* 82/12 (Ottawa: Bureau of Information, Department of External Affairs), quoted in Rhoda E. Howard and Jack Donnelly, *Confronting Revolution in Nicaragua: U.S. and Canadian Responses* (New York: Carnegie Council on Ethics and International Affairs, 1990).

12. Egeland, *Impotent Superpower,* 23.

13. Norway and the Netherlands are usually the world's two leading aid providers on a per capita basis; for most of the past thirty years they contributed eight to ten times more per capita than the United States.

Chapter Nine

1. See http://www.amnesty.org/.

2. For a complete list of HRW's extensive library of reports, see https://www.hrw .org/publications.

3. The Israel-based organization NGO Monitor, which describes itself as "Israel's most prominent watchdog of human rights groups" (http://www.ngo-monitor.org), is a leading source of such arguments.

4. U.N. Doc SG/SM/8277-PI/1428, June 18, 2002, http://www.un.org/press/en /2002/sgsm8277.doc.htm.

5. Lilie Chouliaraki, "The Theatricality of Humanitarianism: A Critique of Celebrity Advocacy," *Communication and Critical/Cultural Studies* 9, no. 1 (2012): 2.

6. Alex de Waal, "Don't Elevate Kony," http://sites.tufts.edu/reinventingpeace /2012/03/10/dont-elevate-kony.

7. W. Lance Bennett, "Branded Political Communication: Lifestyle Politics, Logo Campaigns, and the Rise of Global Citizenship," in *The Politics Behind Products,* edited by Michele Micheletti, Andreas Follesdal, and Dietlind Stolle (New Brunswick: Transaction Books, forthcoming), 2; draft available online at https://www .researchgate.net/publication/252004587_Branded_Political_Communication _Lifestyle_Politics_Logo_Campaigns_and_the_Rise_of_Global_Citizenship.

8. For more information on U.N. efforts, see U.N. Doc A/69/263, August 5, 2014, http://business-humanrights.org/sites/default/files/documents/unwg-report-naps -oct-2014.pdf; http://business-humanrights.org/en/un-guiding-principles; Human Rights Council, "Human Rights and Transnational Corporations and Other Business Enterprises," UN Doc A/HRC/RES/17/4, July 6, 2011, https://business-humanrights .org/sites/default/files/media/documents/un-human-rights-council-resolution -re-human-rights-transnational-corps-eng-6-jul-2011.pdf.

Chapter Ten

1. Carsten Stahn, "Responsibility to Protect: Political or Emerging Legal Norm?," *American Journal of International Law* 101, no. 1 (2007): 99–120.

2. Peter R. Baehr, "Controversies in the Current International Human Rights Debate," *Human Rights Review* 2, no. 1 (2000): 32n75.

Chapter Eleven

1. Alison Brysk, *From Tribal Village to Global Village: Indian Rights and International Relations in Latin America* (Stanford, CA: Stanford University Press, 2000).

2. Margaret E. Keck and Kathryn Sikkink, *Activists Beyond Borders: Advocacy Networks in International Politics* (Ithaca, NY: Cornell University Press, 1998).

Chapter Twelve

1. In U.N. General Assembly resolution A/RES/65/221, adopted December 21, 2010.

2. Human Rights Watch, *In the Name of Security* (2012), https://www.hrw.org /report/2012/06/29/name-security/counterterrorism-laws-worldwide-september -11#406663.

Appendix: Universal Declaration of Human Rights

General Assembly Resolution 217A (III),
10 December 1948

Whereas recognition of the inherent dignity and of the equal and inalienable rights of all members of the human family is the foundation of freedom, justice and peace in the world,

Whereas disregard and contempt for human rights have resulted in barbarous acts which have outraged the conscience of mankind, and the advent of a world in which human beings shall enjoy freedom of speech and belief and freedom from fear and want has been proclaimed as the highest aspiration of the common people,

Whereas it is essential, if man is not to be compelled to have recourse, as a last resort, to rebellion against tyranny and oppression, that human rights should be protected by the rule of law,

Whereas it is essential, to promote the development of friendly relations between nations,

Whereas the peoples of the United Nations have in the Charter reaffirmed their faith in fundamental human rights, in the dignity and worth of the human person and in the equal rights of men and women and have determined to promote social progress and better standards of life in larger freedom,

Whereas Member States have pledged themselves to achieve, in co-operation with the United Nations, the promotion of universal respect for and observance of human rights and fundamental freedoms,

Whereas a common understanding of these rights and freedoms is of the greatest importance for the full realization of this pledge,

Now, therefore,

The General Assembly

Proclaims this Universal Declaration of Human Rights as a common standard of achievement for all peoples and all nations, to the end that every individual and every organ of society, keeping this Declaration constantly in mind, shall strive by teaching and education to promote respect for these rights and freedoms and by progressive measures, national and international, to secure their universal and effective recognition and observance, both among the peoples of Member States themselves and among the peoples of territories under their jurisdiction.

Article 1.   All human beings are born free and equal in dignity and rights. They are endowed with reason and conscience and should act towards one another in a spirit of brotherhood.

Article 2.   Everyone is entitled to all the rights and freedoms set forth in this Declaration, without distinction of any kind, such as race, colour, sex, language, religion, political or other opinion, national or social origin, property, birth or other status.

Furthermore, no distinction shall be made on the basis of the political, jurisdictional or international status of the country or territory to which a person belongs, whether it be independent, trust, non-self-governing or under any other limitation of sovereignty.

Article 3.   Everyone has the right to life, liberty and the security of person.

Article 4.   No one shall be held in slavery or servitude; slavery and the slave trade shall be prohibited in all their forms.

Article 5.   No one shall be subjected to torture or to cruel, inhuman or degrading treatment or punishment.

Article 6.   Everyone has the right to recognition everywhere as a person before the law.

Article 7.   All are equal before the law and are entitled without any discrimination to equal protection of the law. All are entitled to equal protection against any discrimination in violation of this Declaration and against any incitement to such discrimination.

Article 8.   Everyone has the right to an effective remedy by the competent national tribunals for acts violating the fundamental rights granted him by the constitution or by law.

Article 9.   No one shall be subjected to arbitrary arrest, detention or exile.

Article 10.   Everyone is entitled to full equality to a fair and public hearing by an independent and impartial tribunal in the determination of his rights and obligations and of any criminal charge against him.

Article 11.   1. Everyone charged with a penal offence has the right to be presumed innocent until proved guilty according to law in a public trial at which he has had all the guarantees necessary for his defence.

2. No one shall be held guilty of any penal offence on account of any act or omission which did not constitute a penal offence, under national or international law, at the time when it was committed. Nor shall a heavier penalty be imposed than the one that was applicable at the time the penal offence was committed.

Article 12.   No one shall be subjected to arbitrary interference with his privacy, family, home or correspondence, nor to attacks upon his honour and reputation. Everyone has the right to the protection of the law against such interference or attacks.

Article 13.   1. Everyone has the right to freedom of movement and residence within the borders of each state.

2. Everyone has the right to leave any country, including his own, and to return to his country.

Article 14.   1. Everyone has the right to seek and to enjoy in other countries asylum from persecution.

2. This right may not be invoked in the case of prosecutions genuinely arising from non-political crimes or from acts contrary to the purposes and principles of the United Nations.

Article 15.   1. Everyone has the right to a nationality.

2. No one shall be arbitrarily deprived of his nationality nor denied the right to change his nationality.

Article 16.   1. Men and women of full age, without any limitation due to race, nationality or religion, have the right to marry and to found a family. They are entitled to equal rights as to marriage, during marriage and at its dissolution.

2. Marriage shall be entered into only with the free and full consent of the intending spouses.

3. The family is the natural and fundamental group unit of society and is entitled to protection by society and the State.

Article 17.   1. Everyone has the right to own property alone as well as in association with others.

2. No one shall be arbitrarily deprived of his property.

Article 18.   Everyone has the right to freedom of thought, conscience and religion; this right includes freedom to change his religion or belief, and freedom, either alone or in community with others and in public or private, to manifest his religion or belief in teaching, practice, worship and observance.

Article 19.   Everyone has the right to freedom of opinion and expression; this right includes freedom to hold opinions without interference and to seek, receive and impart information and ideas through any media and regardless of frontiers.

Article 20.   1. Everyone has the right to freedom of peaceful assembly and association.

2. No one may be compelled to belong to an association.

Article 21.   1. Everyone has the right to take part in the Government of his country, directly or through freely chosen representatives.

2. Everyone has the right of equal access to public service in his country.

3. The will of the people shall be the basis of the authority of government; this will shall be expressed in periodic and genuine elections which shall be by universal and equal suffrage and shall be held by secret vote or by equivalent free voting procedures.

Article 22.   Everyone, as a member of society, has the right to social security and is entitled to realization through national effort and international co-operation and in accordance with the organization and resources of each State, of the economic, social and cultural rights indispensable for his dignity and the free development of his personality.

Article 23.   1. Everyone has the right to work, to free choice of employment, to just and favourable conditions of work and to protection against unemployment.

2. Everyone, without any discrimination, has the right to equal pay for equal work.

3. Everyone who works has the right to just and favourable remuneration insuring for himself and his family an existence worthy of human dignity, and supplemented, if necessary, by other means of social protection.

4. Everyone has the right to form and to join trade unions for the protection of his interests.

Article 24. Everyone has the right to rest and leisure, including reasonable limitation of working hours and periodic holidays with pay.

Article 25. 1. Everyone has the right to a standard of living adequate for the health and well-being of himself and of his family, including food, clothing, housing and medical care and necessary social services, and the right to security in the event of unemployment, sickness, disability, widowhood, old age or other lack of livelihood in circumstances beyond his control.

2. Motherhood and childhood are entitled to special care and assistance. All children, whether born in or out of wedlock, shall enjoy the same social protection.

Article 26. 1. Everyone has the right to education. Education shall be free, at least in the elementary and fundamental stages. Elementary education shall be compulsory. Technical and professional education shall be made generally available and higher education shall be equally accessible to all on the basis of merit.

2. Education shall be directed to the full development of the human personality and to the strengthening of respect for human rights and fundamental freedoms. It shall promote understanding, tolerance and friendship among all nations, racial or religious groups, and shall further the activities of the United Nations for the maintenance of peace.

3. Parents have a prior right to choose the kind of education that shall be given to their children.

Article 27. 1. Everyone has the right freely to participate in the cultural life of the community, to enjoy the arts and share in scientific advancement and its benefits.

2. Everyone has the right to the protection of the moral and material interests resulting from any scientific, literary or artistic production of which he is the author.

Article 28. Everyone is entitled to a social and international order in which the rights and freedoms set forth in this Declaration can be fully realized.

Article 29. 1. Everyone has duties to the community in which alone the free and full development of his personality is possible.

2. In the exercise of his rights and freedoms, everyone shall be subject only to such limitations as are determined by law solely for the purpose of securing due recognition and respect for the rights and freedoms of others and of meeting the just requirements of morality, public order and the general welfare in a democratic society.

3. These rights and freedoms may in no case be exercised contrary to the purposes and principles of the United Nations.

Article 30. Nothing in this Declaration may be interpreted as implying for any State, group or person any right to engage in any activity or to perform any act aimed at the destruction of any of the rights and freedoms set forth herein.

Glossary

American exceptionalism is the belief that the United States is culturally and politically different from, and usually superior to, other countries. It can be traced to the colonial period and the biblical image of the city on the hill. In the area of human rights, it tends to be expressed in the common American view that the United States in some important sense defines international human rights standards.

Amnesty is any law that retroactively exempts a person or group from any criminal liability for crimes they may have committed in the past. Amnesty policies are often pursued in countries undergoing a political transition after a period of intense human rights violations or abuses, ostensibly to move on from the past. They are widely condemned by human rights activists as promoting **impunity**—the knowledge that, no matter how serious the crimes that rulers may have committed, they will never be prosecuted for those crimes. Amnesty for genocide, war crimes, and crimes against humanity are widely considered to be contrary to international law.

Anarchy, the absence of political rule, is characterized by the lack of authoritative hierarchical relationships of superiority and subordination. In international relations, anarchy refers to the fact that there is no higher authority above states. Anarchy, however, need not involve chaos (absence of order). Thus, international relations have been called an anarchical society, a society in which order emerges from the interactions of formally equally sovereign states.

Apartheid, an Afrikaans term meaning "separateness," was the policy of systematic, official racial classification and discrimination in South Africa. Building on a long tradition of racial discrimination, white South African governments in the 1950s and 1960s developed an unusually extensive, highly integrated system of official discrimination, touching virtually all aspects of public life and many aspects of private life as well. The policy was officially renounced following a (whites-only) plebiscite in March 1992.

Civil and political rights are one of two principal classes of internationally recognized human rights. They provide protections against the state (such as rights to due process, habeas corpus, and freedom of speech) and require that the state provide certain substantive legal and political opportunities (such as the rights to vote and to trial by a jury of one's peers). They are codified in the International Covenant on Civil and Political Rights and in Articles 3–15 and 19–21 of the Universal Declaration of Human Rights (see Table 1.1).

Cold War is the term used for the geopolitical and ideological struggle between the Soviet Union and the United States following World War II. It began in earnest roughly in 1948, waxed and waned over the following forty years, and finally ended with the collapse of the Soviet bloc in 1989. See also **détente.**

The principle of achieving **consensus** has been part of the culture of the United Nations since the 1970s. The idea was to move the organization away from the contentious politics of voting on every measure—where the goal is to simply achieve a numerical majority—to drafting resolutions, programs, and policies that could be adopted by consensus, without a vote. This would promote compromise in the drafting of resolutions and policies, with the aim of achieving consensus at the end. In practice, adoption by consensus is achieved when no one with a vote objects to such an adoption (although they may disagree with some part of it). If there is an objection, then a formal vote is taken.

Contentious jurisdiction refers to the jurisdiction of a court or tribunal that is accepted by the parties to a dispute, which may be compulsory (for example, with the European Court of Human Rights) or voluntary. States that accept a court's contentious jurisdiction agree (in principle) to accept the judgment issued in any such case heard by the court.

Cosmopolitan and **cosmopolitanism** refer to a conception of international relations that views people first and foremost as individual members of a global political community (cosmopolis) rather than as citizens of states.

Cultural relativism (see **relativism,** below).

Détente is a term used to describe the relaxation of tensions between the United States (and Western Europe) and the Soviet Union (associated with the **Cold War**) from the late 1960s through the early 1980s. Its hallmarks were several arms control agreements and the Helsinki Final Act, which settled a variety of lingering post–World War II issues and problems between Western and Eastern Europe.

Disappearances are a form of human rights violation that became popular in the 1970s. Victims, rather than being officially detained or even murdered by the authorities or semiofficial death squads, are "disappeared," taken to state-run but clandestine detention centers. Torture typically accompanies disappearance, and in some countries the disappeared have also been regularly killed.

Economic, social, and cultural rights are one of two classes of internationally recognized human rights. They guarantee individuals socially provided goods and services (such as food, health care, social insurance, and education) and certain protections against the state (especially in family matters). They are codified in the International Covenant on Economic, Social, and Cultural Rights and in Articles 16–18 and 22–27 of the Universal Declaration of Human Rights (see Table 1.1).

Ethnic cleansing is the genocidal "purification" of the population of a territory through murder and forced migration. The term entered international political vocabularies to describe the strategy and practices of Serbian separatists in the former Yugoslavian republic of Bosnia-Herzegovina during the civil war of 1992–1995.

The four **Geneva Conventions** of 1949 (and their additional protocols of 1977 and 2005) form the basis of international humanitarian law in situations of armed conflict. They aim to protect those who are *hors de combat* (outside of combat) despite being in a combat zone. The First Convention protects soldiers who have been wounded or fall ill on land; the Second, those at sea. The Third Convention applies to soldiers who have surrendered or been captured (prisoners of war). The Fourth applies to civilians.

Genocide, in the narrow, technical sense of the term, involves systematic killing and similar methods aimed at destroying, in whole or in part, a people (*genos*) or ethnic or religious group. In a looser sense of the term, it involves targeted mass political killing—politicide—directed against a group that may or may not be defined by common descent.

Humanitarian intervention is **intervention** (see below), almost always involving the use of force, for humanitarian purposes, typically in situations of genocide, armed conflict, or severe humanitarian crisis (especially massive famine).

Human rights, the rights that one has simply because one is a human being, are held equally and inalienably by all human beings. They are the social and political guarantees necessary to protect individuals from the standard threats to human dignity posed by the modern state and modern markets.

The **Human Rights Committee** is a body of eighteen independent experts created by the International Covenant on Civil and Political Rights. Its principal activities are reviewing periodic state reports on compliance with the Covenant and reviewing individual complaints of violations. Compare **treaty monitoring bodies.**

An **intergovernmental organization**—often referred to as an international organization—is a treaty-based organization of states. Prominent global examples include the United Nations and the World Health Organization. The European Union is the most prominent regional example. Compare **nongovernmental organization.**

The **International Bill of Human Rights** is the informal name for the Universal Declaration of Human Rights and the International Human Rights Covenants, considered collectively as a set of authoritative international human rights standards. This title underscores the substantive interrelations of these three documents.

The **International Human Rights Covenants** comprise the International Covenant on Economic, Social, and Cultural Rights and the International Covenant on Civil and Political Rights, which were opened for signature in 1966 and entered into force in 1976. Along with the Universal Declaration of Human Rights, these are the central normative documents in the field of international human rights.

Internationalist and **internationalism** refer to a conception of international relations that stresses both the centrality of the state and the existence of social relations among those states. See also **society of states.**

International humanitarian law is a body of law governing armed conflict. The Hague strand covers the laws of war itself—who can legally wage it, how it is declared, and the laws of surrender and armistice. The Geneva strand—codified especially by the four **Geneva Conventions**—limits the legal use of force to protect those who are outside of combat, and therefore not belligerents. These include soldiers who are wounded, have surrendered, or have been captured and civilians. International humanitarian law has also codified many violations as constituting crimes: genocide, war crimes, and crimes against humanity.

An **international regime** is a set of principles, norms, rules, and decision-making procedures accepted by states (and other relevant international actors) as binding in an issue area. Most international regimes include formal institutions or organizations that are established by treaty or agreement. However, the notion of a regime points to patterns of international governance that are not necessarily limited only to a single treaty or organization.

Intervention, as the term is used in international law and relations, means coercive interference, usually involving the threat or use of force, against the sovereignty, territorial integrity, or political independence, or any matters essentially within the domestic jurisdiction, of a state.

The **like-minded countries** are a group of about a dozen small and medium-size Western countries, including Canada, the Netherlands, and the Nordic countries. They often act in concert in international organizations and generally pursue foreign policies that are more "liberal" than those of the United States, Japan, or the larger Western European countries. The like-minded countries particularly emphasize development issues, and they have tried to play an intermediary role between the countries of the South and the larger northern countries.

Mainstreaming is a process within (especially) the United Nations to incorporate what have traditionally been thought of as "specialty" concerns (such as gender or human rights) into the wider work of the United Nations. Thus, human rights are not merely the concern of the U.N. Human Rights Council or the treaty monitoring bodies but are also incorporated into the work of development, environmental, or security-related agencies as well.

A **nongovernmental organization** is a private association of individuals or groups that engages in political activity. International NGOs (INGOs) carry on their activities across state boundaries. The most prominent human rights INGOs include Amnesty International, Human Rights Watch, and the Minority Rights Group. In some areas, especially international relief, NGOs are frequently referred to as private voluntary organizations.

Nonintervention is the international obligation not to interfere in matters that are essentially within the domestic jurisdiction of a sovereign state. This duty is correlative to the right of sovereignty and expresses the principal practical implications of sovereignty, viewed from the perspective of other states.

Peacekeeping involves the use of lightly armed multilateral forces to separate previously warring parties. Peacekeeping is distinguished from collective security enforcement by a limited mandate, an effort to maintain neutrality, and reliance on the consent of the parties in whose territory peacekeepers are placed.

Quiet diplomacy is the pursuit of foreign policy objectives through official channels, without recourse to public statements or actions. A standard mechanism for pursuing virtually all foreign policy goals, it became a political issue in the United States in the late 1970s and 1980s, when conservative critics of the policy of the Carter administration and defenders of the policy of the Reagan administration argued that U.S. international human rights policy toward "friendly" (anticommunist) regimes should in most cases be restricted *solely* to quiet diplomacy.

Realism (*Realpolitik*) is a theory of international relations that stresses the absence of international government (that is, the presence of international **anarchy**) and the centrality of egoism in human motivation, thus requiring states to give priority to power and security in international relations and to exclude considerations of morality from foreign policy.

A **relativist** believes that values are not universal but are a function of contingent circumstances. **Cultural relativism** holds that morality is significantly determined by culture and history. Marxism is another form of ethical relativism, holding that values are reflections of the interests of the ruling class. Radical cultural relativism sees culture as the source of all values.

The **society of states** conceptualizes "the international community" as a largely contractual community whose principal members are states. See also **internationalism.**

To be **sovereign** is to be subject to no higher authority. International relations over the past three centuries have been structured around the principle of the **sovereignty** of territorial states.

Statist and **statism** refer to a theory of international relations that stresses the centrality of sovereign states. Realism is usually associated with a statist theory of international relations.

Thomism is the philosophy of Thomas Aquinas, which continues to play a central role in Catholic moral and ethical theory.

A **treaty** is an agreement between states that creates obligations on those states. Treaties are one of the two principal sources of international law, along with custom (regularized patterns of action that through repeated practice have created expectations and thus acquired an obligatory character). The two most important international human rights treaties are the International Covenant on Economic, Social, and Cultural Rights and the International Covenant on Civil and Political Rights.

Treaty monitoring bodies is the term of art used for the various committees created under the International Human Rights Covenants and other international human rights treaties to monitor state compliance. Compare **Human Rights Committee.**

The **Universal Declaration of Human Rights** is a 1948 U.N. General Assembly resolution that provides the most authoritative statement of international human rights norms. The Universal Declaration and the **International Human Rights Covenants** are sometimes referred to as the **International Bill of Human Rights.**

Universalism is the belief that moral values such as human rights are fundamentally the same at all times, in all places, or across some particular "universe" of application. It is the opposite of **relativism.**

Utilitarianism is a moral theory (most closely associated with Jeremy Bentham and John Stuart Mill) that holds that the right course of action is that which maximizes the balance of pleasure over pain. This is the most common form of consequentialist ethics, which focus on the consequences of acts rather than their inherent character.

Index